Transforming Infantile Tra in Analytic Work with Ch and Adults

This vivid and moving volume presents the clinical work and writings of Alessandra Cavalli, an internationally known child and adult psychoanalyst who taught and supervised widely, ran infant observation seminars in the UK and Europe and was closely involved in the development of child analysis training in Russia.

Informed by a deep knowledge of theory, each chapter draws on many strands of both psychoanalytic and Jungian thought, integrating multiple analytic languages into a coherent clinical language specific to Cavalli. The book includes 11 of her most important papers about work with children and adults, with an introduction by the distinguished Jungian psychoanalyst Warren Colman.

Her work was primarily concerned with the impact of trauma on the developing self and the importance of weathering emotional storms in search of meaning, and the book will be fascinating reading for clinicians of different psychoanalytic approaches working with adults and children, as well as students of psychotherapy and counselling.

Alessandra Cavalli, PhD, was an internationally known child, adolescent and adult analyst who created a unique clinical model integrating Jung, Klein and Bion. A training and supervising analyst of the Society of Analytical Psychology in London, she taught infant observation seminars and lectured and supervised widely in the UK and abroad.

'This collection of papers by Alessandra Cavalli is both intellectually wide-ranging and clinically impressive. Her deep interest in and attention to early states of mind and body, nourished particularly by her devotion to Infant Observation and her experience of analysing traumatised young children, has enabled her to propose fresh theoretical convergences between Jungian and post-Kleinian concepts of development. Imagination and generosity characterise her clinical writing, and make this book a pleasure to read as well as a stimulus to debate about fundamental psychoanalytic theory. The book is an eloquent demonstration of the creative bringing together of clinical practice with adults and children, in the footsteps of Klein, Winnicott and Fordham.'

Margaret Rustin, *child and adult psychotherapist at Tavistock and Portman NHS Trust, and honorary member of the British Psychoanalytic Society*

'Alessandra Cavalli's work integrating infant observation, child and adult analysis will be of immense interest to clinicians who work with early trauma and its vicissitudes in the psyche of children and adults. Cavalli offers a much needed and comprehensive integration of the work of Jung, Fordham, Klein, and Bion. Her exploration of the nature and meaning of unconscious intersubjective processes is both timely and profound, and will be invaluable to psychotherapists and psychoanalysts.'

Brian Feldman, *PhD, child, adolescent and adult Jungian psychoanalyst, Palo Alto, CA*

Transforming Infantile Trauma in Analytic Work with Children and Adults

The Clinical Writings of Alessandra Cavalli

Edited by Martha Stevns and Lucinda Hawkins

LONDON AND NEW YORK

Cover image: © Getty Images

First published 2023
by Routledge
4 Park Square, Milton Park, Abingdon, Oxon OX14 4RN

and by Routledge
605 Third Avenue, New York, NY 10158

Routledge is an imprint of the Taylor & Francis Group, an informa business

© 2023 selection and editorial matter, Martha Stevns and Lucinda Hawkins; individual chapters, the contributors

The right of Martha Stevns and Lucinda Hawkins to be identified as the authors of the editorial material, and of the authors for their individual chapters, has been asserted in accordance with sections 77 and 78 of the Copyright, Designs and Patents Act 1988.

All rights reserved. No part of this book may be reprinted or reproduced or utilised in any form or by any electronic, mechanical, or other means, now known or hereafter invented, including photocopying and recording, or in any information storage or retrieval system, without permission in writing from the publishers.

Trademark notice: Product or corporate names may be trademarks or registered trademarks, and are used only for identification and explanation without intent to infringe.

British Library Cataloguing-in-Publication Data
A catalogue record for this book is available from the British Library

Library of Congress Cataloging-in-Publication Data
A catalog record for this book has been requested

ISBN: 978-1-032-21465-8 (hbk)
ISBN: 978-1-032-21467-2 (pbk)
ISBN: 978-1-003-26853-6 (ebk)

DOI: 10.4324/9781003268536

Typeset in Times New Roman
by Apex CoVantage, LLC

Contents

Acknowledgements vii
About the author viii
Editors' biographies ix
Editors' note x

Thinking the unthinkable: Trauma, defence and early
states of mind in the work of Alessandra Cavalli 1
WARREN COLMAN

1 Casper or 'the cabinet of horrors' 19

2 Power cut in the countertransference 34

3 On receiving what has gone astray, on finding
  what has got lost 49

4 Transgenerational transmission of indigestible facts:
  From trauma, deadly ghosts and mental voids
  to meaning-making interpretations 60

5 From affect to feelings and thoughts:
  From abuse to care and understanding 76

6 Clinging, gripping, holding, containment:
  Reflections on a survival reflex and the development
  of a capacity to separate 89

7 From not knowing to knowing: On early infantile
  trauma involving separation 105

8	Giving voice to psychic pain: The British-Mexican connection, on the vicissitudes of creating a home for street children	119
9	Identification – obstacle to individuation, or: On how to become 'me'	131
10	Noah's Ark: Technical and theoretical implications concerning the use of metaphor in the treatment of trauma	146
11	Continuous becoming or the experience of coming into being	161
	Index	171

Acknowledgements

The author's photograph is used by permission of Kay Marles.

The introduction is an edited version of a paper presented at the Second International Conference in Jungian Child Analysis, Online, March 12–14, 2021.

Chapters 1, 2, 3, 4, 5, 6, 9 and 10 have been previously published in the *Journal of Analytical Psychology*, John Wiley and Sons Ltd, and are used by permission of the publisher.

Chapter 7 has been previously published in *Transformation* (Karnac, 2014; Routledge, 1918) and is used by permission of the publisher.

Chapter 8 has been previously published in *From Tradition to Innovation: Jungian Analysts Working in Different Cultural Settings*, Eds., C. Crowther & J. Wiener. New Orleans: Spring Journal Books, 2015. Republished as *Jungian Analysts working across Cultures: From Tradition to Innovation*, Eds., C. Crowther & J. Wiener. London and New York: Routledge, 2021, and is used by permission of the publisher.

Chapter 11 is the transcript of a talk given at the conference on Childhood by The Alpine Fellowship in Venice, 28 June 2018, and is used by permission of the Alpine Fellowship, London. The talk is available on YouTube.

About the author

Alessandra Cavalli PhD (1957–2020) was a child and adolescent, and adult analyst, who was internationally active and influential. A training and supervising analyst of the Society of Analytical Psychology in London, she drew from many traditions, integrating Jungian and psychoanalytic language into a coherent clinical model.

Born in Italy, she did undergraduate and postgraduate studies in Germany. She worked in Munich and Brussels before moving to London where she did her analytic trainings. Fluent in several languages, she taught and lectured internationally and shared her profound belief in the importance of early life in infant observation seminars in the UK and Denmark. She did supervision in Hungary and Bulgaria, and in Mexico supervised therapeutic work with children in care. She was closely involved in the development of child analysis in Russia and was one of the organizers of the first international conference for Jungian Child Analysis, held in Russia in 2019. The second international conference, held in England in 2021, was dedicated to her memory.

Editors' biographies

Lucinda Hawkins is a Training Analyst of the Society of Analytical Psychology in private practice in London and a member of the editorial board of the *Journal of Analytical Psychology*. She was an editor at *Studio International* and *Grove Dictionary of Art* and is co-author of *Michelangelo* (1991). With Alessandra Cavalli and Martha Stevns, she co-edited *Transformation: Jung's Legacy and Clinical Work Today* (Karnac 2014/Routledge 2018).

Martha Stevns is a Training Analyst of the Society of Analytical Psychology in London and works in private practice in Cambridge, UK. She teaches, supervises and runs Infant Observation Seminars. She was an editor at the Swiss art magazine *du*. With Alessandra Cavalli and Lucinda Hawkins, she co-edited *Transformation: Jung's Legacy and Clinical Work Today* (Karnac 2014/Routledge 2018).

Contributor's biography

Warren Colman is a Training and Supervising Analyst of the Society of Analytical Psychology in London. He is a former UK Editor-in-Chief of the *Journal of Analytical Psychology* and remains a member of the Journal's Editorial Board. He has published numerous clinical and theoretical papers on topics including couple interaction, the self, archetypes, analytic process and symbolic imagination. His book *Act and Image: The Emergence of Symbolic Imagination* was published in 2016.

Editors' note

Our friend and colleague Alessandra Cavalli was an extraordinary person, full of ideas and energy, with a great passion for life and work. In addition to her extensive practice in London working with children, adolescents and adults, she taught, supervised and lectured internationally. Her untimely death in 2020 was mourned by friends, colleagues, patients and students in the UK and abroad.

She was an intrepid traveller, both external and internal. Her spirit and energy were fed by nature, from sea swims to mountain hikes and walks on Hampstead Heath. She wrote poetry and had broad cultural interests, particularly classical music, but was also deeply involved with the world outside. Her experience of working with homeless children in Mexico influenced her efforts to help child refugees in England.

Alessandra published widely, and the vivid and moving accounts of her clinical work are supported by her deep knowledge of theory, drawing on many strands of psychoanalytic and Jungian thought. This broad approach informed the book we commissioned and edited together, *Transformation: Jung's Legacy and Clinical Work Today* (Karnac 2014/Routledge 2018).

Alessandra was planning to publish a collection of her papers, and we hope this book is a fitting tribute to our friend and colleague and will ensure the legacy of her unique contribution to clinical work and theoretical thinking.

Thinking the unthinkable

Trauma, defence and early states of mind in the work of Alessandra Cavalli

Warren Colman

Introduction

I feel honoured to be asked to introduce this collection of Alessandra Cavalli's papers as I did not know her well except through her writing, having worked with her on the editing of several of her papers. Of the 11 papers included in this volume, four were published in the *Journal of Analytical Psychology* during my editorship between 2007 and 2013; in addition, I worked with her on an early draft of what turned out to be her final paper ('Noah's Ark'), which was eventually published posthumously. Ours was a mutually fruitful relationship. Alessandra was bursting with ideas from which I always learnt a great deal, but when it came to putting those ideas into a theoretical form, she often struggled with turning intuitive imagination into theoretical coherence. It is fascinating to look at how much some of her papers changed through the editorial process, and this will be one of the ways by which I hope to illuminate her clinical and theoretical aims in this introduction.

I have been told that there were certain matters on which Alessandra held very fixed views. This was not my experience of her. There were several instances where I questioned some of her ideas or the concepts she used – usually because I didn't understand what she was saying – to which her response would often be simply to drop them from her revised version, often coming up with another new idea in the process. So it is especially valuable to have her papers gathered together in this collection since it is only when they are considered as an overall body of work that some of the unifying themes become clear.

One of these themes – her interest in what she called 'the archetypal law of the mind' clearly reveals her embeddedness in the Jungian tradition, something that was not always immediately apparent since the main orientation of her work usually appears to owe more to Kleinian psychoanalysis. This theme was present in the unpublished versions of her final paper 'Noah's Ark' (Chapter 10) but, failing to recognize its significance, I edited it out of the version that was published in the *Journal of Analytical Psychology* after Alessandra's death. My editorial *faux pas* has been corrected in the version published here, but it nevertheless serves as

DOI: 10.4324/9781003268536-1

a good introduction to unpacking Alessandra's theoretical model which, as in this case, was often implicit and not clearly spelt out. I aim to clarify that model in this introduction, but my previous error is also *caveat emptor* for the rest of my comments on Alessandra's work. These may serve the reader as an introduction – a taster, perhaps – but they are only one view; for the main meal, the reader needs to go to the primary source and allow themselves to experience directly the unique creative vitality that informed all of Alessandra's work and is so vividly in evidence throughout this book.

The translating function and the archetypal law of the mind

In the first version of 'Noah's Ark', Alessandra referred to two mental functions – the transcendent function and the translating function both of which she regarded as 'archetypal'.

> This organisation, 'the translating function' (Intro. Matte Blanco 1975) co-exists in a correspondence with *the archetypal law of the mind*, what Jung (1916) called 'the transcendent function,' that binds together opposites each of which is unconceivable in isolation, unless mysteriously related to its antithesis.
>
> [And a bit later]: Fordham (1985) thought that by definition experiences that are integrated into the self have a representable form. This is due to *the archetypal structure of the mind*. Each experience that has been integrated has for the individual a meaning and can be represented symbolically. [italics added].

In my response to her, I queried what she meant by 'translating function'. This was a term I didn't know at the time which, in Matte Blanco's work, refers to the translation of symmetrical to asymmetrical aspects of mind, something roughly similar to the transition from body to mind that could also be related to Fordham's concept of deintegration/reintegration[1] – both concepts to which Alessandra regularly referred. Nevertheless, in her amended version, Alessandra simply dropped the idea and must have decided to explain what she meant in other ways. This was the version she submitted to the *Journal of Analytical Psychology* for peer review. Here is the same passage from that version:

> The capacity to integrate experiences into mind (Fordham 1985, p. 61) consists then in the complex capacity to translate bodily events into thoughts, and in *the archetypal law of the mind* to bring and bind together opposites (Jung 1916; Klein 1935) belonging to the same experience. When experiences are integrated, they are representable for mind by definition (Fordham 1985, p. 57). [italics added]

This turned out to be the last version that Alessandra produced. The paper was sent out for peer review and accepted subject to addressing various issues raised by the reviewers (which is the journal's usual procedure) but Alessandra died before she could undertake the revision. As it was too valuable to remain unpublished, I was asked to work with one of the current *Journal of Analytical Psychology* editors, Nora Swan-Foster, to edit the paper posthumously (and, with the aforementioned amendment, this is the version that is published here). We aimed to do this while maintaining Alessandra's own idiom and avoiding any substantive changes or additions as far as possible.[2]

However, I had difficulty understanding the passage I've quoted, and when I looked up the Fordham reference, it was hard to recognize which bit of it Alessandra had in mind.[3] So I decided to gloss her meaning by replacing 'the archetypal law of the mind' with an elaboration of what Fordham says.

Here then is the version published in the *Journal of Analytical Psychology*. My elaboration of Fordham is in square brackets:

> The capacity to integrate experiences into mind consists then in the complex capacity to translate bodily events into thoughts, and to bring and bind together opposites belonging to the same experience (Jung 1916; Klein 1935). [In this regard, Fordham links Klein's view that symbolization lies at the root of the infant's mental life, with the Jungian view of archetypal forms being present at birth which regulate the infant's behaviour and have the potential for mental representation (Fordham 1985, p. 61). However, Fordham also makes clear that this process requires a mother who holds her baby in mind: 'in a state of maternal reverie, she relates directly to her baby's protomental life and helps in the transformation of beta into alpha elements' (ibid., p. 57).] When experiences are integrated in this way, they are representable for mind by definition.

But now, not only had the 'translating function' disappeared but along with it 'the archetypal law of the mind'. I had failed to see that this was important to Alessandra because I didn't understand it and didn't realize it was an idea to which she frequently refers but never discusses. However, I now consider that Alessandra firmly believed in the 'archetypal law of the mind' or, as she also mentioned in the original version, 'the archetypal structure of the mind' (and I will say more about this later). I now see that what she had in mind was two archetypal functions that are inherent in the structure of the mind – the function of translating bodily events into thoughts and the function of transcending opposites, especially the splitting of good and bad experiences as discussed by Klein. In her own mind, Alessandra had developed a theoretical synthesis that was never fully articulated – one that integrated Klein, Fordham, Bion, Matte Blanco and Ferrari in an archetypal structure that was firmly rooted in Jung. I think this informed all her work but was so embedded in her clinical work that she did not, or perhaps could not, ever fully express it. Each paper is an instance of one or other feature of a theory which is primarily concerned with the impact of trauma on the developing self and how this can be ameliorated through the analytic process.

In view of this, I now regard my deletion of 'the archetypal law of the mind' as a serious error and, with this in mind, I must point out to the reader the possibility that in this introduction too I may be misrepresenting the dead. Alessandra isn't here to speak for herself, and her true meaning may be lost in translation. Maybe Alessandra was relaxed about this because she spoke so many different languages and knew how inexact the translating function always was. As she once wrote to me, 'Sometimes I have good thoughts, but the English is still what it is' (email, 25/05/2011). The psyche too speaks many languages and none – translating that original language of raw primitive affect into representational form was at the heart of Alessandra's project but was always a work in progress. This too is therefore a provisional statement by definition.

'Love hurts' – Casper and the 'martyr to psychotherapy'

Child analysts are much more directly exposed to early states of mind, and these are usually expressed by a level of disruptive behaviour that seems extremely daunting to adult analysts like me who can usually expect to sit quietly in our chairs. Yet even for child analysts, some of Alessandra's clinical accounts were hair-raising and controversial, especially those in her earlier papers where she describes being subjected to quite extreme levels of physical and mental violence. These early papers also display a radical courage and depth of engagement that characterized all her subsequent work. She wrote about this with passion laced with ironic humour, notably in her first paper ('The Cabinet of Horrors') where her young patient, Casper, a severely deprived and neglected 9-year-old, subjected her to regular outbursts of violence that frequently left her bruised and in tears. It was, as she says, 'not a joke':

> It is impossible for me to cope with it. I feel paralysed, afraid of dying. . . . [It] is so unbearable that at times I imagine that I could give up, this case being too difficult for me. I fear I will die if I go on, a martyr to psychotherapy.
> (Cavalli 2007, p. 619)

But she does not give up. She somehow manages to go on thinking about the meaning of Casper's violence, and as she is able to communicate this to him, he begins to develop a capacity to reflect on his own experience. One particularly moving aspect of this is her understanding that, for Casper 'love hurts' (ibid., p. 617); his violence is a means of destroying the agonizing possibility of love and the pain of abandonment and rejection that it so often entails. Through this understanding, Casper begins to refer to Alessandra as 'a woman of feelings'. We will see a great deal more of this woman of feelings in Alessandra's subsequent work. In her conclusion, she explains,

> From looking at the world from his bottom, [Casper] had to learn to look at it from his mind. Casper needed to trust a good holding other, an analyst on whom he had to become dependent. From there thinking could begin to develop.
>
> (Cavalli 2007, p. 621)

This simple statement remains at the heart of her work. Although from a theoretical point of view, she writes more about the shift from body to mind – a central theme that she explores in all her papers – the need for a 'good holding other', the woman of feelings who knows that love hurts yet is never afraid to go on loving, is always a fundamental ground to her analytic way of being.

And what about the woman who dies a martyr to psychotherapy? Alessandra certainly gave an enormous amount to her work, and her willingness to exceed conventional limits and boundaries sometimes met with disapproval and controversy. Yet all analysts are wounded healers who are only able to heal if their own psychic wounds have been sufficiently processed through the psychic equivalent of the alchemical *vas* and thus transformed into therapeutic gold. This process does not occur only in our own personal analysis. It continues throughout our analytic career and is the source of a deep gratitude towards the patients with whom we are able to go on working on issues that continue to preoccupy us and remain a vital source of our creativity. When that is no longer the case, it's time to hang up our hats and retire. This means that while some may have seen concerning elements of omnipotence in Alessandra's work, these are best regarded as aspects of her particular form of inspirational creativity: they were two sides of the same coin.

Transforming the unthinkable trauma of abandoned children

It is obvious from her clinical writing that Alessandra was deeply concerned with early infantile trauma. She had an acute sense of the tragic isolation of children and parts of the self that, left without the containment provided by shared understanding, had become lost and abandoned. Deprived of the possibility of mourning and meaning, these parts of the self are exposed to incomprehensible storms of chaotic affect or else become split off and shut away, thereby depriving the self of the vitality that comes from being rooted in the world of feeling. Casper, who seems to have been one of her first training patients, becomes emblematic in this respect. She describes him as a feral child whom she compares to the story of Kaspar Hauser, a mysterious savage child who had been cast out and, for as long as he can remember, had lived in a black hole that he calls a 'cave', never seeing another human being. Many of the children she writes about in later papers have similar qualities in the way they seem to have dropped out of the normal world of childhood as a result of early abandonment traumas.

Several of them were brought to therapy before the age of 4 – one whose mother had a double mastectomy when he was 9 months (Alef in 'Identification', Chapter 9), another who was abruptly weaned at 7 months when his over-stressed mother had become unable to maintain a 'mindful capacity in which feelings could be metabolized' (Gigi in 'On Receiving What Has Gone Astray', Chapter 3) and, finally, Paperino whose sudden loss of hearing at 9 months was not recognized until he was nearly 2 years old ('Noah's Ark', Chapter 10). In addition, there is an adolescent whose mother left her at a few months old ('Clinging, Gripping, Holding, Containment', Chapter 6, Cavalli 2014c) and an adult woman whose mother had become ill in her early months and whose care was transferred to a strict and rigid relative, leaving her early self split off and left behind in a comatose state ('From Not Knowing to Knowing', Chapter 7, Cavalli 2014a). And then there was the project for the lost and abandoned street children of Mexico for whom Alessandra provided supervision for over a decade (Chapter 8). These examples make it abundantly clear that she not only felt a deep compassion for such children but also possessed a remarkable capacity to understand and relate to them. Here she displayed an openness to psychotic and borderline states of mind and a passionate commitment to redeeming them through translating un-mentalized states into the containment offered by shared symbolic meaning.

This is the *leitmotif* that runs through all her papers and is also the underlying theme of her theoretical model, especially in relation to the transformation of unprocessed, unmetabolized proto-thoughts (*beta* elements) into thoughts capable of being represented and elaborated in a thinking mind (*alpha* elements) (Bion 1962) – something which can only occur through the analyst's attuned understanding. Some papers describe particular instances of this process such as the one on transgenerational trauma (Chapter 4, Cavalli 2012); others describe the clinical expression and theoretical formulating of a particular aspect such as the one on identification (Chapter 9), whereas 'Noah's Ark' focuses on a methodological aspect – the use of metaphor. It is notable that several papers have the idea of from/to in their titles, implying the idea of *transformation*, which was also the title of the book she edited with Lucinda Hawkins and Martha Stevns (Cavalli, Hawkins & Stevns 2014):

- 'Transgenerational Transmission of Trauma. From Trauma, Deadly Ghosts and Mental Voids to Meaning-Making Interpretations' (Chapter 4).
- 'From Affect to Feelings and Thoughts: From Abuse to Care and Understanding' (Chapter 5).
- 'From Not Knowing to Knowing' (Chapter 7).

The same theme is apparent in two other titles:

- 'On Receiving What Has Gone Astray, on Finding What Has Got Lost' (Chapter 3).
- 'Giving Voice to Psychic Pain' (Chapter 8).

Although it is likely that something like this takes place in any analytic process, it is clear that Alessandra's interest was in healing (or at least ameliorating) the kind of early trauma that cannot be put into words because it cannot be known about; it is either unconscious or, particularly with children, it is unformulated and is therefore largely expressed through action. The patients with whom Alessandra was concerned could never provide an answer to what, in some form, is often the therapist's first question: 'What ails thee?'

What is also special about Alessandra's papers is the close interweaving between theory and practice. My impression is that her ideas arose directly from the particular cases she discussed: I never got the feeling that she first had an idea and then looked around for a clinical example to illustrate it. She was a terrific storyteller; the clinical accounts in her papers rarely needed much in the way of editing and were always what made the papers vivid and memorable. In fact, the clinical material was *so* vivid, it's easy to forget about the theory, although, as I mentioned earlier, I think this would be a mistake – there is a consistent theoretical model that is being elaborated through the various cases she describes.

Her clinical writing takes us right into the emotional experience of the patient on the one hand and her own response on the other. The latter is more explicit in the early papers when she was still learning her craft – following the violence of Casper, she wrote vividly about the impact of a 'power cut in the countertransference' (Chapter 2, Cavalli 2010) with a child and an adult who would suddenly switch from love to hate, violently cutting off the connection between them without warning. Here is her account of the power cut with 5-year-old Bianca:

> Her wish to destroy was total, real, a matter of life and death. Her method was: destroy everything, do not leave anything out, including my hair, my face, my body. Her attacks were instantaneous and totally unpredictable. To say that I was left unable to think is an understatement. I was cut out, in the dark, unable even to know what was going on.

Then, in 'On Receiving What Has Gone Astray' (Chapter 3), there is the deeply moving account of the love affair between her and 3-year-old Gigi. Although Gigi could speak with apparent fluency, his speech was incomprehensible to anyone else. Thus he was unable to communicate in words.

He spent the first six months of his analysis playing under the couch with Alessandra lying down on the floor so that they were 'on the same level, face to face, at a pre-verbal stage' (Cavalli 2011, p. 6). The pivotal moment in Gigi's analysis arose out of a countertransference reverie when Alessandra found herself recalling a session with a depressed mother and her baby in which the baby had picked up a stone and bitten it. Out of this, Alessandra 'understood that what had remained split off was his primitive aggression, his incapacity to manage the internal pressure to bite and his fear of damaging the object' (ibid., p. 8). She shared this understanding with him in the next session, and this all came to fruition two weeks later.

> For a long, long time we gazed at each other in silence. The intensity of this aesthetic experience moved me deeply, and almost in tears I looked at this creative child who had taught me so much with his silences. Suddenly Gigi talked to me. Although I did not understand him as usual, his voice seemed rather normal to me. Yes, I realized unexpectedly that his voice had lost the strange vibrations, it was not booming anymore. . . . Suddenly, out of the blue, he sprang out from underneath the couch. . . . Before I could understand what was going on, he had attacked me and bitten my arm. We stood for a moment there, looking at each other full of surprise. Then we both began to laugh. This laugh, although a bit manic, was very important. I felt we were both relieved: Gigi because nothing had happened, I because I felt something unthinkable could finally be expressed and understood in a very concrete way to start with, which I hoped would lead to something more symbolic.
>
> (ibid., p. 9)

This clinical account produced several raised eyebrows when it was submitted for publication. On a theoretical level, it was accepted that something had been reintegrated, but it was questioned whether a 'magical' event like this would reliably lead to symbolization. Since one of Gigi's main problems was his incomprehensible speech, Alessandra specifically addressed this in her revision of the paper, showing that, after this event in the analysis, he began to talk normally and comprehensibly at home and that this improvement was maintained over time. Clinically, though, others remained concerned at what they saw as Alessandra's omnipotence, expressed in the comment that nothing had happened, and they had both survived the biting. They felt that this would not help the child.

Perhaps, though, after the violence and destructiveness of the patients described in her first two papers, Casper and Bianca (Chapters 1 and 2), Alessandra may have felt that a little nip on her arm was, quite literally, child's play. In any event, to me, this account describes the work of a gifted analyst whose unconscious intuitive attunement (reverie) opens the way for a 'moment of meeting' that is transformative. Gigi's incomprehensible way of speaking was perhaps due to the fear that his dangerous aggression would be revealed. Alessandra had drawn the sting of his terror through her attunement, her courage and directness and her radical emotional engagement.

How then did Alessandra herself understand what had happened in the theoretical account that frames the clinical story? Originally, the paper was written as a joint paper with Marica Rytovaara with the title 'In Search of a Lost Archetype: A Study of Mutative Intervention in the Therapy of a Young Child and an Adolescent'. They asked for my help in developing it, and I questioned whether the idea of a 'lost archetype' was the right idea for the task. Unsurprisingly, they dropped that idea, and the paper came back as a formal submission a few months later with an entirely different title 'The Transcendent Function and Transformative Moments in the Therapy of a Young Child and an Adolescent'. While most of these concepts turn up again in Alessandra's work, at this point, they were still not sufficiently developed.

In this version, the incident with Gigi was briefly referred to as a moment of meeting (Stern et al. 1998), which it certainly was. However, the work of the Boston group and, more generally, concepts arising from infant research studies are conspicuously absent from Alessandra's writing and the term disappeared from the final version (along with the co-authorship). She always remains faithful to her direct theoretical heritage, especially Fordham's work on deintegration and reintegration and Bion's work on transforming *beta* elements into *alpha* function through containment. Klein is always there in the background, of course, and remains a rich source of theoretical metaphors but there are some subtle but important differences from a traditional Kleinian approach. For one thing, her emphasis on trauma always sets the patient's defences more directly in the context of what has happened to the patient, rather than being the outcome of purely internal instinctual forces. And, while she does not use the idea of moments of meeting, she does refer to attunement as an essential requirement for the process of deintegration and reintegration.

A year or so later, the paper came back for a third time, now under Alessandra's sole authorship. The clinical story was now framed in terms of failures in the deintegrative process that can be repaired through the analyst's attunement to what has been lost and gone astray.

> The analytic relationship requires the capacity of two minds, the analyst's and the patient's, to be in tune if access to this unbearable event is to be found. . . . [T]he analyst makes use of his own mind in order to think what is unthinkable for the patient.
>
> (Cavalli 2011, p. 1)

This enables unconscious psychic events that cannot be known consciously to be 'born into mind by the analytic couple' (ibid.). Interestingly, this phrase turned up again in 'Noah's Ark where it was not clear to me whether Alessandra might also have meant 'borne in mind' in the sense of being held in mind by the analyst until the unthinkable thought can be born between them. Both aspects of this poetically ambiguous phrase are implicit in the title of the final chapter in this book, 'Continuous Becoming or the Experience of Coming into Being (Chapter 11). For it is through being borne in mind that the unthinkable thought can be born into mind, thus making it possible for the nascent self to come into being. This central theme is clearly expressed in 'On Receiving What Has Gone Astray'.

> The analytic couple will be at work in modifying what had been previously unthinkable: the two minds engaged in 'dreaming' may prove adequate in thinking the unthinkable thought.

Alessandra's explanation of what has happened to Gigi refers to the loss of his mother's capacity to be in tune with him, and this is linked with mentalization, deintegration and second-skin defences. Referring to the need 'for un-mentalized bodily events to be born into being' she says,

> When bodily contents have failed to become mind, a thinking skin has failed to grow and with it the capacity to understand. For this to change, it is necessary for analyst and patient to be attuned to one another, in a way similar to mothers and their infants at the beginning of life. This primitive capacity to be in tune makes it possible for the unfolding of a process which aims at the transformation of unmetabolized psychic events into symbolic thoughts. Instead of affecting and disrupting the development of the patient, they can hopefully emerge as thinkable emotions. In this way, unintegrated and split-off deintegrates become re-integrated and the naturally spontaneous process of deintegration/reintegration can re-commence.
>
> (ibid., p. 11)

This is an extraordinary condensation of a series of theoretical ideas that reverberate through all of her subsequent papers.

- Un-mentalized events – the need for bodily contents to become mind.
- The need for attunement for this to be possible.
- A 'thinking skin' without which a protective (second) skin is needed.
- The development of a capacity for symbolization ('thinkable emotions').
- And this is also how deintegration and reintegration work.

In other words, deintegration/reintegration, mentalization and the process by which bodily events become thinkable emotions *are all aspects of the same process*, a convincing fusion of an array of theories. To understand what a *tour de force* this is, we need to add references to the transformation of *beta* elements mentioned earlier in the paper and to recognize that when Alessandra refers to the body becoming mind, she is tacitly referencing the work of Matte Blanco and the Italian analyst, Ferrari – two additional sources whom she would have learnt about through a long period of supervision with Richard Carvalho who also wrote the theoretical commentary on her first paper, 'Casper and the Cabinet of Horrors' using that theoretical model (Carvalho 2007).

In that commentary, Carvalho also acknowledges his debt to Peter Fonagy, whose work Alessandra never actually mentions, although the connection between her approach and that of mentalization was equally clear to me when I wrote my commentary on 'Noah's Ark'. My own speculation about this is that Alessandra didn't respond to the scientific literalness of infant research and the theories arising from them. She preferred theories which enabled her to think *metaphorically*, theories that lent themselves to reverie and imagination and which she could therefore use in the consulting room. That's why her theory-writing in her original drafts appeared to be chaotic and slapdash – because she was using the same approach that enabled her to think so creatively and imaginatively in the consulting room where theories emerge in a kaleidoscopic, piecemeal, almost dream-like way in response to the flow of clinical material. But by the same token, that's also at least one reason why her clinical stories are so vivid and provide such illuminating examples of the ideas she wants to convey. In fact, both the clinical accounts and the theory are metaphorical stories expressing the archetypal truths of the unconscious mind in different registers.

This is one of the things that places Alessandra squarely in the Jungian tradition. In describing the reverie of the baby with the stone that enabled her to grasp Gigi's split-off need to bite, she writes, 'I treated my reverie as *traditional mythology* applied to children and thought of it as Gigi's unconscious communication now becoming accessible to me' (ibid., p. 8). In the previous version, this read, 'I thought of it as Gigi's *unconscious infantile phantasy* now becoming accessible to me'. Alessandra was certainly not the first to recognize the similarity between Klein's unconscious phantasies and Jung's derivation of archetypes from mythological motifs, but it seems significant to me that she chose the notion of mythology in preference to unconscious phantasy. This suggests that she used theory in much the same way that other Jungians use mythology – as metaphorical images that provide symbolic conceptions of unconscious meanings. She subjects her own reverie to the same process as her patient's unmetabolized bodily affects – something to be transformed through the containment of symbolic meaning. Similarly, in my paper 'Symbolic Conceptions' (Colman 2007), published a couple of years earlier, I had argued that psychoanalytic theories are themselves symbolic conceptions which, like mythological narratives, seek to communicate and comprehend psychic reality through imaginal forms.

From the Oedipus complex to affect and feeling

I know that Alessandra had read this paper because she referenced it in an early version of another paper that went through several versions and was originally called 'Further Thoughts on the Oedipus Complex'. After a critical editorial review, Alessandra had to be encouraged not to give up on it, and it eventually re-emerged as 'From Affect to Feelings and Thoughts: From Abuse to Care and Understanding' (2014a) (Chapter 5). Once again, the clinical material remained virtually the same but the theoretical structure around it was transformed, providing a much clearer statement of Alessandra's core theoretical model involving the development of the capacity to think and feel about unthinkable, unbearable trauma. Nevertheless, the abandoned attempt to provide a reformulation of the Oedipus complex in terms of the capacity for differentiated thought provides a valuable insight into Alessandra's way of thinking.

12 Thinking the unthinkable

In the original theoretical introduction, she linked the capacity to transform *beta* into *alpha* elements with a capacity for otherness, difference and differentiation. It was hard to follow her meaning in this raw form, so here is the whole passage:

> The Oedipus complex could be seen as an archetype that begins to be constellated in the psyche only when there is enough capacity to bear an affect . . . which can . . . be split into good and bad. . . . In this frame, the Oedipus complex is constellated by a self which is capable of processing otherness. . . . If this otherness is not contained, the affect becomes a persecutor from which the unity of the primary self is defending: deintegration to this primary self is experienced as disintegration. Nevertheless the guiding voice of the archetype, the inborn Tiresias, is pointing towards differentiation which can be reached by 'marrying' the affects and by 'killing' the previously existing unity while staying in the relationship with another. . . . A resolution is possible only if in the external world the infant is met by an Oedipal breast with a mind which feels and thinks in tune with him while the difficult operation of integration and differentiation is taking place.

Peer reviewers and editors alike were baffled by this description with one significant exception. Giles Clark, whose own work explored the same difficult terrain of borderline personalities struggling with unbearable affect, thought it an important and seminal paper that was well thought out and clearly presented. However, even Giles questioned Alessandra's conceptualization of 'archetype' and 'archetypal' in such phrases as 'the guiding voice of the inborn Tiresias'.

But if for a moment we ignore the theory and focus on the imagery, aren't some of these images like the oedipal breast and the inborn Tiresias rather fascinating? And doesn't it take a particularly creative and free imagination to entertain such flights of fancy? So here again we can't subtract Alessandra's somewhat cavalier attitude towards ordinary limits from her exceptionally creative intuition. She must have been undertaking, within her own mind, the same process she describes in her theoretical model: transforming untamed, undifferentiated affects and crazy intuitions into communicable and shareable symbolic thoughts. And she was not only cavalier about the ideas she entertained – she seems to have been equally cavalier about dropping them. Her impossibly abstract and metaphorical reformulation of the Oedipus complex disappeared almost entirely from the revised version of the paper, apart from a brief discussion of Jung's paper on psychic conflicts in a child at the beginning and a single reference to triangulation at the end.

In retrospect, this passage from the original version is another indication of how important the notion of the archetypes and the archetypal was to her. Just as I had questioned whether calling the aggressive wish to bite 'archetypal' added anything meaningful, so Giles Clark thought the use of archetype and archetypal 'somewhat redundant, perhaps an unnecessary nod to Jungian terminology'. As I mentioned earlier, though, I now think it was nothing of the sort. Alessandra had quite a fundamentalist view of the mind: she was interested in identifying basic functions of processing affective and bodily states into thinkable symbolic thoughts via engagement with a thinking and feeling other person. She considered that such functions must necessarily be universal features of the human mind and were therefore 'archetypal'. The idea of the 'inborn Tiresias' was a typically Jungian way of personifying functions of the mind – in this case, the capacity for differentiated thought.

Abuse as a defence against (the pain of) containment

'From Affect to Feelings and Thoughts' was controversial for another reason – her main thesis, illustrated by a detailed account of the sexual abuse suffered by her adolescent patient, was that, in the absence of emotional containment, abuse could become a way of managing unbearable states of mind experienced as 'nameless dread'. She describes a system of defences in which the uncontained affect itself is perceived as intrusive and abusive. As a result, she says,

> neglected children can be seduced by external abuse in the hope of being protected from affect that threatens to feel abusive from within. Paradoxically these children are drawn toward abusive situations in the hope of finding some ongoing shelter from unmanageable affect.
> (Cavalli 2014b, p. 31)

If this proved difficult to digest in theory, the clinical evidence was even more difficult to stomach. The patient, Mary, had been sexually abused by her mother's partner at the age of 8 and had only disclosed the abuse when the abuser (Mr X) began abusing her younger sister as well. In her therapy some years later, Mary admitted

> that she always felt that Mr. X was not ok, but she was seduced by the fact that she was feeling special, chosen by him. This is why she allowed him to do what he did.
> (ibid., p. 37)

Alessandra comments, 'By allowing Mr. X to abuse her, Mary was looking for an abusive way of looking after unmanageable feelings that her mother had not been able to contain' (ibid., p. 38).

For some readers, the idea that Mary had 'allowed' the abuse, implying some kind of choice on her part, was verging on the outrageous. Fortunately, although initially discouraged, Alessandra stuck to her guns, as she had done in the clinical work itself. For it is only by recognizing the horror, pain and suffering of sexual abuse that the unbearable reality of nameless dread can be understood as something even *worse*. Alessandra had the courage to think the unthinkable here and that made it possible for her patient to eventually know about it as well. One statement from the original draft that didn't make it into the final revised paper sums this up brilliantly: 'Containment is . . . feared as abuse because of the dread of the affect that needs to be born'. In other words, *containment feels abusive, and abuse feels containing.*

The brilliance of this insight required a kind of ruthlessness and determination that is plainly evidenced by the clinical material. Only by demonstrating that she herself was not afraid to confront the worst in her patient could Alessandra help Mary to bear the unimaginable storms of her chaotic infantile affect in the hands of an unstable mother who had been unable to protect her children from abuse.

As Mary began to get in touch with her unbearable rage towards her mother and her guilt for having disclosed the abuse and rejected her family, Alessandra does not take refuge in sympathetic understanding. Instead, she gives an unflinching transference interpretation saying,

> Mary felt I was like her mother and was not able to protect her from the pain of seeing with her own eyes how many contradictory feelings she was experiencing, some belonging to the past, some belonging to the present.

Mary started shouting that Alessandra was sadistically abusing her and began banging her head on the radiator. At this point, Alessandra had become equated with Mary's foster mother whom she believed was poisoning her food and trying to kill her by banging her head on the radiator. This unconscious equation between Alessandra and the foster mother on the one hand and between having her head banged on the radiator and banging her own head on the radiator indicated a psychotic state of symmetrical undifferentiation, as described in Matte Blanco's theory of 'infinite sets' to which Alessandra had referred in her theoretical introduction. In symmetrical states of mind, affects are infinite, and there is no differentiation (asymmetry), so everything becomes equated with everything else. By contrast, Alessandra suggests that

> a limited space with boundaries – that is an asymmetrical finite universe in which feelings could have a particular place – seems to offer protection from such potential overwhelmingness. Bion's notion of containment (Bion 1962), . . . can be understood as the function that translates infinite affect into finite feeling.
>
> (ibid., p. 32)

This incident illustrates what she means. For in the next session, Mary announced that the holy spirit had helped her understand that Alessandra was right. In a complex explanation, not included in the original version of the paper, Alessandra suggests that

> while the psychotic episode may have been an attempt to seek refuge in the infinite magnitude and complete symmetry of the unconscious (Matte Blanco

1975) ... the emergence of her newly acquired capacity for reflection and differentiation had led Mary to locate in the holy spirit what we might call hope. I read Mary's communication as ... indicative of a conscious move towards differentiation between herself and her objects, and between affect and abuse, with a consequent increase of ego strength and capacity to create meaning for herself. ... *What my patient was attributing to the 'holy spirit' was her own capacity to resolve psychic conflict.*

(ibid., p. 40)

Doesn't this version of the 'holy spirit' sound rather like what, in the original version, Alessandra had called 'the inborn Tiresias' whose influence can only be released through interaction with an attuned other capable of transforming unbearable affect (*beta* elements) into *alpha* function?

Conclusion: Alessandra's credo and *modus vivendi*

The published version also contains a succinct statement of what I understand to be Alessandra's theoretical and clinical credo, her *modus vivendi* in a nutshell.

> The capacity to transform affect into an emotional experience that can eventually be thought about requires a mind and a body which are linked together and can work together. This is what Bion calls container contained and it brings about the capacity to have an experience that can be lived and known about. Put in these terms the intercourse between mind and body could be seen as the realization of an archetypal potential that can only be constellated when, through interaction with another, enough capacity to bear affect has been established.

(ibid., p. 33)

In addition, Alessandra's clinical work focuses on the powerful defences of the self that are instituted in the absence of containment in order to ward off the infinite magnitude of nameless dread. In other papers, she discusses some of these powerful defences.

So, for example, in Chapter 9 on identification, she describes 'the use of identification with aspects of a lost object as a defensive strategy to cope with traumatic loss' (2017, p. 187), illustrating this through 3-year-old Alef's omnipotent identification with his mother's lost breast through the magical fantasy that his pooh was a nipple that was capable of producing 'wonderful pooh-milk' (ibid., p. 193). At the same time, his pooh was also a nipple that could kill, obliterating any awareness of the psychic pain of losing his mother's breasts too soon (his mother had a double mastectomy when he was 9 months old). Once this fantasy decreased, the more murderous aspects of his rage against the mother he had lost came to the fore and could then be worked through, enabling the unbearable loss to be mourned.

In Chapter 8, 'Giving Voice to Psychic Pain', she offers a similar understanding of the street children in Mexico who repeatedly run away from the homes provided for them and go back to living on the street. Alessandra sees their running away as an idealized defence:

> A perverse way of thinking according to [which] when things don't go well, one runs away. Many of these children manically hope to reunite with their parents forever and reject what the good but limited home has to offer. Remaining attached to idealisation makes them denigrate and run away from what they have, unable to value what is really possible.
>
> (2015, p. 242)

More generally she suggests,

> Children who are deprived of parents who can look after them physically and mentally tend to develop strong defences against the pain of having been deprived of what is archetypally expected. Survival anxieties give rise to omnipotence, the child becomes the invincible hero. . . . *These children cling on to an internal object that promises them blissfulness.*
>
> (ibid., italics added)

And once again the 'antidote' to these powerful defences of omnipotence and idealization is found in the experience of another mind that can think about them and hold them in mind, enabling them to begin to be able to think about the unthinkable loss of parents, home and family.

In Chapter 6, she draws on the work of Hungarian analyst Imre Hermann, linking his proposal of a 'clinging reflex' in infants to the use of 'gripping on' as a defence against failures in early holding (in Winnicott's sense).

> If an experience of being held has not been good enough, at separation the infant 'loses' his mother instead of being able to let go of the experience. A representation of himself being held by her cannot become internalized because the experience has not been nourishing. The baby feels empty inside and resorts to gripping onto a version of his mother.
>
> (Cavalli 2014c, p. 557)

In her final paper ('Noah's Ark'), she returns to this theme but adds the important caveat that these defensive ways of dealing with unthinkable pain are

> not only a regressive narcissistic defence against growth, *but also a confused manifestation of bodily turmoil and mental growth at the same time.* It is a representation of how an incomprehensible experience has been shaped so far.
>
> (Cavalli 2020, p. 791, italics added)

Here we can discern Alessandra's Jungian heritage in the recognition of a purposive self, however undeveloped, that seeks to order experience, however traumatic but can only do so in the presence of a responsive and attuned other.

Alessandra knew that attunement meant a lot more than sympathetic care and that an essential component of love was a tough determination to pursue the truth at whatever cost. At times, this may have expressed itself as a kind of dogmatic certainty, but we would do well to remember that the psyche is a *complexio oppositorum* in which everything has a dual aspect, just as she described in the tension between narcissistic defence and mental growth. What's more, the brighter the light, the darker the shadow, as Jung himself knew well. Nevertheless, it was her capacity to stay close to unbearable states of mind and to do so with great warmth and intensity alongside her intuitive brilliance that made her so deeply valued by patients, supervisees and colleagues alike. For me, as her sometime editor, she was a joy to work with and inspired a love and respect that is quite remarkable considering how little I knew her in other contexts. I hope I have succeeded in conveying what that love and respect were based on, and I commend you all to go on enjoying and learning from the rich *oeuvre* contained in this volume that she has left as her bequest to us all.

Notes

1 One author has related the translating function to a process of positive disintegration (Laycraft 2017).
2 Some of the unanswered issues and questions raised by the peer review were addressed in a commentary (Colman 2020).
3 Assuming that the reference was correct, which it may well not have been.

References

Bion, W.R. (1962). 'A theory of thinking'. *The International Journal of Psychoanalysis*, 43, 306–10. Also in Second Thoughts. *Selected Papers on Psychoanalysis*. Abingdon and New York: Routledge, 2018.

Carvalho, R. (2007). 'Woman of feelings: reflections on Alessandra Cavalli's Casper or "the cabinet of horrors"'. *Journal of Analytical Psychology*, 52, 625–33.

Cavalli, A. (2007). 'Casper or "the cabinet of horrors"'. *Journal of Analytical Psychology*, 52, 5, 607–23.

———. (2010). 'Power cut in the countertransference'. *Journal of Analytical Psychology*, 55, 4, 485–501.

———. (2011). 'On receiving what has gone astray, on finding what has got lost'. *Journal of Analytical Psychology*, 56, 1, 1–13.

———. (2012). 'Transgenerational transmission of indigestible facts: from trauma, deadly ghosts and mental voids to meaning-making interpretations'. *Journal of Analytical Psychology*, 57, 5, 597–614.

———. (2014a). 'From not knowing to knowing: on early infantile trauma involving separation'. In *Transformation*, eds. A. Cavalli, L. Hawkins, & M. Stevns. London: Karnac Books.

———. (2014b). 'From affect to feelings and thoughts: from abuse to care and understanding'. *Journal of Analytical Psychology*, 59, 1, 31–46.

———. (2014c). 'Clinging, gripping, holding, containment: reflections on a survival reflex and the development of a capacity to separate'. *Journal of Analytical Psychology*, 59, 4, 548–65.

———. (2015). 'Giving voice to psychic pain: the British-Mexican connection. On the vicissitudes of creating a home for street children'. In *From Tradition to Innovation: Jungian Analysts Working in Different Cultural Settings*, eds. C. Crowther & J. Wiener. New Orleans: Spring Journal Books.

———. (2017). 'Identification – obstacle to individuation, or: on how to become "me"'. *Journal of Analytical Psychology*, 62, 2, 187–204.

———. (2020). 'Noah's Ark: technical and theoretical implications concerning the use of metaphor in the treatment of trauma'. *Journal of Analytical Psychology*, 65, 5, 788–805.

Cavalli, A., Hawkins L., & Stevns, M. (eds). (2014). *Transformation: Jung's Legacy and Clinical Work Today*. London: Karnac Books; Routledge 2018.

Colman, W. (2007). 'Symbolic conceptions: the idea of the third'. *Journal of Analytical Psychology*, 52, 5, 565–83.

———. (2020). 'Commentary on "Noah's Ark" by Alessandra Cavalli'. *Journal of Analytical Psychology*, 65, 5, 806–17.

Fordham, M. (1985). *Explorations into the Self*. London: Academic Press.

Jung, C.G. (1916/1958). 'The transcendent function'. *CW*, 8.

Klein, M. (1935). 'A contribution to the psychogenesis of manic depressive states'. *International Journal Psycho-Analysis*, 16, 22–48.

Laycraft, K.C. (2017). 'Positive disintegration as a process of symmetry-breaking'. *Nonlinear Dynamics, Psychology, and Life Sciences*, 21, 2, 143–58.

Matte Blanco, I. (1975). *The Unconscious as Infinite Sets*. London: Butterworth.

Stern, D.N., Sander, L.W., Nahum, J.P., Harrison, A.M., Lyons-Ruth, K., Morgan, A.C., Bruschweilerstern, N., & Tronick, E.Z. (1998). 'Non-interpretive mechanisms in psychoanalytic therapy: the "something more" than interpretation'. *International Journal of Psychoanalysis*, 79, 903–21.

Chapter 1

Casper or 'the cabinet of horrors'[1]

This chapter is a presentation of clinical material from the first 18 months of a four-times-a-week analysis with a 9-year-old boy who had been severely neglected from birth and could be described as a feral child. The aim of this chapter is to challenge the reader to reflect upon the theoretical implication of the developing clinical material. I will therefore give an account of the analysis as it gradually unfolded, including my own observations, thoughts and feelings. These should be understood as my reverie, as well as the anchor in my mind, which helped me in my search to give meaning to what was happening in the analysis.

With the same intention, I also turned to a book that I had read some years before, *Kaspar Hauser*, a documentary account written in 1828 by Anselm von Feuerbach, counsellor of the Court of Appeal of Bavaria. Von Feuerbach had been appointed to make an enquiry and find the secret behind Kaspar Hauser, a feral boy who had made his appearance in his hometown, Nuremberg, on 26 May 1828. In relating to my patient, I felt I had to accomplish a similar task to his: my patient was mysterious and strange to me, and I could not find similar cases described in specialized literature. In my account, I will interpolate Anselm von Feuerbach's notes, tracing his observations and discoveries about Kaspar Hauser and comparing them with mine of my modern-day Casper.

Case presentation

My patient was born in another country. His father had been disabled from when the boy was two, and his mother had already begun to suffer from myalgic encephalomyelitis, commonly known as ME, before he was born. My patient's birth and later her husband's disability precipitated the mother's condition to the point that she was literally unable to leave her bed for weeks as she was in a semi-comatose state. She could not pick her son up when he was a baby, and by the time he was 2, she could not even touch him because she had very severe attacks of nausea and vomiting whenever she came close to him. The boy grew up, abandoned in a very rural environment without contact with other children and only sporadic meetings with adults, apart from his ill parents who were unable to look after him properly. When he was 5, his parents decided to come back to England, where they had lived before their marriage, and he was sent to nursery school. In a state of constant alarm, he used to stab children with pens whenever they came close to him. He was alarmingly described by professionals as a child 'with low language skills, learning disabilities and an IQ of 69. . . . Casper has no friends, is fascinated by fire, urinates in a little corner of his bedroom, suffers from encopresis daily, and has no sense of empathy or remorse. He is reported to have killed his hamster. . . . School life tires him out so much that he has to recover almost every week by missing school days'. The parents of my patient asked for help, but it took three years before the case was allocated to me for four-times-a-week analysis and before a location close to his house could be found where the analysis could take place. At this point, the patient had just turned 9.

The analysis

First meeting

Kaspar Hauser does not seem to know more than 50 words . . . his look is as dull as an animal's can be . . . his walk, like a child's, is in between the upright position and falling down. To cry he twists his mouth in a terrible grimace, if happy for some reason his face lightens like a little child's. . . . As long as he can remember, he has always lived in a black hole that he calls a 'cave'. He never saw a human being or an animal, but every morning when he woke up, he found food and his body had been looked after, his clothes having been changed and his nails cut. He has never been ill, nor has he ever known pain.

Casper is quite tall and robust. He has blond hair and beautiful blue eyes, but he seems strangely lonely and melancholic. I look into his eyes, and I feel a veil over them, then suddenly the veil is lifted, and I feel the possibility of going deep down, almost endlessly deep. I am very surprised. He gives me a casual look. I watch him walk. He does not seem to have much sense of balance, his upper body leans forward, and his feet point inward. He seems neglected as his school uniform is not very clean, his trousers are too long, and his nails and hair are unwashed.

He does not seem to know how to tell the time or to be interested in learning how to. From the first moment with him, I talk as I usually do with children in a session. But I hear my voice coming back to me like an echo, like a record played at the wrong speed. I show Casper his box full of different toys and material and tell him the box is for our work together; we will be meeting in this room four days a week from now on. He does not seem very interested, and altogether he seems detached. Nevertheless, he takes out of the box I am presenting to him the play dough. He smells it, gives it to me to smell, touches it, gives it to me to touch, makes a flat cake with a mouth and two eyes, screws them up, stands up and walks on it. Then he runs to the lavatory, and when he comes back, after a while, there is a persistent smell of faeces in the room. I suppose that he has defecated in his pants. His hands have not been washed, and, as I later discover, he has left the toilet in a mess. He talks to me using monosyllabic words, like 'smell, touch, eyes, mouth', or short sentences, like 'don't know, let's run'. The session is over, and the carpet is full of play dough traces and the toilet full of faeces.

Some hypotheses

Kaspar Hauser's behaviour displays the psychology of a child of 2 or 3 years of age in the body of an adolescent. The seclusion undergone did not provoke either idiocy or madness in Kaspar. After having been freed, he behaves, although with some limitations, like a person who can think and understand.

It is difficult to attribute a chronological age to Casper. His incontinence, his language and his lacking sense of balance make me think of a very young child in the body of a 9- or 10-year-old. However, Casper is not interested in relating to me in the way a young child would do. He seems to be defending himself against me. I sense it already when I look into his eyes. Either he protects himself from my look by rejecting it, or he allows my look to penetrate his eyes, but then it gets lost in an endless space. The same happens with my words. Either they bounce back to me, or they get lost, somewhere inside him, where they cannot be related to. Who am I to him? A sort of impersonal play dough, flat archetypal face? Maybe his response to my interest in him is to squash me with his foot and then to go to the lavatory where he recharges himself and his smell. At the end of the session, I write in my notes,

> Have felt to be with someone who lives outside time, almost immune to new experiences, as he does when, after having touched and smelled the play dough with me, he goes to the loo to get rid of this experience and re-finds himself through his smell.

Casper, unlike Kaspar Hauser who was kept imprisoned, is living in an imaginary cage. He looks, full of mistrust, at the world outside. Is there an entry? Will he be interested in coming out of it? Will I be able to interest him enough for him to open the door?

Although Kaspar Hauser was alone in his cave, there seemed to have been someone there who mysteriously looked after his physical needs. Sadly, it seems to me that there is no one to look after Casper, to wash him, to cut his nails, nor does he seem to be able to look after himself. Will I be able to look after his emotional needs when he seems to be deprived of even the most basic physical care?

The first month of analysis

Kaspar is anything but happy outside his former home, his cave. There he did not suffer from headaches, and nobody tormented him. By torment, he means the pain inflicted on him by the different colours, smells and people he is constantly confronted with. As far as he can remember, in his hole he could not hear noises either of humans or of animals, nor could he distinguish night from day. The flood of impressions must be unbearable to him.

Whenever I try to make contact with Casper, he reacts by looking away, saying, 'Shut up', 'Don't look at me', and then he leaves the room repeatedly because he needs to go to the toilet, often getting there too late and bringing the smell of his faeces back into the room. Casper is probably not used to being with a person who is concentrating on him fully for so long. Near the end of every session, he walks on the play dough leaving me to clear a messy room full of squashed play dough shit.

It is difficult to make real contact with him at this stage. Nevertheless, I understand his avoidance as his inability to process too much sensory input, just like Kaspar Hauser. It takes one month before my sense that my voice sounds like a record played at the wrong speed disappears. By now, Casper is showing more interest in our meetings. Although intrigued by my presence, he seems to prefer his own smell, which is probably reassuring to him.

Second and third months of analysis

Kaspar Hauser doesn't take anything for granted until he has experienced it himself. When I told him that soon we would have snow and everything would be white, he expressed joy, but let me understand that to believe it, he needed to see. When the first snow fell, he ran outside, full of joy but then crying complained that 'the snow had bitten him'. Whatever he thinks, believes or knows is the result of his sensorial experience, which builds his actual capacity for understanding.

In my work with Casper, I am the one who cannot take anything for granted. I have to learn from him how the world looks like in his mind. What I learn from him is surprising to me. He seems to have given a meaning to his early experience, interpreting reality in a way which is totally alien to me.

At this stage at the core of the sessions is the play dough that he uses to teach me how he sees the world from inside his cage. We throw the play dough at each other in the form of one, two or many balls. A ball of play dough can be thrown very softly or terribly violently. Inevitably my breasts are a target or my head or my 'privates', which I learn from him take the form of a penis. 'Ah, ah, got your penis', he says excitedly when he succeeds in throwing the ball close to my genitals. He seems to be embarrassed when he lets me know that making love means 'penis to penis'. Two 'balls-us' is when each of us throws a ball at each other at the same time so that the 'we-balls' meet hitting each other in the air. This is terribly exciting to him, and I wonder if he sees our meetings as a concrete 'penis-to-penis' collision. A ball can also become a baby that he caresses, saying 'baby', but then throws away and squashes. The two balls can also become two breasts that he calls 'boobies'. He puts them under his pullover and then reveals to me:

'Women wear them'.

'Where?'

'Under their bras'.

'And then?'
'They take them off'.
'When?'
'When they go to sleep'.

And then the boobies become poos: he throws them on the floor and walks on them. Inevitably, the one, the two or the many balls become poos and everything is reduced to the same substance: excrement. He laughs, pleased, and if I try to differentiate, he attacks me by punching or kicking me. I realize he can become very violent, and every week I count a few new bruises on my legs and arms. To give me a clear picture of his understanding of a relationship, he conducts a demonstrative experiment for me and leaves two play dough balls-us over the weekend in a container full of water so that when we meet again, there is only a melted, muddy substance. I interpret that 'Mum and baby are one'. If the difference is obliterated between us, we become one. With great difficulty, we recreate two balls out of the sludge, but a lot of play dough is lost in the process. If mother and baby separate, so much is lost, and the 'separation' takes so much away. Our first break is approaching. He leaves one container empty overnight and a big ball of play dough in another container, and I interpret that he is showing me how it feels to be separate from a ball-mother-me who goes away and leaves an empty baby-him. Does he feel that I take everything away from him by going away? His response is to make the play dough into a huge penis, which he sticks onto his 'privates' and sucks as if it were a breast. 'I am sucking my milk', he keeps repeating, ignoring me. If I go away and leave him, he does not need my 'shitty boobies', he has his poos and his own milk to feed himself with, in the form of his pee. His bodily products in the absence of his real Mum have clearly been idealized.

The last two weeks before the break are terrible. He smashes everything in the room, kicks and punches me, targeting my breasts and my head. As soon as I close the door at the beginning of each session, I feel we are entering a Roman arena. He is trying hard to pervert the therapy by getting me involved in a fight. One day, he breaks the cup he uses to drink from, first saying that the water was poisoned and then denying that the cup is now broken. Then he leaves the play dough mass overnight in so much water that it dissolves and has to be thrown away. The break feels 'irreparable'. He doesn't allow me to talk. 'Shut up! Zip up your stinking mouth! Your breath smells!' I call my words 'milky words' and tell him that they seem to make him very afraid of being poisoned because they mean 'not meeting for two weeks', and this feels terrifying to him. I, like the play dough ball, have to be destroyed before my leaving him destroys him. Indeed, for Casper, a relationship with another is profoundly dangerous.

Nevertheless, in one of the last sessions, he says, 'I wish I had millions of sessions with you'. He discovers the paper punch and what he describes as the 'beautiful dots', the little discs of paper inside the punch. When punching a dot out of a sheet, he seems to be describing his increasing realization of the beauty of our being together and the danger that a relationship represents. Will the me-sheet be destroyed if he sucks all my milk-dots-words? Am I withholding my dots from him during the break because I need to survive his greed? Regularly at the end of the sessions of the last week, I feel a terrible sense of nausea, similar to seasickness, which lasts for several hours. Perhaps this is Casper's response to being left after the regularity of our meetings during the week, which feels to him like losing his precarious sense of balance. Or maybe he expects me to feel sick of him when I leave him for the weekend like his Mum felt in reality when he was a baby.

In his emergent relationship with me, Casper still cannot leave his 'imaginary' cage, but he is letting me know why he has to live there. He is protecting himself from the terror of living outside. His poo, the play dough and now the dots are the concrete symbols of his experience and his beliefs.

From Easter to the summer

Kaspar Hauser's curiosity and his thirst for knowledge, let alone the iron perseverance he shows whenever he seems to decide that he wants to learn or to understand something, are beyond imagination and yet moving at the same time. . . . His mind is learning how to think. It is easy for him to learn from sensorial perceptions. However, one day, Professor Daumer made him understand that thoughts are not visible. This discovery left him marvelling.

Casper's relationship with me compels him to test his vision of the world. Although he seems to 'know' that I spend my 'holiday in South America enjoying my boobies', he then attempts to recreate them for himself with the paper punch. We spend session after session punching holes in sheets of paper and collecting the little paper discs in a big container.

At every new session, he examines the dots, puts them on the desk, touches them, smells them, divides them into two mountains and puts them back in the container. They are never enough, and we punch and punch and punch. He says, 'I cut the bras and make more dots in the jar', showing me how needy and greedy he is, and how angry he is with the bras for withholding the 'boobies'.

Casper starts to regress; he asks for milk at every session, which I give to him in the form of a glass of water, but then he vomits the water I offer him and re-drinks his own vomit, or the mucus from his nose, which he puts in his sandwich brought from home, saying, 'Delicious', and then the dots become pee, which he pours onto the floor. The desired milk is as good as real vomit or real mucus; therefore, the pretend milk-dots can be turned into pee. It is difficult for me to keep thinking. Why should he want my milk if he has his own vomit? In doing so, he doesn't need to value me any longer, nor has he to cope with the feelings that dealing with me bring about: I leave him at the end of each session. Despite his effort to turn me into vomit, being with me is great fun, and what I have to offer is better than poo. This new experience seems to elicit his curiosity and desire to know.

'Why do you have brown eyes?', he asks me, looking at me and acknowledging my difference from him with his blue eyes. He then touches my breasts. 'I want to know if you have boobies'. Then he tries to feel my bottom. 'I want to see if you have a hole'. It seems that Casper is beginning to want to know and to give up his fundamentalist beliefs.

'Where does the baby come out?', he asks me one day hiding the play dough mass inside his pants. 'What do you imagine?' I ask. 'From the bottom'. If my bottom has a hole, he might like to get inside so he need not be separate, and all the differences can be obliterated. This phantasy doesn't seem to work because every time he plays with this thought an invisible man, the 'Banana man', appears in the sessions in the form of a hallucination. Suddenly Casper screams, hiding somewhere in the room protecting his genitals with his hands: 'Help, the Banana man! Help! Police! Police!' He is terribly afraid of him, an imaginary phallic Daddy who disapproves of his love for me and will punish him by castrating him. The 'Banana man' transforms the me he wants to be melted with into the 'other' me, the me who is separate from him. Immediately after the imaginary but scary appearance of the 'Banana man', Casper attacks himself, trying to cut his nose, his hair, his 'willy' as he now calls his privates. He has a sort of implicit knowledge that he will be punished for not wanting to let me go and becomes himself identified with the Banana man, who appears at times as 'Banana head', a big man whose head has the shape of a banana.

The summer is approaching and with the summer another break. Casper becomes more and more violent. He really wants to kill me by breaking my neck. Suddenly, in the middle of a nice interaction, he throws the chairs at me, toys, everything he can reach, making me feel lost and afraid that I will not survive the session. It is not a joke. Being together is not safe. Then he attacks himself again. It seems he wants to kill me because he does not want to be separate. At the same time, he needs to be separate from me; otherwise, he will be destroyed by the Banana man, which is also me, the me who abandons him, and this threatens to destroy him.

'I see you double', he says one day, first caressing my face, then pulling my hair and really wanting to make me bald. He sees me double, the good me he wants to possess and the 'other' me he wants to destroy. When with me he has my boobies, has me, but when I take myself away from him, when I become different, which means separate, this provokes violent feelings in him, and he tries to violently destroy me before my going away harms him. Did he experience the abandonment of his ill mother as a threat to a total destruction of his self? And did he feel he had destroyed his mother when she got ill and abandoned him?

Casper starts spending long periods of time in the session masturbating or 'making love' to an imaginary person. 'It is nice', he repeats, behaving as if he were having an orgasm. It is difficult and dangerous to be dependent on a me who has so much and cannot be controlled. His pooing and his 'sex-making' in the sessions are a defence against me, as well as a way to show me that he also has so much. If I am not interested in his poo, I might be more interested in his newly discovered penis. By now the episodes of incontinence have become rare. Shortly before the summer break, he makes money, big discs that he cuts out of sheets of paper. He writes their values on them, 'infinite'. The extraordinary experience of meeting another who is available to him and whose presence he enjoys has provoked a new thought in Casper: is it safe after all to live outside his cage?

While Kaspar Hauser seems to be able to learn from experience, ordering it in containing but abstract new thoughts, Casper is operating on a much more concrete level, using his body and hallucinations to give form to his emotions and phantasy. Is this proto-thinking?

From September to Christmas

To begin with, Kaspar used to play with little tin soldiers. Every evening he used to spend several hours with his soldiers . . . but then he discovered writing and drawing. He is so eager to learn, and this is moving. He is learning so fast that it is almost pathological. Today he wanted to copy the mayor's etching which is in his room. He made more than 40 attempts, the first being similar to children's drawings but increasingly he was able to improve each feature.

Kaspar spends hours and hours in his room practising drawing and writing. A few days ago he told me he had decided to write his autobiography. This was his first attempt to give a form to his thoughts. Today he has given me to read what he wrote. It only has value as the testimony of a still very young and infantile spirit from whom education had been withheld for a very long time.

Casper does not play with toys like normal children. They do not interest him. He prefers his body. After the break, he moves around in the session as if he were a spastic. Maybe he is covering his sense of inadequacy. He could not stop me from leaving him for four weeks. I see hate in pure culture on his face and it seems to appear out of the blue. Then he spits and kicks me, leaving me feeling paralyzed. I do not feel safe with him, constantly expecting to be kicked or beaten up. Banana man no longer comes into the sessions. This may be because we have wasps trapped in the room. Casper screams, hysterically terrified that they will bite his 'willy'.

He then spends an enormous amount of time sitting on a revolving chair spinning around, his head bent backwards. I name this position 'looking in reverse' and understand this as not wanting to think. Or is he communicating to me how difficult it is for him to adjust to my way of thinking? 'I make myself dizzy', he says spinning around on the revolving chair, looking, his head bent backwards.

'You want to look in reverse and this makes you sick'.

One day, he tells me about Alfie, his ghost friend, who died when he was a boy of seven. 'I have a ghost in my house. He comes to play with my toys at night. He sits on my bed and asks me how things are going in school. He came into my house to help me. There was another ghost before him, an evil one who scared me every night'. Alfie the ghost is his only friend; his imaginary companion. Children at school bully him and call him names. It is the first time that Casper tells me what upsets him. The ghost seems to represent the archetypal expectation of a companion, of a guiding parent. Perhaps meeting me has helped him to introject something benign which protects him from terror, which he can only describe in the form of a hallucination, the evil ghost.

He spends long periods of time lying on the desk, pretending to make love to someone and to have orgasms. Just as he used to try to pull me into his poo-world of excrement, now he is trying to pull me into his sexual world. The therapy becomes, 'Let's make sex'. He talks about highly pornographic material, claiming that he saw it on the Internet. It might interest or impress me. Then he admits how scary this is for him, 'Revolting, disgusting!', he says. I repeat, 'Casper does revolting and disgusting things. Can he be a loveable boy if he does revolting and disgusting things?' We start using words like 'disgusting' and 'revolting' at times to describe what he is doing, at times just as a joke between us. The more we talk about disgusting and revolting things, the less sick I feel at the end of the week when I leave him after the last session.

Casper has moved on in his development. His interest in sex and his violent outbursts are aspects of vitality. A lot of psychic energy has been mobilized; he is never tired. Like Kaspar Hauser, he is discovering that words can be a good container for emotions and feelings. As much as drawings.

One day, he makes his first drawing. 'Get me some paper', he commands, and on the white sheet I hand over to him, he draws a circle, a face with one eye, which he then angrily crosses out with a black pencil because he does 'not like the eyes', as he says. He then starts again, this time taking my eyes as a model.

Looking intensely at me and smiling, he draws the face of a boy as a much younger child would have done: blue eyes, a little orange nose, thin red lips and red cheeks, a lot of hair. Proud of it, he gives it to me. 'Put it in my box', he orders. Through my eyes, he sees himself as alive and full of vitality. Two weeks before the Christmas break, he dictates to me the story of a boy called Alfie, like his imaginary companion, the ghost. Alfie and his parents were happy together, but then the boy disappeared into the world of the Elves. It was a terrible world there. No one perceived that he was there. He was simply unseen, so he had to run away, but in his flight, he was wounded. Found by the 'mystical man', he needed to be healed. It was a difficult case, but finally, the mystical man found the right word in his mystical book. The healing word was 'reverse', and the little boy was healthy again. The last words spoken by the mystical man were, 'Alfie, you are not a monster anymore'.

I realize that he can reflect about himself as a boy who became invisible to his own parents and was deeply wounded. The therapy can heal him. Its symbol, the word 'reverse', can repair Casper's confused state of mind. The story of the invisible boy seems to show that Casper has really moved on in his development. He has reached a stage where symbolization can take place. Like Kaspar Hauser, he seems to be able to organize his thoughts around his real experience and to find in drawing and writing a satisfactory form to contain and transform them.

Shortly before the last session before the Christmas break, I realize he can tell the time. 'I knew it already!' he says, annoyed. But then he adds, 'I wish I'd learned it earlier'.

From January to Easter

One night after looking at the most beautiful sky he has ever seen, Kaspar sank into his thoughts, like a statue, immobile, his eyes fixed on nothing. When he came back to himself, he asked why he had been kept captive for so long, the possibility of seeing such beauty been withheld from him. What had he done wrong to deserve such treatment? And he started to cry inconsolable tears. From that day Kaspar started to reflect on his own destiny and to understand day by day the great losses in his life. Why hadn't he a family, a mother, a sister? To sustain him in his precarious psychic equilibrium it was decided that riding would be beneficial to his health. Kaspar loved horses.

After the Christmas break, Casper hugs me, kicks me and then hits himself. When I say my going away felt like his ill Mum having abandoned him and how painful this is, the furniture flies all around the room. 'Stop talking about my parents!' He throws his shoes at me screaming and crying, 'I want to kill myself because I had a bad life. Everybody hurt me, including my parents. My life was only bad'. Casper's despair feels irrecoverable. It becomes isolation because he is unreachable and seems to believe nobody wants to understand him.

Session after session, I have to deal with Casper's violence. He is so cruel and brutal that at times I can't help crying in the middle of sessions when an unexpected pain is inflicted on me. 'Ah, ah, you are crying, you are weak!' It seems he needs to know what I do with the pain, as if he had always been left alone with it, and now he needs to learn how to deal with it. Then inevitably he arrives the day after with a wound.

'What happened to you?'

'I hurt myself'.

'You hurt yourself? But Alessandra doesn't like it when Casper hurts himself. Why did you do it?'

'I wanted to feel the same pain as you'.

Casper spends long periods of time during sessions making sex on the desk to an imaginary other, talking about pornography and wanting me to look at his penis, which I interpret as his way to stop my going away by seducing me. I keep saying the reason why we are here is to understand his feelings. By now he calls me 'vagina woman'. 'Stop talking about my feelings, vagina woman!' By now some difference between us has been acknowledged and accepted.

One day he comes in with an idea. He wants to draw an alien. With a lot of difficulty and fear about not being able to do it, Casper draws a big alien, a bold head, big eyes, animal ears, a long tongue like that of a chameleon, long and sharp claws on his feet and hands, asexual. When after a few weeks the drawing is finished he says, 'Oh, this alien looks really true', meaning that the drawing expresses something true about himself. 'I love you. I really love you', he says, then he hurts me, and then he hurts himself. 'Love hurts', I say softly. He talks about my breasts full of milk. He has a real image of it, sweet and white and juicy milk. Then he turns into Dracula. I say he is afraid of having sucked his Mum dry when Mum got ill, and now he is afraid of sucking me dry, maybe sucking my milk-life. Is this why intimacy is unsafe?

He regularly brings his pencil case for the last session of the week, and we look at his 'treasures'. Every week he has a new object in it: a new pen, a perfumed rubber, a new marker, a glittery pen. We carefully clean the pencil case; sometimes we wash pens and pencils. 'Wash them again, I said. You didn't wash it properly! Look here', he commands me. He then goes to school after the session proud, and everything is tidy and neat. 'Casper is full of beautiful things inside, like the pens in his pencil case', I say waving bye-bye. Is it possible that creative, clean pens have replaced a dirty, pornographic penis? His interest in pornography increases, and a very pornographic Casper seems to compete with me, twisting intimacy into pornography. 'I saw a lady sucking a man's penis. "How refreshing", she said!' He is perverting me into a baby sucking his maternal penis. One day he sits on my lap and says, 'Let's talk like businessmen', and then passes the Sellotape a few times around the arms of the chair where we are sitting so that neither of us can get up. I feel safe, without the fear that he will suddenly hit or kick me. He wants my milk. I say, 'Alessandra has no milk, only milky words for Casper. This is why Alessandra talks so much'. He kisses me softly.

Then the next day, he brings a pornographic magazine into the session. It belongs to a friend, and he is afraid of being found out. How can he give it back? He asks me to talk with his father, which I do after the session in his presence and eventually it emerges that Casper is involved with a gang of children. He was sharing floppy disks that he downloaded from the Internet while they passed porno magazines to him. Perhaps he felt that the only resources that he had to exchange were bad stuff, disgusting stuff. To be disgusting and revolting is not pleasant. He wants to become a normal boy. Can the therapy transform his alienation into normality? For Casper is ready to make an 'act of faith' and trust me by giving up his faecal messes and pornography. He allows change. He now hopes to find real love. Unfortunately, another period of being bullied in school begins.

We now play shop. Session after session I have to rob his shop of his goods and then sell them in my own shop until one day he comes in with a sword. I have to steal his sword, and when he finds out I am selling his sword in my shop, he decapitates me saying, 'I regret having told you about the pornographic floppy disks'. Now I have taken away his contents, which he equates, to the floppy disks. At a very concrete level, they are his value, but also his do-it-yourself defence. I have left him naked. He would like to decapitate my mind and my capacity to think. Now he is vulnerable, dependent on me.

The violent outbursts increase. He really wants to kill me. I try to stop session after session by pulling him out of the room, but it is always too late. Again I cry during the session. He says, 'Now you cry!' I reply, 'You are cruel to me, the way the other children are to you. You do not believe I can suffer as much as you do when they are cruel to you'. He gently caresses my face.

In his pencil case, there are more and more nice new pens as if he were afraid he would not be able to get hold of his good internal resources because of his cruelty. I feel distress and experience doubts about the feasibility of this therapy, but I do not want to give up. I dream of him emerging out of mud and fire.

Before the break, he confesses he is planning to run away during the holiday. He will go to Italy, probably looking for a better Mum-me, a fantasy about how to deal with the pain of separation.

Once outside their respective cages, Casper and Kaspar Hauser are confronted with suffering. How to give it a meaning?

From Easter to the summer

On the 15th of August Kaspar had a dream. . . . He cannot have seen anything alike here in Nuremberg. Dreams do not create anything new. They are a mere re-elaboration of motives externally absorbed. . . . Only one plausible hypothesis can be drawn, or, better said, a moral certainty, which is: he must have seen what he describes in his dream before having been imprisoned.

Kaspar Hauser's psyche is processing what was taken away during the time he was imprisoned: once free his capacity for remembering, ordering, and understanding is set in motion again. His dream is a demonstration of it. Although Casper's psyche is functioning on a much more concrete level, he seems to be dealing with his most primitive experience: the violence of his mother's abandonment, which he has never been able to understand is transferred in his relationship with me. His first relationship has moulded his way of relating to others.

After the summer break, the violence explodes again. It is impossible for me to cope with it. I feel paralyzed, afraid of dying. I can only try to prevent it and then stop the session. But it is always too late. Nevertheless, I start thinking more clearly about the violent outbursts as being of two different types. One type takes place after his having had the feeling of being in a nirvana state with me and it having to finish, while the other type occurs because we are too much in tune, as if he was afraid I could take him over. An example of type one takes place when I am preoccupied with thinking, and he asks, 'What have you done with your big smile?' and then kicks and spits on me. This is when he feels he cannot control me because there is a third element, represented by my thinking or by the end of the session, and this arouses such oedipal rage that he hates me and wants to destroy me.

An example of type two occurs when we are enjoying being together, and I have the deep feeling that I am in tune with him. Suddenly out of the blue, he takes a chair and throws it at me. I understand this violence as a way of reclaiming himself, as if he could lose himself in me. This second type is totally unpredictable, and it feels like abuse to me. It may represent his experience of having felt left empty, as if his Mum had taken him away from himself when she abandoned him because of her illness. This second type is so unbearable that at times I imagine that I could give up, this case being too difficult for me. I fear I will die if I go on, a martyr to psychotherapy.

A new game begins. He finds in the clinic where the analysis takes place, a toy called crazy marbles. It is made of different tubes, which, once put together in different ways, allow the marbles to roll through. It has to be built vertically, has 'feet' on which the tubes are fixed and 12 different 'diversions' to allow different tubes to communicate with others built on another foot. Session after session, he builds and rebuilds the toy in different shapes. I interpret the marble as food going through his body and coming out as poo, or as a thought or a feeling. One day, he builds the tubes into a human being, with two heads and two exits, but only one body, a symbol of our relationship as I suggest. He listens to that. A few weeks later, it has two entries and two exits, two separate bodies in one structure. Two balls run in two different directions. As I say so, he stands up, kicks and destroys it and then harms himself by banging his hands on the wall. I understand this as a desperate wanting and not wanting to come to terms with separation and differentiation from another.

The situation in the school is getting out of control. Casper is bullied and refuses to go now for fear of having to confront other children. One day, he comes to the session in a state of total anxiety. He runs out of the room and breaks the fire alarm. He keeps exclaiming, 'Anxious, anxious!' When the firemen arrive, he is told off. He was asking for help, but the fire brigade made him even more anxious. Once in the room, he says, 'It was a joke' and denies having called the fire brigade, denies that the firemen arrived.

'It was a joke'.

'No, Casper, it was real'.

'Are you having sex with me?' is Casper's answer to my thinking. He seems to have become psychotic. There is no difference between real and imaginary, between sex and thinking. After this episode, he starts doing crazy things, like licking the whole desk with his tongue and saying he is making sex with himself by putting his penis into his bottom. I interpret, 'Children are doing crazy things to Casper, but Casper doesn't want to see that they are bad to him. He wants to see them as good, and this is twisting the truth'.

Casper kisses me in a very innocent way, recovering from a borderline state because he was able to find the truth in my words. For the first time, Casper's father becomes active in his child's education and takes him out of school. A few weeks later, he decides to move to another borough. The father wants to give his son a better chance by enrolling him in a better school.

The holiday is approaching again, and Casper now regresses to playing a baby who wants milk and nappy changes. Out of the blue, he starts harming himself and then looks at me and says, 'Come on, stop me!' I become identified with a good mother and he allows me to meet his needs. The difference between poos, penis and breast is established.

'I am moving house. I am worried', he says shortly before the holiday.

'What worries you?'
'That I will not see you anymore', he says.
He can think about the holidays and the possible loss of the therapy.
'Take all the bad feelings away', he asks me, acknowledging the reason why we are meeting.
'If you move house, we will move the therapy close to the new house', I reassure him. From now on he starts calling me 'woman of feelings'. Some differentiation between a breast me and a thinking me is also possible.

In one of the last sessions before the break, he takes the play dough again, puts a Lego brick inside the play dough mass, makes a ball with it and throws the ball violently all over the room until the ball breaks and the brick comes out. I understand this brick as his violence, kept hidden inside. Now the violence has come out, raw, without a container. Will we be able to transform it? The experience of being a disgusting baby in his mother's eyes has been a real experience for us. Casper needed to know that I could survive it. He does not need to punish himself anymore for assuming the guilt of having destroyed his mother, who in reality is much better. She says her ME has been healed.

Conclusions

There is strong evidence that Kaspar spent the first years of his life in a free, healthy and loving milieu, and only much later was imprisoned as a way to protect him from sure death.

Kaspar Hauser was probably imprisoned when he was a very young child, after having lived a happy life in a wealthy and caring environment. He must have known a language and elementary rules of personal hygiene. The person who imprisoned him (a servant? his doctor?) must have been moved by the desire to protect his life from intrigues and conspiracy. Once freed, the rapid development of Kaspar's mental faculties was almost pathological. Two years after he regained his freedom, Kaspar does not stand out as an odd creature. Everybody who meets him finds himself confronted with an intelligent, cultivated, well-mannered young man, strangely innocent and melancholic. His lost infancy seems to follow him like a frightening ghost. The awareness of his unhappy destiny seems to have devastated his soul.

According to the Bavarian penalty code, the following crimes have been committed against him: (a) unlawful imprisonment, (b) abandonment and, if our codex would contemplate it, (c) crime against the soul, with Kaspar having been deprived of his freedom and of the destiny of his soul.

Casper did not have the good fortune to grow up with a mother who was in tune with him, responding in a meaningful way to his affects and emotions. His ego could not develop out of his self. He did not have the opportunity to introject a capacity for understanding. Rather he developed its contrary, a misunderstanding filter that defended him against the terror of being alone in a hostile world. This 'filter' (his body?), protected him from differentiation, separation, clarity and order. From early on, he was left having to rely on a 'do-it-yourself' way of coping.

Analysis has been a terribly intense experience for him, a turning point of 180 degrees. For everything had to be 'reversed'. From looking at the world from his bottom, he had to learn to look at it from his mind. Casper needed to trust a good holding other, an analyst on whom he had to become dependent. From there thinking could begin to develop.

Kaspar Hauser's imprisonment arrested his already well-established basic development. Once freed, he seemed to have been able to build upon an already well-functioning psyche. Once he had adjusted to his new environment, he fell into a severe depression. Apart from condemning his jailers, nobody was able to help him to cope with his destiny, as it was felt to be an unbearable crime.

My patient, Casper, was imprisoned in an undifferentiated way of functioning. He could not develop in reality. The low IQ, the incontinence, the poor sense of balance and the incapacity to relate were the major symptoms of his mode of functioning. These symptoms have now disappeared. He seems to have discovered that he has a mind and can start thinking about himself and the world around him. Analysis has freed him from his cage, which was created by neglect. Will he ever recover fully from his imprisonment? Analysts have little in common with lawyers. Although they, too, are preoccupied with understanding and reparation, their work focuses on the question of internal resources, development and making sense of one's life. These questions in themselves though remain mysterious.

Postscript

This material refers to the first 18 months of four-times-a-week analysis. Since then a lot has happened, and four years have passed. His analysis finished a year ago. Casper, now 15 years old, lives with his family in another borough and goes to a boarding school for adolescents with special needs. He has settled down in the boarding school where he is experiencing positive feedback, especially in computers and cooking. He has been able to make some friends, and thanks to the intelligent support of the teachers, he has been made into the key boy, the person in charge of showing the school to newcomers. He is very affectionate with his parents, who are coping much better with their own lives. When Casper comes back from school, he cooks for them, and his cooking seems to be excellent.

Note

1 First published in *Journal of Analytical Psychology*, 52, 5, October 2007.

Reference

Feuerbach, A. von (1835). *Kaspar Hauser. Beispiel eines Verbrechens am Seelenleben des Menschen*. Nuremberg: Selbstverlag (later, Klett 1963).

Chapter 2

Power cut in the countertransference[1]

Introduction

Fordham (1995, p. 71) considered deintegration to be the dynamic which makes it possible for the self to grow and unfold, and for consciousness to arise. When a new adaptation is required, the self responds by deintegrating. Deintegration refers to the energy going outwards towards objects and reintegration to the energy returning to the self after the experience (Astor 1995, p. 50). A deintegrate is 'a readiness for experience, a readiness to perceive and act' (ibid., p. 228), and is followed by assimilation and integration of the new experience into the self with its good and bad aspects, provided a suitable environment is available. If this is not the case, the deintegrate cannot be assimilated; it remains split off and distorted (Fordham 1985).

In this chapter, I describe and discuss what happens when the split-off experience is not reintegrated but actively defended against. When failures in the deintegrative process (the meeting of internal and external forces) repeatedly occur in early infancy, the infant's readiness for adaptation to experience remains unmet. If the environmental mother is absent or not in tune with the infant, the infant has to deal alone with violent affects coming from within which accompany the meeting of the new situation, what Bion (1962) calls 'nameless dread' and Bick (1968) 'catastrophic anxiety'. In these cases, the experience becomes persecutory; its integration threatens violation of the self (Fordham 1995), and the infant resorts to what Fordham (1985) calls 'defence of the self', the more or less violent attempt to deny the experience again and again and the violent emotions arising from it. One may think of the infant resorting to all types of manoeuvre to keep split off an experience which would, in itself, contain enough energy to come back into the self for reintegration, but is perceived as annihilating the self. The attempt here is to describe and discuss how to understand and work with a specific and powerful defence of the self, that I call 'power cut'. From the infant's point of view, it might be helpful to think of these early failures of containment and lack of adequate responses by the caregiver as meetings with an object perceived as stripping away the baby's contents in an evil way. A possible identification with this object may then occur so that every new experience is violently pushed away by the subject in

DOI: 10.4324/9781003268536-3

such a way that the object ends up feeling depleted of its contents. I will show how the analyst relating to patients resorting to this kind of defence feels incapable of thinking and feeling. Although rejection and failures are perpetrated, and growth becomes impossible, it is important to understand this defence as being on the side of life: destruction as the only way of being.

I will now present some extracts from a baby observation to show how a baby from the beginning of life outside the womb reacted by rejecting her mother and by denying the experience of the birth as if it had not happened. I will then show how the split-off experience of the birth could be recovered when the mother was able to separate from her infant's anxiety and violence. Although infant observations always contain a speculative aspect due to the observer's countertransference and fantasy, these observations can be of help in understanding how the 'power cut' as a defence can 'happen'. I will then present clinical material from my work with a young child and with an adult patient, modelling extracts from their analyses on the extracts from the baby observation. While there are other ways of theorizing infant experience from infant research, infant observations use the same kind of imaginative construction of the infant's experience from the combination of careful observation and the observer's countertransference that is used in clinical analytic work and can therefore be particularly valuable in guiding the analyst in their work. I hope to show not only how the 'power cut' defence manifests itself in childhood and adulthood but also the enormous demand that is made on the analyst's capacity to be able to understand and contain the vicissitudes of primitive anxieties and powerful destructive, unmetabolized, explosive affects in the patient. If the analyst (like the mother in the infant observation) is able to withstand the attacks, contain them and separate from them while retaining a capacity for thoughts, an early failure in deintegration can be overcome, and with it, integration of primitive and disturbing experience can begin.

Baby Claire: from hatred of the breasts to mourning the womb and loving the breasts

Baby Claire was born between 25 and 17 days prematurely. The birth happened very quickly, in two hours, much to the puzzlement of the mother, Claire being her first baby. From the very beginning, Baby Claire did not seem to want to feed but preferred to curl herself in a perfect semicircle oblivious to the world. When obliged to feed, she ended up chewing the nipples. Claire's Mum was very anxious; Claire was losing weight, and Claire's Dad had to be present at each feed to support his wife in her almost unmanageable task. The feeding took hours. Claire's Mum felt very uncomfortable about 'being seen' by the observer: her capacity to be a good mother for her baby was deeply undermined by the feeding difficulty.

This is a brief extract from the observation when Claire was seven days old: 'Dad said that Baby Claire had fed very little but was now tired. Baby Claire was settled down, nestled right in with her back bowed almost into a semicircle in the cot. Dad said: 'This is her favourite position'. It looked like a very foetal position. At one point, she tucked her head right down and appeared to be sucking her finger. When I asked, Dad said she often puts her whole hand inside her mouth. And added that in her pre-birth pictures, she was sucking her feet. She looked as if (and this is the observer's countertransference) she was communicating loudly: 'I want it to be just how it was before when I was safely in the womb'.

One week later, Baby Claire had lost more weight; Mother was upset and frustrated, and the anxiety had reached unmanageable levels, to the point that the family had gone twice to the hospital to seek help from the midwife. 'Dad started talking about the feeding and how Claire seemed now to prefer the left breast. . . . I was struck by her long limbs, her skin hanging off, her head nestled in between Mum's breasts. She looked tiny, as if she wanted to disappear. She gradually went to sleep and moved into the foetal position. I felt envious of her being able to be so oblivious of the world around (again the observer's countertransference). . . . Mum said she seemed to have needed quite a lot of reassurance about her mothering from professionals. . . . She then added that, in the last few days, Claire got into a habitual way of crying: 'She gets very red in the face, with an ear-splitting yell and nothing will make her ok until she seems to forget whatever it is and falls asleep''.

In the following week, the situation had not changed. 'Dad is holding the baby, and Mum is upstairs. Daddy is very upset and tells me that his wife's nipples are all chewed up by Claire. His wife wants to keep breastfeeding and each feeding takes hours: Baby Claire keeps falling asleep in her foetal position. . . . At the end of the observation, Mum comes downstairs, goes close to the baby and says with a loving but firm voice, 'You are going to get your act together or they are going to be putting you on a drip''. The observer was surprised by mother's firmness and reaction.

The following week: 'Claire's face looks fuller. She is now seven pounds. Both parents are happy, and the atmosphere in the house has changed. After the feed, Claire seemed very content. She yawned a few times but wasn't sleepy as she apparently is after a feed. She looked around and seemed quite absorbed in the sensations going on in her digestive system. For the first time, I saw her face: how lovely!'

Discussion

Baby Claire was born prematurely and very quickly, without having had the time to come to terms with the total change that her birth was bringing about. She was not able to open up to the new environment and reintegrate her birth, probably because the birth had been too traumatic for her; she seemed to have remained in the womb, as if the birth had not taken place, at least this is the observer's fantasy. Claire began to misuse the breasts, biting them as if she had lost her capacity to suck properly. She was losing weight and was behaving as if she wanted to defend against life outside the womb. Her mother felt rejected by her newborn baby's behaviour and was initially not able to receive her baby's anxiety because of her own preoccupation with being a good mother. Claire's attacks must have reinforced her mother's insecurity, making it impossible for her to disentangle herself from her baby's reaction. She could not receive her baby's anxiety and could not think about her baby who was born too early, not yet totally ready for the birth.

This might provide some insight on how power cut as a defence begins to operate. Mum's trust in herself was first seriously undermined as she perceived herself as not good enough once her daughter was born. The countertransference response of the observer seemed to mirror something of this: the observer felt envy for this baby who seemed to be so happy in the 'imaginary' womb. She evoked envy, although her state (close to death) was far from being enviable. Despite the temptation to give up, Mum kept trying to meet her baby's needs by offering the chewed breasts and cuddling her when she was in the foetal position. Claire slowly began to acknowledge the change. Perhaps her repeated cry, every day at the same time for a few days, was a sort of mourning of the womb, the realization that a major change had taken place, could not be avoided but had to be accepted. It was only when Mum found the strength to disentangle herself, to separate her own anxiety and fears of not being a good enough mother ('Get your act together!' seems to represent this) that her baby opened up to the world outside, discovering not only how to suck properly but also becoming aware of the noises of her digestive system. Then the observer could see her face: finally, Claire was born, willing to relate to her mother and to herself.

Theoretical implication

The baby was able to recover from the reality of the birth, and from the loss of the womb (a place of safety), only when her mother was able to mother her by offering the breasts, by giving her child enough time to adjust to the change and finally by performing the 'paternal function' (Williams 2004) for her baby by setting a limit to the child's dislike of the change, acknowledging the baby's responsibility to open up to reality. By doing so, she was becoming aware of having a lot of goodness to offer to this baby. By using the mother's breasts as a container for her experiences, the infant first attacked them to express her hatred of the change; later, by feeding only from one, she seemed to be able to begin to find a way of expressing that she was becoming aware of a more complex range of experiences, good and bad ones, outside the womb. This might have allowed the baby to slowly recover from the loss of the womb and mourn it and begin to discover some pleasure in her new status, outside. The split-off experience of the birth could be reintegrated when the infant could bring together the experience in the womb and at the breast in relation to the same person, her mother: at first, they seemed to represent in her mind two unrelated states. Baby Claire gave up being in identification with the womb which was felt to have violently rejected her: similarly, she rejected the breasts and her new status as a newborn. This shift in the baby's attitude was possible only when her mother stopped feeling rejected by her infant's attacks on the breast and started to believe in her capacity to be a good enough mother.

I will now move on to some clinical material. I hope that the extracts of the baby observation will help to clarify where the patients I am going to present are in relation to the finally new born Claire.

Similarities

Both patients were born to mothers who were successful in their careers and left their babies very early and for long periods in order to go back to work. Both mothers projected their own value onto their capacity to be good at their jobs, without being in touch with their baby's emotional needs. Although the mothers came from very different backgrounds, culturally, economically and ethnically, each asked their child from very early on to adjust to a cultural model they had in mind as acceptable for their child: one was left with relatives, the other with a childminder. In reality, both were asking the child to be emotionally self-contained and in no need of them.

First patient: attack the 'breasts' before they attack you!

Bianca was 4½ when she started treatment with me. She was born with a genetic disease which had made both parents terribly anxious about their own performance. The disease was under control, although it needed constant monitoring. Always dressed like a boy, it was difficult to know anything about her. What was her character? She gave me the impression of holding herself together by nerves.

Being with Bianca

Being with Bianca was like being with a tornado. I saw her in a private institution as an intensive patient. During the first months of treatment, each session would begin on the staircase: Bianca would run upstairs, throwing the display leaflets onto the floor, her mouth wide open in a grimace, her body all tense. She then paused to throw her blanket down the stairs and, while her mother was saying softly, 'Be a good girl, Bianca', she would run into the kitchen, throw all the napkins on the floor, steal sugar, open the library door, scream loudly for interminable periods, hide in the waiting room and eventually run to the consulting room. By the time I arrived, she would already have trashed the room: drawers, pens, paper sheets and toys on the floor; she would be scribbling on the walls or on the desk with an urgency that left me puzzled. Her wish to destroy was total, real, a matter of life and death. She would then say, 'Hi Alessandra!' with a big grimace, then 'sorry', casually, as if she had pushed me inadvertently on the bus. Before I was able to collect my thoughts, to know how and what I was feeling, she would take the scissors, cut some paper and with it if I was not careful my skirt, or my socks. 'Don't worry', she would say, 'it's nothing', or 'Let me repair it for you', and she would Sellotape the cuts, patting my shoulder or face: 'You see, it's ok'. She would then climb on the desk, open the window, throw pens and paper out, run to the loo, lock herself in it and come out, ten minutes later, leaving the water running, toilet paper everywhere. Back in the room she would take a pen, scribble on the desk, destroy all the soft plastic animals, tearing them apart, cutting them, biting them, throwing the wooden bricks at me or on the floor, run out of the room into the waiting room and so forth until the end of session, which seemed to come terribly quickly, as if it had lasted only a few minutes. Her method was destroy everything; do not leave anything out, including my hair, my face, my body. Her attacks were instantaneous and totally unpredictable. To say that I was left unable to think is an understatement. I was cut out, in the dark, unable even to know what was going on. For me to say something only fuelled her destructive greed. What caused the disturbance seemed to be the very fact that I was trying to relate to her. The rapidity and power of her behaviour was so intense that I did not feel anything. No hate, no anger. I was simply made incapable of thinking, feeling, reacting. After the sessions, an intense feeling of surprise, puzzlement pervaded me. It was as if she had total control of me, and of my capacity to stay in a relationship with myself.

Several months later, having learnt in myself that the only way to recover from her attacks was to keep a certain internal distance from her manoeuvres, I tried something out. In the middle of one of her destructive assaults, I said, 'You have lovely hair', hoping to make contact with her in a positive way. It made no difference. She was not listening to what I was saying; it was the very fact that I was saying something that she wanted to destroy.

Discussion

Bianca resorts to destruction in order not to feel destroyed by powerful affects and emotions which, coming from within, might feel like destroying her when she relates to another. So she attacks any attempt at relationship first. Her behaviour could also reflect the phantasy that she is destroying boundaries. If not contained, she could at least violently control and annihilate another, and therefore she would not feel separate, which in her mind equals rejection.

In this first period of work with her, I used to feel annihilated, but I would become aware of it only in retrospect. While it was happening, I could not feel, could not think, I was not. It was only afterwards, when I had regained the awareness of my being, that I was I again. This experience was so powerful that it is best described as a power cut; it is dark before one feels the surprise and with it the awareness of what happened.

We can speculate that, in the presence of another, Bianca felt so violently unwanted that she sought to create a state in which there is no distance, no space and where she would not feel attacked by powerful disturbing emotions. With her destructive manoeuvre, she manages to empty another of their emotions, cutting off the relationship this other has with their mind. We can see how Bianca identifies with an object which does not want to know and understand, and by attacking beforehand the relationship, she leaves the other unable to know and understand. This is similar to what Rosenfeld (1987) calls 'destructive narcissism' and Bion (1962) 'attacks on linking'. A theoretical discussion is beyond the scope of this chapter; nevertheless, it is important to stress here that while both authors come to understand destructiveness as an omnipotent defence against envy projected onto an object perceived as uncontrollably overpowering, I understand it as the result of a real experience of internal and external violent disruption and violation of the self's integrity which could not be mediated and is therefore defended against because it threatens the self's survival.

Some developments: can a 'good breast' and a 'bad breast' coexist? Only after a year and a half, when I had become able to watch her making a mess of things and feel rather 'bored' by her activity, could she collapse and stop her mania. Finally, she discovered the couch, on which she could rest and regress into a little baby who wanted me at her side, feeding her and singing songs to her. Bianca was rediscovering moments of a good relationship with her mother in which she was loved. These sessions were wonderful, touching, a real love experience for us. For some time in every session, she would lie on the couch and ask me to tell her a story. First, I used to tell her her own story. Now she could hear what I had to say about her as a baby, her love for her Mum, her Mum having gone to work and left her very early, her fear of having been thrown away by her Mum, her disease, her difference, her orthopaedic shoes. But because she could not hear about her desire to destroy her Mum, and the distance between her and her Mum, or me in the transference, I introduced a fictional 'my cat' and started telling her interesting stories about my cat which she seemed to identify with. Two years into her analysis, after the Christmas break, Bianca came in and asked, 'How is your cat?' Then added, 'I will kill you, so your cat will be sad'! She then went on, 'I will cut your pimples', explaining to me that pimples were 'the little things on your boobies'. She then threw her toy box on the floor, stamping on it and saying, 'Sorry'. I replied that she was not sorry but was showing me how much she hated me for having left her during the break. The next session, she destroyed her toy box saying, 'I am sorry. I liked your box'. I said that she had destroyed the box because it was beautiful and full of interesting things, all things she couldn't possess but had to leave in the room at the end of the session, at breaks, like me and what is inside me. To this she answered, 'I was a seed. Were you a seed too?' 'Yes', I said, 'I was a seed too. My Daddy put me into my Mum's tummy, like your Daddy put you into your Mum's tummy when you were a seed'. In seconds she had trashed the room. I said that she was thinking about the possibility of making my tummy into a shabby place so that no Daddy would ever want to put a seed into it. Then my tummy room would be only for her. To that she became furious, prey to the destructive mania.

Some sessions later she asked, 'Do you love me?' 'What do you think?' I answered. 'No, you do not love me because I am nasty'. I answered, 'Yes, sometimes Bianca is nasty, but she needs a lot of love because if she is not loved she becomes nastier and nastier'. This explanation seemed to be right.

She kissed me and then sat down and drew a Valentine's card for me calmly. The room was filled with love and peace. 'Do you like this silence?' she asked, enjoying it. A few minutes later, it was the end of the session, and out of the blue, she pulled my hair and kicked me with her heavy shoes. Recovering from the shock, I said, 'Now it is the end of the session, and Bianca is afraid that Alessandra doesn't love her any longer, so she also stops loving her'. Another power cut.

Discussion

For more than a year, Bianca showed me that badness was the only reality. It was only when I could disentangle myself from her manoeuvres that a big shift in our work became possible. Bianca was able to recapture with me moments where she felt loved. She became beautiful; all her best qualities were discovered in our work. I am loved because she is loved. She does not need to destroy me/herself any longer because there is something good in me that she recognizes in herself, and this is beautiful and nourishing. But the moment I cannot sustain the present goodness, when I leave her and she becomes aware that my goodness is not only for her, that she has to share it with others, everything becomes bad. If I am not totally good, I must be totally bad. Rage at my imperfection destroys her totally, and it seems that no love survives. I become the person who doesn't care about her at all. Why should she care about me? Then all the good feeling in me or in her is lost. I become all bad, and she feels I am identical to her. The imperfection spoils the beauty of our relationship which cannot be tolerated because of its complexity. Rejecting me gives her the illusion that we are identical, and this restores the illusion of oneness that is broken by separations.

Her incapacity to hold onto the good me and good her in moments of distress makes me doubt the possibility of transforming her identification with an object which keeps stripping away meaning, despite my capacity to bear her attacks and to give meaning to her emotions.

Three years later

Bianca is now 7½. She is a beautiful girl, with long blond hair, a captivating laugh and a good sense of humour. She is doing well in school, has friends and is active. She wears heavy orthopaedic shoes and seems to inhabit her body with a certain degree of acceptance. But the work is not yet complete. 'Out of the blue', her parents complain, she switches mode, and from a lovely child, she becomes an awful girl. These 'turns' last a few days and disappear as suddenly as they have come. I understand them as the remains of her destructiveness, something that analysis had not yet transformed. Let us see what they look like in the session:

Today she asks me to help her to split the toys into two groups, the good and the bad ones; then she wants to put all the toys together again and creates a play for me, about a 'bad girls' school'. Only very nasty girls go to this school, and once there, one is a bad girl forever. She shows me how they behave. They enjoy terribly being nasty: pulling hair, putting their fingers in their noses, touching their vaginas, calling names, etc. She shows me how much they enjoy being bad, and she stresses that they are confined there forever. For a moment, I feel totally helpless. She is right; there is nothing one can do but keep them locked up there, how terrible! In myself I understand this thought as my countertransference response to her incapacity to deal with her destructiveness: enjoying it makes her feel she does not need to take any responsibility for it.

Two months later, two sessions before the Christmas break, we have a lovely session in which we enjoy being together. Three minutes before the end, she is helping me to put all her toys in the box, and suddenly she smears a handful of play dough on the carpet, saying in a caring voice, 'Have you seen the film Flushed Away?' and then adds full of contempt, 'It is nice that you entertain me'. Again I am completely taken aback: another of her famous power cuts. It takes me a moment to recover, and I say, 'When you are afraid that I do not care for you, you want to destroy the beautiful room, the beautiful session, and me. Everything becomes bad, including you. But I wonder, is there something we can do to save the beautiful room, the beautiful me and the beautiful you? Or does it have to stay nasty forever if we cannot be together forever? What shall we do now?' I add, crossing my arms and waiting for her response. She rushes to the loo, comes back with soap and paper, and we manage to clean the carpet. I feel rather enthusiastic about hope. The carpet can be cleaned, on a very concrete level, to start with. She says with real empathy, 'It's nice when friends work together'.

Discussion

In these sessions, Bianca seems to be thinking about the possibility of seeing good and bad aspects of the same object and of herself as belonging together. This thought has a major impact on her. I now understand Bianca's withdrawal into badness as a defence against separation, depressive feelings, love and reality. The power of her defence made her believe that nastiness is enjoyable and that goodness does not exist; therefore, it does not need to be sought, cherished and protected. She seemed to be trapped in an early experience which became perhaps a phantasy according to which goodness was stripped away from her and that she was left only with badness, from which she could not recover. Like Baby Claire, Bianca now seems to begin to know that good and bad belong to the same experience. She needs to take responsibility for her actions and mourn the loss of a perfect good object that will never leave her. I, like Claire's observer, hope to see her 'rebirth' soon.

Second patient: refusing the breasts in the hope of finding better ones

Bruna, a beautiful African woman, was 30 when she started a four-times-a-week analysis with me. She had made a suicidal attempt in her twenties, and while dangerously promiscuous and alcohol addicted for some years, she started a relationship with a solid man with whom she had a baby. The responsibility for a new life, born from her, made her seek help. She had never achieved anything in life and was convinced that nobody wanted her to progress. She saw the outside world as responsible for all her failures, including her suicide attempt. In her phantasy, all the badness was outside, and the goodness was seriously under attack by the virulence of the badness. Whenever she tried to defend herself from the attacks of the outside world, she felt the world was retaliating, threatening her life. She was trapped in this phantasy. We can see how this defence in an adult patient becomes more sophisticated, more difficult to contain and more dangerous.

Being with Bruna

During the first four months of analysis, my patient didn't use the couch. She sat in front of me, looking at me incessantly, controlling every single movement I made. I felt as if I were dazzled; it was very difficult to think while she was trying to destroy me. She would comment on my shoes, my clothes, my haircut, the way I looked, teasing me for wearing the same pair of shoes every day, wanting to know my age, everything about my private life. She knew I was a trainee at the time, and she complained that I was not experienced enough; I was a second-rate therapist for her, a black patient. She referred to me as a table, a piece of furniture, a wall, a painting, a statue, a doll, a ballerina, not available, a jolly Italian, girlish, a me who was using her for the purpose of finishing my training. I was an Italian Fascist therapist, stupid, I was a racist and my 'mission' was to humiliate her.

The sessions were very noisy, a total experience: my patient used to jump from one topic to the next. Her attacks were vicious, and it was extremely difficult to keep thinking in the sessions. It was only after the session that I could re-find myself and my thinking. She was attacking my capacity to make links in myself to what she was saying, as my way to show her my care for her was my capacity to understand her. I used to leave the room in a state of total confusion. During sessions, she would say one thing and immediately afterwards the opposite. She was crippling my thinking. And she said,

> 'You are a crippled child. How can you be my therapist if you are crippled?'
> One day she talked about her wish to destroy me.
> 'I'd like to do crazy things'.
> 'For example?'
> 'I am only inventing, passing from one story to the next. Everything is meaningless. When I was a child, I was afraid of the devil'. She cries. 'No,

I was not crying. I was inventing. But it is true, it is all true. I was inventing for you a way to understand'. She went to the loo, and when she came back, she laughed at me in a chilling way. 'You are not bright. You are simply stupid. You talk like a book. You are perfect. Inaccessible.'

'Like an absent mother who cannot bear the pain of her child'.

'No, you do not deserve my hate because you mean nothing to me. I want to destroy you'.

On many other occasions, she used to say, 'I enjoy attacking you', or 'I want to corrupt you'.

After these initial sessions, she began to look awful, uncared for, unwashed, wearing trainers, very untypical of her, as if she felt I was retaliating for her attacks, as she had experienced others in the past, her father, teachers, peers, all telling her off, driving her to suicide and then to drink.

Discussion

As I learnt to recover from the surprise and power of her attacks, Bruna was able to begin to reflect with me about her life, her fear of a relationship and chiefly about the way she was abusive to herself. She abused herself by two kinds of deprivation: first by enviously stripping away anything that could be given to her; secondly by punishing herself for wanting and allowing herself to know what she needed. This second deprivation seemed to come in the form of retaliation from outside. She was identified with an absent mother who was constantly stripping away whatever she was given and kept punishing her for wanting and needing anything. In our relationship, it was me who she first destroyed and then felt was coming back to her by telling her, 'How do you dare to wish anything from me? You do not deserve anything. I will destroy you'. Abuse felt safe, and perhaps she felt at one with me in those moments, identifying with the abuser.

Some developments: the discovery of the good and the bad breast I became gradually more able to stand her attacks. I addressed her wish to destroy me, her hatred of me and her envy not only of me but also of herself and the goodness in herself and in me. This enabled her to give up these defences in a dramatic way. She started a course and realized she was intelligent, talented and able to think. She also discovered that she had a lovely husband and a delightful daughter, things she did not cherish before. I was also becoming of invaluable importance to her. After three years of analysis, she returned from the Christmas break feeling very cross with me for having left her. She said, 'I did not miss you because I met Amalia, a wonderful singer and I fell in love with her'. The pain of having to come to terms with a me who was capable of caring for her and was imperfect felt unbearable to Bruna.

'Amalia was so nice to me. We spent hours talking together, and I felt she cares for me'. I said, 'It is difficult to hold onto a me who leaves and is somewhere else. It is easier to rubbish the me and the you who are attached to each other and pretend a break can efface it, making us strangers to each other'. She could not hear my interpretations and, prey to a sort of mania, she had already left me.

One month later, she met a famous psychoanalyst at a talk and subsequently asked to begin an analysis with him. The psychoanalyst agreed, and Bruna came to her next session saying that she was going to have analysis with a famous psychoanalyst. It was all sorted.

This news came as a 'power cut' and left me unable to react, with a splitting headache for one whole day. Before I was able to find a way of understanding what was going on, Bruna had already 'split', with me as 'the bad breast' (unpleasurable experience) and the famous analyst as 'the good breast'. She wanted to be with 'the good breast' all the time. She did not want to think about the emotional impact of her manoeuvre, but, already in love with her new analyst, she started to spend her sessions with me talking about him, like an excited and cruel wife telling her husband how wonderful her lover is. When I recovered from my headache and the surprise of her behaviour, I was able to say to her that she was behaving like a child who had lost all hope with her mother. I added that the only alternative to accepting me and my imperfection, my holiday, was to become adhesive to the new analyst and have verbal sex with him. If she left, she would miss the opportunity to work through with me what she could not work through with her mother: the imperfection of a mother who had loved her but also abandoned her very early for her work, as she felt I had done with my holiday. Bruna did not want to hear any of this but continued using her sessions to praise the new analyst, using her love for him to make me feel humiliated. I kept interpreting:

> 'Why don't you want to try to find out the meaning, what makes you run away from me?'
> 'The fact that you are inadequate'.
> 'Or the fact that you cannot be grateful to me for all the improvement you have made here? Fewer attacks on thinking, for example'.
> 'I am grateful to a certain extent'.
> 'Which is?'
> 'That I love you only to a certain extent, but this is all'.
> 'So, why are you running away from loving me?'
> Long silence . . . 'because if I had to love you, I had to love myself as well, and I don't want to love myself . . .'
> 'And don't you think you will face the same problem with your next analyst?' She did not answer.
> A few sessions before her departure she asked, 'If the new analyst does not understand me, can I come back to you?'
> 'You have used the new analyst as an insurance policy with me. You did not want to feel anger and pain at my independence but preferred to leave me, convincing yourself of my inadequacy. Now, just before going away from me, you would like to sign another insurance policy with me. And what if the new analyst is also inadequate? At least you hope to have me, but this is

not possible. You have to leave me without an insurance policy. If you do not want to work out with me what you need to work out, you hope you will do it with the new analyst'.

In one of the last sessions, she told me that the husband of a friend had died of cancer. The doctor did not recognize it.

'I wonder if you are also telling me that the doctor me is not seeing something terrible and is letting you leave with it'.

'What do you mean? The famous psychoanalyst?'

'Yes, the madness of going to see him'.

'Yes, I know a bit, it is madness. I had a perfect dream last night. I discovered a pool, cold and deep'.

'Tell me, why was the dream perfect?'

'Because the dream is about the famous psychoanalyst. He is deep and cold, but he will help me to understand my feelings. . . . I am sure I will miss you, but I need another therapist in order to miss you'.

'Are you telling me that you are running away from the opportunity to learn with me how to mourn and accept loss?'

'Is analysis about learning to mourn? [Silence.] 'Yes, I need time to do that, it is too early for me now'.

Discussion

Bruna was not able to accept the good and the bad belonging to me and to her as intrinsic parts of us but preferred to keep them far apart, maintaining the experience of good and bad split into two different persons. By running away from me she was running away from her fury, her wish to destroy the good me and all the good she had achieved in herself. The good would be preserved only if she had a perfect mother analyst who would never upset her. She had the phantasy that goodness could be sustained only in such an ideal circumstance. Bruna had identified me with her defence against the pain of dependency. She was trying to deny the imperfection and limitation of love and care, and by running away from me, she had hoped to obliterate the pain of having to deal with these realities.

Fortunately, before leaving me, in glimpses of sanity, she could see that the good and bad aspects of me and of herself belong together. Hopefully, she will be able to work through with the new analyst what she could not do with me and come to terms with the good and bad aspects of herself and of another, stopping herself from destroying understanding and meaning and beginning to want to know about herself and another and their relationship.

Conclusion: implication for technique

I hope to have been able to show how a failure in the early deintegrative process can seriously impair development and how the split-off part needs to be addressed and worked through until it can be converted into a deintegrate or an experience which can be lived through and possibly integrated. For Baby Claire, Bianca and Bruna, an early maternal failure obstructed the path to normal development: a too quick a birth and a very anxious mother for Claire and a too absent mother for Bianca and Bruna. Because they were not received and contained by their absent mothers, they came to believe that the only way to survive was to become identified with a rejecting object. By constantly attacking and therefore losing their relationships with another and with themselves, and by performing what I have called a 'power cut', they resorted to the phantasy of being at one with a rejecting object, protected from abandonment first and from the resulting feelings of anxiety and pain. By resorting to this type of defence, they were defending against a primitive experience which must have felt to be a violation of their existence at an early stage of life. I hope to have been able to show how this defence can be modified if the analyst is willing to receive and at the same time separate from the bomb-like affects the patient sends.

Their purpose is not only to show to the analyst how the patient feels whenever he attempts at relating but also to perpetrate (for survival purposes) a status quo: the sabotage of meaningful communication between himself, another and their (mutual) internal worlds. These patients hope to survive the loss of their external object by identifying with it and by perpetuating the loss.

By taking the infant observation as a template, I hope to have been able to show that integration is possible when the experience stops being perceived globally but can be broken down into its many aspects and facets, including a wide range of emotions connected with it. The self is capable of containing opposite poles of an experience and ordering them (Fordham 1985, pp. 56–60) into their good and bad aspects. The closer they are in the conscious psyche, the smaller will be their antagonistic opposition in the unconscious (Jung 1957, para. 75). The work with these patients aims at reaching a deep emotional understanding of a primitive traumatic experience which is constantly pushed away from consciousness because it is too indigestible.

Analogous to the mother of the infant observation, the analyst working with patients presenting this type of defence can survive their attacks only if he is able to reach a position of simplicity and modesty contrary to masochism or sadism. Holding tightly on to his attributes, but aware of his limitations, this analyst might be able to look at the patients' manoeuvres as desperate attempts to convince themselves and the analyst that destruction is the only possible way of existence.

T.S. Eliot (1944) describes in *Four Quartets* a space which he calls 'suspended in time' as a new 'internal space' of its own making, existing in a time that never existed, reconciling and unifying sets of opposites. Perhaps the analyst's internal attitude could find some inspiration here, aiming at reaching a state of mind in which the patient's present experience can be held in mind and linked with the patient's past, its good and bad aspects and the resulting violent feelings. Kradin (2007, p. 10), quoting Jung, speaks of a position of 'mindful attention' similar to what Buddhists call 'meditation' (vipassana). According to Kradin, when the analyst is able to observe the manoeuvres of the patient, allowing the material to unfold, and without wanting to know beforehand, the patient feels that the analyst is truly interested in getting to know him and gradually stops projecting onto the analyst his unresolved complex (ibid., p. 10). It requires a great deal of resilience and trust from the analyst who, constantly attacked, may feel propelled to join in the destructive manoeuvres of the patient. The analyst needs to be able to maintain an analytical attitude and a separate mind from which to assess his and the patient's limitations. It is indeed a rewarding experience for both parties when new insights and changes are brought about.

Note

1 First published in *Journal of Analytical Psychology*, 55, 4, September 2010.

References

Astor, J. (1995). *Michael Fordham: Innovations in Analytical Psychology*. London and New York: Routledge.

Bick, E. (1968). 'The experience of the skin in early object-relations'. *International Journal of Psycho-Analysis*, 45, 558–66.

Bion, W. (1962). 'A theory of thinking'. *International Journal of Psycho-Analysis*, 43, 306–10.

Eliot, T.S. (1944). *Four Quartets*. London: Faber and Faber, 2001.

Fordham, M. (1985). *Exploration into the Self*. London: The Analytical Press.

———. (1995). *Freud, Jung, Klein and the Fenceless Field*. London and New York: Routledge.

Jung, C.G. (1957). 'Two essays on analytical psychology'. *CW* 7.

Kradin, R. (2007). 'Minding the gaps: the role of informational encapsulation and mindful attention in the analysis of transference'. *The Journal of Jungian Theory and Practice*, 9, 2, 1–13.

Rosenfeld, H. (1987). *Impasse and Interpretation. Therapeutic and Anti-therapeutic Factors in the Psychoanalytic Treatment of Psychotic, Borderline and Neurotic Patients*. London and New York: Tavistock.

Williams, G. (ed) (2004). *Exploring Feeding Difficulties in Children. The Generosity of Acceptance*. Vol. 1. London and New York: Karnac Books.

Chapter 3

On receiving what has gone astray, on finding what has got lost[1]

Introduction

Intra-psychic trauma resulting from external trauma or from constitutional psychic fragility is currently understood as unintegrated, unbearably painful emotions (Urban 2003). The experience of being overwhelmed by conscious and unconscious events leads to misperception of reality (Urban 2003) of another and of oneself. The question of the most adequate technique with patients who suffer from intra-psychic trauma is paramount. The analyst is compelled to engage with the patient in an experiment which is designed within the analytic frame to throw light on intra-psychic 'events' which are not conscious and cannot be described verbally (Mancia 2007, p. 60) although their 'shadow' is present and represents a double bind: the only way the patient is able to express the traumatic event, as well as the pathology of the patient.

In this chapter, I discuss what is required from the analytic relationship in terms of the capacity of two minds, the analyst's and the patient's, to be in tune if access to this unbearable event is to be found and how the analyst makes use of his own mind in order to think what is unthinkable for the patient. The concepts of deintegration, primitive identity and the mechanism of projective identification will be briefly discussed as useful theoretical containers for the mental operations happening in the patient and in the analyst, while clinical material from the analysis of a child patient will be presented to support the theoretical introduction.

Different authors who conduct infant observation seminars (Proner 2000; Urban 2006) describe how newborns and their mothers work hard at attuning with one another, so as to create a state of synchronous response, which creates the illusion of oneness that brings mother and baby together in an orchestrated attunement (Proner 2000). This instinctual synchrony acts as a catalyst for the mother's capacity to be fully aware of her infant's existence outside the womb and to be fully attentive to his external and internal movements, 'matching' them (Urban 1998) with an appropriate response. This process is the prerequisite for the mother's mind to perform what Bion (1962b) calls 'reverie': the ordinary capacity to listen, contain, make links and understand emotional states. For the infant, this experience might incarnate the archetypal expectation of finding another outside

DOI: 10.4324/9781003268536-4

the womb who can understand him. Esther Bick (1968) calls the formation of this awareness in the infant 'skin', attributing to the physical skin that contains the body a mental (izing) capacity (Proner 2000). Elizabeth Urban has shown (1998) how hard babies work in order to bring their mothers to this level of attunement, postulating that although their intrinsic basic knowledge of differentiation and otherness is already there at birth, without this attunement, they cannot unfold: babies need their mother's capacity to understand them in order to develop their own capacity to understand themselves.

Urban's observations draw upon Fordham's model of the self. According to Fordham, the ego develops out of the psychosomatic unity of the infant that he describes as the original or primary self (Astor 1995, p. 237).

Development occurs via the functioning of deintegration and reintegration which are spontaneous activities of the self. The self deintegrates (opens up, is ready to relate) in order to gather objective data about the world and the infant himself. Once the data has been collected, it needs to be related back to the self, but if it appears irreconcilable, it remains as an unintegrated deintegrate (Fordham 1985), an experience that cannot be related to the self.

Such a deintegrate is a container of bodily mental contents that appear inimical to the self. Fordham thought that, although the potential capacity of the self to integrate collected data is inborn, because of its complexity, the availability of the mother's help is paramount. Her own capacity to be attuned to her infant is required to metabolize the infant's various experiences, thereby facilitating the integrative process.

Although Fordham emphasized that the infant is primarily separate from his mother, he nevertheless felt that 'mutual identity between mother and infant may help an understanding of the state of close intimacy between the couple' (1985, p. 43), thus facilitating the most primitive capacity of two people to get in tune with each other's states of mind. Identity between mother and infant is necessary before more complex forms of communication can become operative.

Primitive identity fosters the illusion of oneness between infant and mother, which is broken by the emergence of bodily and sensory emotions (Carignani & Romano 2006; Ogden 2009): if the mother responds appropriately to her infant's emerging emotions in time, her understanding will work as a binding element, 'a thinking skin', and through maturation and good mothering, the infant will gradually recognize the difference between self and not self (Astor 1995, p. 152), internal and external. If this is not the case, the infant will not be able to integrate new experiences in a meaningful way. When a deintegrate has not been assimilated into the self, there will be no 'thinking skin' to contain such an experience. The experience cannot be understood and remains unintegrated, creating a state of confusion between subject and object (Fordham 1985, p. 152). In this situation, the emerging bodily and sensory event will remain unknown, while the infant will unconsciously employ all sorts of manoeuvres to get rid of the disturbing events that constitute what Bion calls 'beta elements' (Bion 1962a). According to Fordham, the mechanism of projective identification will be prominent (Fordham 1985, p. 152) in these cases as the mechanism of evacuating beta elements.

A review of the historical genesis of the mechanism of projective identification (Regazzoni Goretti 2007) is beyond the scope of this chapter. I will, however, briefly refer to Ogden's understanding of this concept as the mechanism by which a person is able to experience himself in accord with the mental state of another person by means of the real interpersonal pressures that accompany somebody else's unconscious communications (Ogden 2009). Revisiting Klein and Bion, Ogden (2009, Chapter 6) understands the mechanism of projective identification as the forceful unconscious communication of one person who manages to bring another to feel or think in accord with one's own feelings and thoughts. The implicit purpose of this mechanism is to get rid of sense impressions arising from the incapacity to manage difficult emotions in oneself when relating to another. Bion stressed the healthy aspect of projective identification as an unconscious way of communicating to another person the mental process one is experiencing, in the hope of being helped to gain insight into one's own mental state. If this occurs, a thinking skin can grow, and integration of unmetabolized beta elements can take place. When the mechanism of projective identification is at work, the person who is projected into loses touch with the logic of his previous thoughts (Ogden 2009, p. 98), and participates in the unconscious emotion-thought of another (Bion 1959). If this person is able to shake himself out of the psychic reality engendered in him, he is in a new position: he has been changed by the new experience and can try to understand what has happened to him from a new vertex (Ogden 2009, p. 99). Following Bion, Ogden (2009, p. 98) is interested in the interpersonal dimension of this mechanism. By being affected by the patient's intra-psychic conflict and by re-emerging from it, the analyst is gaining insight into the conflict of the patient: this will not itself resolve the conflict for the patient but will strengthen the patient's own capacity to resolve it.

Ogden is interested in exploring what kind of processes the analyst's mind is performing in these cases and how un-verbalized and unthinkable experiences in the patient can affect and be transformed by the analyst. Ogden (2009, p. 17) describes this as the capacity of the analyst to 'dream up' the patient, his own mind free to wander in a sort of free association mode, which he calls 'talking as dreaming' (Ogden 2009, p. 24). By doing so the analyst will be performing his transcendent function (Jung 1957/1979, para. 146) that Bovensiepen has described as the use of a 'symbolic attitude' (Bovensiepen 2002) which links and names the emotional, sensory and physical data that the meeting with the patient has evoked in him. This capacity of the analyst will influence the patient and help him to begin to develop his own rudimentary capacity to 'dream himself into being' (Ogden 2009, p. 24).

Bion (1962b, p. 89) and Jung (1957/1979, paras. 131–93) recognize that the human personality is equipped with mental operations that generate symbolic meaning, dreaming being an integral part of this capacity. Dreaming occurs continuously, both while we are awake and while we sleep (Ogden 2009, p. 112). If the analyst is willing and able to engage with the patient in the process of 'dreaming his patient's un-dreamable experience' (ibid., p. 113), the analytic couple will be at work in modifying what had been previously unthinkable: the two minds engaged in 'dreaming' may prove adequate in thinking the unthinkable thought. This operation will work like a binding skin so that unassimilated mental contents can be integrated: a concrete unconscious bodily event will come into being and can become symbolic (Astor 1995, p. 237) through being transformed into a thought. Only in this way can it be integrated into the self. Bion's comment, 'It takes two minds to think a disturbing thought' (Ogden 2009, p. 97), refers to the willingness of the analyst to be affected by the patient's unconscious communications (performed through the mechanism of projective identification) and to bear in himself sensory data, emotions and feelings that the encounter with the patient engenders in him until he is capable of putting them into words, giving them life. When this is the case, the analytic couple participates in a process which hopefully results in the patient finding his own transcendent function, bearing himself into being.

Thanks to the capacity of the analyst and the patient to attune, it becomes possible for them to engage in this experiment in which unintegrated primitive bodily events can be hopefully metabolized and integrated. The capacity of the analyst to match the patient's archetypal expectation of being understood, attune to the patient, be affected by the patient's manoeuvre to get rid of beta elements, and his own capacity to dream and transform what is unthinkable for the patient, might allow a disturbing event to come to life so that thinking oneself into being might become possible for the patient too. Although the transcendent function and the process of deintegration and reintegration are 'natural' and hence archetypally grounded as Jung and Fordham maintained, they do not work spontaneously (Bovensiepen 2002). Traumatic events can obstruct the harmonious development of the personality. Sometimes the encounter with a receptive other can work at mending the obstruction so that the natural process can be reinstated. Case material from the analysis of a child will now follow to illustrate this theoretical introduction.

A child's case

Assessment

I met with Gigi when he was 3½. He was referred to me with a diagnosis of autistic features: notably speech delay and difficulty in relating to his peers. I felt as if I was in the presence of a deaf child who had learnt to pronounce sounds with extreme difficulty. Gigi could 'speak', but I soon realized that Gigi's 'language' was undecipherable to human ears, including those of his mother. It was not only the strange sound of his voice, which puzzled me (it was as if his voice was coming from an enclosed space and re-echoed), but his words held absolutely no meaning for me. I could not single out any sound which sounded familiar to me.

For our first meeting in my consulting room, Gigi arrived carrying a big metal bus in one of his hands. Once in the room, he sat quietly on the floor and explored what was inside the box full of toys that I had put out for him in the room. He played for a while by putting a little car he found in my box inside his bus. His bus had a door, and my car went swiftly inside. He seemed amused with that. He quickly closed the door of the bus and spent the rest of the session playing with the car, putting it inside and taking it out of the bus. When it was time to go, I noticed that my car was still in his bus. 'I wonder if you would like to go away with my baby auto in your Mummy's bus', I said. Gigi blushed and gave the car back to me.

For the second meeting I had arranged for his assessment, Gigi started a curious search inside the box of toys I had prepared for him and found a kangaroo with a little baby kangaroo in its belly. He seemed fascinated by it, rushed out of the room and got his mother to come and see. Mother came in, sat on the floor and Gigi, after having shown the kangaroo to her, started playing on the floor, pushing his head inside his mother's belly and later in between his mother's legs. When I pointed out that Gigi was trying to go inside his mother like the little kangaroo, mother said, 'Oh that's right'.

In the following two sessions that I had planned for the assessment, Gigi spent most of the time with his head underneath the couch, his body outside. He was happily enjoying himself there, talking to himself from time to time, oblivious of me.

Nothing significant could be found in Gigi's history, apart from the fact that he was abruptly weaned at around seven months when the family changed houses, and the mother was preoccupied with the move and burdened by the emotional and physical stress arising from this.

Theoretical assumptions

After the initial assessment, the following considerations could be made. Gigi seems to have lost his mother's attention when he was weaned. The loss of the maternal breast coincided with the loss of mother's capacity to be mindful of him so that his hypothetical depressive and aggressive feelings could not be metabolized once his breastfeeding mother 'disappeared'. Gigi seemed to 'articulate' this dramatic loss as a lack of psychic skin, which prompted him to develop autistic defences, resulting in a phantasy of hiding in his mother's womb, showing that he had no means of using his mind to understand himself. It seemed that he had given up hope of being understood. Gigi did not seem to believe that this loss could be mended; he had adjusted to his condition of being inarticulate, of not having a mental 'skin', and sought protection in his own self, as if in his mother's womb. The question of attunement with him might be of paramount importance, as a prerequisite to understanding how the formation of a 'missing psychic skin' could be accomplished so that what he was defending himself from could be born into being.

First six months of analysis

Soon after the beginning of his analysis, Gigi started to disappear under the couch, not only with his head but with his whole body. He did not respond to my attempts either to describe what he was doing or to interpret what I thought he might be doing. I, therefore, decided to stay with his defence, which I treated as a communication, implying that Gigi was telling me that language was not making sense to him and that I had to find a way to understand him without the intrusion of language (Urban 1989). I decided therefore to lie down on the floor, at a certain distance from the couch: we were on the same level, face-to-face, at a preverbal stage. I began to understand the couch as a defence against something that was preventing language, a split-off experience. Although Gigi was at times turned on his back, playing with the springs from underneath the couch, or turned onto his belly, playing with the carpet, he would start by spending most of the session looking at me in silence. These were moving moments of great intensity. These sessions were a true aesthetic experience for both of us. We were gazing at each other in awe. I was often propelled to think of the meeting of a mother and her baby soon after birth, and the beauty and intensity of this moment. I imagined this having been Gigi's and his mother's experience.

From the second month of his analysis before going underneath the couch, he would wrap himself up in one of the rugs he found on my couch. A couple of months later, instead of using the big and thick rug, he started to wrap himself up in a thin and transparent piece of fabric which was in the box of toys. This new rug was easier to manage. I began to think of the rug as a skin, a link between the 'inarticulate' experience he was defending against and the possibility, I hoped, of getting hold of it in our work. I knew that I only had to wait. Around this period, his mother reported that he had had a series of nightmares. She thought that Gigi was dreaming of something dangerous coming out of the dark and attacking him.

Session A

When Gigi and his mother arrived, she reported that Gigi had had another nightmare the night before, and she had spent more than half an hour calming him down.

Gigi went to the loo and made a poo. He came into the room talking to me in an agitated and a slightly alarmed way. Although his voice by now sounded perhaps less booming (closer to normal in sound), I understood practically nothing. I wondered in myself what he was trying to tell me. I said that it was very upsetting wanting to be understood and Alessandra not understanding him. He took a soft teddy from the box and put it underneath the couch: then he began his routine; he wrapped himself in the soft and transparent fabric, after having flattened it on the couch. I said, 'Your Mum said that you had another nightmare last night. She said you were very afraid that something was coming out of the dark to attack you. And now, what if your poo is coming out of the dark loo and attacks you?' He looked at me with an intense and fearful look and then laughed. I said, 'You laugh, but I thought you were afraid it could happen'. I was referring to the poo as the 'inarticulate' experience he was trying to get rid of and understood the nightmare as this experience becoming 'dreamable', the dream as the precursor of a possible integration.

Gigi went underneath the couch with the fabric and started a long conversation with the teddy. The teddy has a long soft white nose, culminating in a black spot, and for some reason, I started to think of it as a breast and a nipple. While Gigi was absorbed in his conversation with the teddy, I lost myself in reverie. A few days before I had seen a 6-month-old baby with a depressed mother who, despite being emotionally cut off from her baby, had been physically available to the baby. She breastfed her baby regularly, was physically very close to her baby without fearing the intense physical contact, but she was offering her body to her baby as if it was dead. I was struck by the way the baby was treating the breast, actually as an insensitive object. During one of the sessions with the baby and her mother, while the mother was looking out of the window pensively, baby in her arms, the baby grabbed a stone from the windowsill of my consulting room. The mother commented on this, came closer to me and sat down, the baby on her lap. In slow motion, the baby brought the stone onto her mouth and bit and bit it. The mother and I were both struck by the baby's activity. 'What are you doing?!' The mother repeated this several times. Slowly, the baby let the stone go, and I suggested that the baby was trying to tell us something about her experience of the breast.

Later in the session, the baby wanted a feed, and Mum generously put her to the breast. The baby sucked for a little time and then bit the breast with the same intensity as she had bitten the stone, leaving the mother speechless for a second, until she started to scream. 'Perhaps she wants to make sure that the breast is not a stone, but can feel. . . . I said. The intensity of that experience came back to me, and slowly in my mind, I tried to make sense of my countertransference. I treated my reverie as traditional mythology applied to children and thought of it as Gigi's unconscious communication now becoming accessible to me. I looked at Gigi. He was kissing the teddy, caressing it; then suddenly he bit it and threw it out from underneath the couch. It was the end of the session. I tried to organize my thinking. I thought of Gigi hiding under the couch as his way of showing me in a concrete way his phantasy. He did not seem to be able to link a past experience he had had into his self. This experience remained out of reach while he was 'pretending' to himself that he had found a 'safe place', protected from it.

After this session, I understood that what had remained split off was his primitive aggression, his incapacity to manage the internal pressure to bite and his fear of damaging the object. Perhaps he expected his objects to be incapable of containing such pressure. I wondered if what had remained split off had been his experience as the result of an abrupt weaning. I also wondered if his mother had been depressed at that time of the move, and this coincided with the weaning. Perhaps Gigi's biting in this session was the closest way for him to re-experience and make sense of his primitive wish to bite, integrate and live out his archetypal necessity to be angry with his mother for weaning him and possibly being absent-minded at the time. Like the baby who was moved by a desire to know and learn something about the breast, Gigi seemed to want to test out something in relation to another when he finally found the courage to bite the teddy. Finally, I wondered if Gigi was relating to language as to a concrete object: he could 'not bite into' it, as he did not seem to be able to bite the breast at the time.

I started to feel clearer in myself.

Session B

In the following session, Gigi took the teddy with him under the couch and bit it again. This time, he did not throw it away, but kept it with him, talking to it and playing with it. At this point, I said to him that the teddy reminded me of a mum's breast, and I wondered aloud with him if, a long, long time ago when he still was a baby, he had felt the urge to bite it but had stopped himself from doing it because he had been afraid of destroying his Mum's breast . . . or was it the fear of being bitten back? I asked him if he had then decided to spend all his life hidden in a place where nobody knew of his desire; did he hope nobody would understand it? I then said that Alessandra had understood it despite his tactic, and Alessandra felt that it was ok to bite the teddy; it was all right.

Gigi listened silently to this.

Session C: two weeks later

Gigi came in and wrapped himself as usual in the transparent fabric before going underneath the couch. This time he went there on his own, without the teddy. From there he started to look at me. I positioned myself on the floor at the usual distance. For a long, long time, we gazed at each other in silence. The intensity of this aesthetic experience moved me deeply, and almost in tears, I looked at this creative child who had taught me so much with his silences. Suddenly Gigi talked to me. Although I did not understand him as usual, his voice seemed rather normal to me. Yes, I realized unexpectedly that his voice had lost the strange vibrations; it was not booming anymore. I became aware that Gigi was laughing and talking to me like to a friend. His conversation to me sounded perfectly natural and normal. Unfortunately, I did not understand his language.

In some way, our conversations were similar to what is called 'motherese', a sort of proto-conversation between mothers and babies, when speech is imitated but not yet fully acquired. We smiled at each other, and again he spoke to me, long sentences which made no sense but seemed perfectly coherent. Suddenly, out of the blue, he sprang out from underneath the couch, still wrapped up in the fabric, while, in a sort of mirroring behaviour, I sat up. Before I could understand what was going on, he had attacked me and bitten my arm. We stood for a moment there, looking at each other full of surprise. Then we both began to laugh. This laugh, although a bit manic, was very important. I felt we were both relieved: Gigi because nothing had happened, I because I felt something unthinkable could finally be expressed and understood in a very concrete way to start with, which I hoped would lead to something more symbolic.

'So', I said, 'That was it! You just wanted to see if Alessandra was strong enough to bear it! And look, you have done it and nothing has happened. Alessandra is not biting back, but I must say . . . your teeth are strong. Hi!' And 'now I understand why you were throwing the teddy away . . . you were afraid the teddy would bite you back, like in your nightmares, like the poo, when you were afraid the poo would come out of the water and attack you!' Gigi kept laughing, showing me his teeth; then still with the fabric on his shoulders, he took the tiger from the toy box and attacked me in pretence. 'Ah, Gigi cannot stay underneath the couch anymore. No more under the couch – belly – mummy'. He smiled and started to play with soldiers.

Two weeks after this session, a long summer holiday began which separated us for eight weeks. One week before coming back to his analysis, Gigi spontaneously began to speak. In the middle of a walk with his extended family, he told them a story about a bird he had just seen, leaving everybody speechless. This was only the beginning of a new era. Gigi was able to speak, and soon afterwards, he allowed himself to try to speak in the foreign language of the country the family was living in.

In the first session after the break, Gigi looked at me in a timid way, almost ashamed of his improvement, but then overcame his embarrassment by taking the measuring tape out of the box of toys and using it to measure every single object in the room, including himself. I said he wanted to show not only to me but to himself too that he had grown, not so much in height, but inside, now that he could trust that it was possible to be understood. Gigi spent the rest of the session dividing the toys into two groups, the kind and the frightening toys, as a way to show me that he had become aware of a more realistic way of seeing his object, perhaps a mirror of his perception of himself with good and bad qualities, less afraid of being only 'bad' and dangerous.

Discussion

The incapacity to manage the internal pressure of an archetypal primitive need to bite and the external reality of the loss of his mother who, in the form of a breast, was weaning him, were perceived by him to be unable to contain such pressure and perhaps retaliate, propelling Gigi to leave 'inarticulate' a part of himself, the capacity to speak. Gigi adopted some autistic defences as a way to stop his development, which must have felt dangerous to him. The loss of his mother's capacity to be in tune with him coincided with the loss of her feeding breast. This experience must have felt as if she was mentally dead, leaving Gigi 'skinless' with no choice but to hide inside himself, a protected space which must have felt similar to his maternal womb. During his analysis, Gigi could find a space where he recreated and lived out this 'lost' experience. From being under the couch with a thick rug-skin to a transparent fabric: we were reconnecting to an unmanageable link with the private archaeology of his mind. Finding a mind able to attune with and willing to deintegrate with him in order to receive his inarticulate experience allowed him to give up his defences (a protective skin) and find his own mental skin (articulating) while he was finding another able to think with him about his unmanageable traumatic early emotions.

In the process of transformation, the unthinkable experience appeared in the form of a nightmare, as if no container could possibly have been available for it. Slowly in the course of the analysis, I became aware in my mind of his concrete and inarticulate desire to bite until the non-symbolic act of biting could be experienced. The transformation of this event into a symbolic thought could happen (emotional data could become mind) only when Gigi was able to gain some knowledge about it, followed later by his capacity to integrate his experience into his self. By biting, he was able to translate from an unconscious into a conscious mode. The more he allowed himself to reintegrate his split-off experience, the more his rug-skin shrank to a transparent fabric. His desire to know made it possible for him to transform something unspeakable into something that could be spoken about. The awareness of his aggressive impulse allowed him to translate his unconscious phantasy into a concrete experience. Language could finally become humanized: Gigi could finally use language to communicate following the general rules humans attribute to language. He did not need a private incomprehensible language in order to communicate his distress. Gigi wanted to change, and the change, in Gigi's case, was lasting. This is not always the case with children with autistic defences (Meltzer 1986). An undifferentiated bodily mental act could be born into being, providing a way for body and mind to differentiate.

Conclusion

Drawing from mother-infant interactions and exploring the concept of primitive identity and the mechanism of projective identification, the author has presented a few sessions from the analysis of a young child with the purpose of showing what is required from the analytic couple for un-mentalized bodily events to be born into being. When bodily contents have failed to become mind, a thinking skin has failed to grow and with it the capacity to understand. For this to change, it is necessary for analyst and patient to be attuned to one another, in a way similar to mothers and their infants at the beginning of life. This primitive capacity to be in tune makes it possible for the unfolding of a process which aims at the transformation of unmetabolized psychic events into symbolic thoughts. Instead of affecting and disrupting the development of the patient, they can hopefully emerge as thinkable emotions. In this way, unintegrated and split-off deintegrates become reintegrated and the naturally spontaneous process of deintegration/reintegration can re-commence.

Understanding is not an act of will but occurs through the meeting of an internal archetypal necessity (to be understood) with an external receptivity: the analyst allows his mind to be affected by the patient's unconscious communication, and the patient allows his mind to participate in the analyst's understanding. The process of understanding is beautiful every time it is accomplished anew. The analyst-patient couple becomes a creative couple: each participates in the realization of an innate archetypal unformed vision. Understanding is the actualization of this vision throughout the analytic process. As the poet says, 'Words before coming to light are deposited in you as mud awaiting to become light' (Merini 2009). Analysis is the place where the patient is able to transform mud into light.

Note

1 First published in *Journal of Analytical Psychology*, 56, 1, January 2011.

References

Astor, J. (1995). *Michael Fordham. Innovations in Analytical Psychology*. London: Routledge.
Bick, E. (1968). 'The experience of the skin in early object relations'. *International Journal of Psycho-Analysis*, 49, 484–86.
Bion, W. (1959). *Experiences in Groups and Other Papers*. New York: Basic Books.
———. (1962a). 'A theory of thinking'. *International Journal of Psycho-Analysis*, 43, 306–10.
———. (1962b). *Learning from Experience*. London: Heinemann.
Bovensiepen, G. (2002). 'Symbolic attitude and reverie: problems of symbolization in children and adolescents'. *Journal of Analytical Psychology*, 47, 2, 241–57.
Carignani, P., & Romano F. (2006). *Prendere corpo (To Be Embodied)*. Milan: Franco Angeli.
Fordham, M. (1985). *Explorations into the Self*. London: Academic Press.
Jung, C.G. (1957/1979). 'The transcendent function'. *CW*, 8.
Mancia, M. (2007). *Feeling the Words*. London and New York: Routledge.
Meltzer, D. (1986). 'Psychotic illness in early childhood'. In *Studies in Extended Metapsychology*. Perthshire: Clunie Press.
Merini, A. (2009). *Padre mio (My Father)*. Rome: Frassinelli.
Ogden, H.T. (2009). *Rediscovering Psychoanalysis*. London: Routledge and The New Library of Psychoanalysis.
Proner, K. (2000). 'Protomental synchrony: some thoughts on the earliest identification processes in a neonate'. *International Journal of Infant Observation*, 3, 2, 55–63.
Regazzoni Goretti, G. (2007). 'Projective identification'. *International Journal of Psychoanalysis*, 88, 2, 378–405, and Letter to the editors from J.S. Grotstein, 'On "Projective identification"' and, 'Reply to Dr. Grotstein' by G. Regazzoni Goretti, *International Journal of Psychoanalysis*, 88, 5, 1289–90.
Urban, E. (1989). 'Childhood deafness: compensatory deintegration of the self'. *Journal of Analytical Psychology*, 34, 144–57.
———. (1998). 'States of identity: a perspective drawing upon Fordham's model and infant studies'. *Journal of Analytical Psychology*, 43, 261–75.
———. (2003). 'Developmental aspects of trauma and traumatic aspects of development'. *Journal of Analytical Psychology*, 48, 2, 171–90.
———. (2006). 'Unintegration, disintegration and deintegration'. *Journal of Child Psychotherapy*, 32, 2, 181–92.

Chapter 4

Transgenerational transmission of indigestible facts

From trauma, deadly ghosts and mental voids to meaning-making interpretations[1]

Trauma

Victims of trauma are left to pick up the pieces of a blown apart self and reassemble them together into something similar to a former self. One of the major casualties of this disintegration is the capacity to think. Different authors (Auerhahn & Laub 1984; Garland 1999; Brown 2011) have described the traumatic organization of the psyche as characterized by a self-enclosed system split off from ordinary reality that allows no new ideas in. There concrete thinking prevails; repetitive enactments reinforce a traumatic view of the world, while trauma becomes timeless and cannot be historicized (Baranger, Baranger, & Mom 1988).

In working with traumatized patients in analysis, the analyst is required to increase his own capacity to tolerate affects (Garland 1999; Brown 2011), to withstand the identification with the patient (Fraiberg 1980; Laub & Podell 1995; Faimberg 2005), to help the patient to give a form to the traumatic event enhancing symbolic thinking (Faimberg 2005; Moore 2009; Gerson 2009) and, finally, to help the patient to integrate the traumatic event into the person's sense of identity, enabling the patient to achieve what is called 'bearing witness'(Poland 2000; Laub 2012; Gerson 2009), which means separating from the narrative of others and integrating the traumatic event in a subjective and coherent form into the self. Only in this way can the trauma be 'forgotten', and 'remembered', instead of being always present. The challenge in working with traumatized patients is well described by Garland (1999). She postulates that in cases of trauma, primitive anxieties are reactivated. They keep the ego away from the traumatic event. The traumatic event becomes a phobic object which generates dissociation (Bolognini 2011), or is equated with death (Gerson 2009), similar to what Bion (1962) calls 'nameless dread'. As long as this deadly object is split off, self and ego feel safe, annihilation anxieties are kept at bay and the illusion of protection is fostered (Garland 1999). The lost life before the trauma becomes equated in the internal world with loss of goodness and hope (Laub 2012; Gerson 2009; Garland 1999). Reintegrating the traumatic event into the self puts at high risk the so-far-achieved internal organization of the self; therefore, the self puts in place defence mechanisms to avoid contact with it. It is to this particular state of mind that I want to

DOI: 10.4324/9781003268536-5

refer in thinking about transgenerational transmission of trauma and particularly how to work with it in clinical practice.

Angela Connolly, in her paper 'Healing the Wounds of Our Fathers' (2011), has paid particular attention to what it is that is transmitted inter-generationally in the case of trauma. Referring to Eli Wiesel's internal attempt at making sense of his experience in Auschwitz (Connolly 2011, p. 611), Connolly elaborates on three fundamental aspects in inter-generational transmission as described by Wiesel: death of time, death of language and death of narrative. Quoting an impressive number of authors who have worked extensively with patients affected by inter-generational trauma, Connolly pictures a relationship of the first generation to the second and the third that put me in mind of Green's (1986) concept of the dead mother. According to Green, the patient's feeling of emptiness, his constant re/enactments and despair are linked to maternal deprivation and to the incapacity of the mother to contain and respond to the infant's emotional needs. Because of growing up with an emotionally 'dead mother', the child ends up living in a 'deadly deserted universe' (Green 1986, p. 167). When the psychological matrix provided by the mother is lacking, and with it her capacity to differentiate, order and give meaning, everything is then felt to be 'deadly' and paralyzing. Differentiation is possible only if the infant does not feel 'abandoned' by his mother's mental absences, but achieves a state of separated-ness from her: acceptance of the passing of time, the achievement of language and the recognition of an individual narrative are the result of a well-established differentiation that, taken together, create a sense of self (Knox 2011). Laub (2012, p. 44) believes that a similar dynamic is true not only for infantile symbolic maternal loss but also in the case of trauma at any age. Trauma would create an internal condition in which the already achieved capacity to order, process, think symbolically and trust collapses. Following Garland (1999) and Laub (2012), it is possible to postulate that it is this internal condition that is transmitted inter-generationally and creates further trauma in subsequent generations.

First clinical case: Anna

I will now present some clinical material to show how, like a ghost (Fraiberg 1980), the trauma of the first generation shadows the development of the second generation, while the third generation assimilates it into themselves in such a way that it becomes part of the self. While a traumatic event has the capacity to destroy the internal organization for the first generation, the second generation grows up under its influence and forms a sort of attachment to it. In the third generation, it becomes assimilated into the self. I will try to give a 'three generational' illustration of how 'the deadly' can generate a mental void that the third generation has to absorb in the difficult task of giving meaning to what seems absolute meaninglessness. I will then discuss the clinical material linking it with the theoretical framework discussed earlier and expand on it. My aim is to think about a way of interpreting which has an anti-traumatic value and creates meaning. My hypothesis is that the interpretation has to be 'three generationally constructed', for it to differentiate the undifferentiated that has been transmitted and that time, language and narrative have to be contained within it. The analyst's attention and her capacity to tolerate anxieties work as an anti-traumatic value: the possibility of bringing 'the deadly' to life generates hope in the possibility of a real goodness and, with it, the capacity of the self to create order and become integrated is activated.

Anna's grandmother

Anna's grandmother was 16 when she was deported to Auschwitz where she spent two years. After the liberation, she went to live in another country, married and had a daughter. Anna's grandmother never mentioned her past but began to suffer from terrible nightmares, screaming during the night. Since she was a little child, Anna spent all her holidays in Grandma's house and shared Grandma's bed.

Anna's mother

Anna's mother became anorexic and was tube-fed when she was 20, which left a scar on her abdomen. Anna only recently discovered its origin. Anna's mother married a non-Jewish man. She is not religious, and her Jewishness was never mentioned in the family. When Anna was 11, she was sent to a Jewish school where she was confronted with the Holocaust and with her Jewish identity. Anna and her mother do not talk; things happen without explanation, without questioning. Anna's mother eats alone and eats different food from what she prepares for the family. Links between things, states of mind, events are not made in her family.

Anna

Anna became bulimic when she was 8, and her condition deteriorated when she was 15. She asked for help because 'my condition has taken over. I am becoming the eating disorders'. She referred herself to her school counsellor because she had little social life, just managed to go to school and spent most of the time doing what felt familiar: stuffing herself and making herself sick. At the beginning of our work, Anna was obsessed with the thought that she was bad, and it became clear that she was trying to vomit out all the badness and nastiness she felt inside. She repeatedly told me that she felt that this badness could kill her, and it was necessary to get it all out of her system. This nastiness was a confused state, an agglomerate of undigested facts, a negative, deadly, non-representation. She felt she would have died if she had not vomited it. It was difficult to understand and sort out what this badness could have been and why she was confused with it. Vomiting seemed an attempt for her to become alive, but, at the same time, without it, she felt lost. While she wanted to free herself from it, it felt to her that this vomiting was her only sense of self. I felt trapped with her in a system that seemed to have a homeostatic function. There was no way in. In despair, I suggested that we increase the number of sessions to four a week. She returned to therapy with a burn. She told me that she had deliberately burned herself with the iron to show me how much she was suffering, but also to leave a mark for me to see. Although this mark was terrifying, it was from this mark that our work did begin. This mark was the first representation of a chaotic and deadening mental state which needed to be undone, digested and ordered.

It was around that stage, about 14 months into therapy, that Anna began to talk about her grandmother and her mother. We began to understand Anna's eating disorder (she specifically ate bread) as her way of attempting to get rid of a confused mass of personal and transgenerational facts that she had absorbed and had never been understood before. We began to understand her eating disorder as a very primitive infantile attempt to expel the 'deadly' she felt filled with which needed psychic attention she was unable to provide. At the same time, it felt to her that this deadly mass was her own self. The deadly and its transmission: theoretical implication I refer to the 'deadly' as the result of the incapacity of the mind to digest, understand and find a representation for bodily and psychic events as extensively described in psychoanalytical literature (Ferro 2010). Such a capacity for representation, a prerequisite for mental health, is initially dependent on the containing function of the parents. When the environment is not able to fulfil a containing function, it leaves a void, an irrepresentability. This void is felt as deadly and has a traumatic value because it generates anxieties which have no name. Events become experiences when they become meaningful, have a name, become known. Put it in these terms, experience needs a matrix, a representability to become known. In the absence of a matrix, there is not its loss, but its negative (Botella & Botella 2005, p. 156), a non-representation. As Yael Moore puts it, 'According to Botella and Botella (2005) creating "figurability" represents an anti-traumatic value, essential to psychic recovery. This is achieved by creating contact with the irrepresentable in the vacuum' (Moore 2009, p. 1379). Otherwise, a situation similar to Green's 'dead mother' is established in the relationship between the generations (Laub 2012; Gerson 2009). As Gerson puts it, 'The enduring presence of an absence within the psyche may best be conceived of as a dead third' (Gerson 2009, p. 90). This third, made of undigested facts which create annihilation anxieties, shadows like a ghost the development of the second generation, who creates an attachment to it. It is this attachment that the third generation seems to absorb into their selves. This is how I began to understand Anna's badness and her incapacity to rid herself of it. While she was debating within herself between wanting to rid herself of it and wanting to identify herself with it, I began to think of her eating disorder as an attempt to re-enact an internalized 'disorganized attachment' as if, paradoxically, she had developed an attachment towards this 'deadly' disorganization.

The incapacity of the parents to tolerate and process affects and behaviours generate anxieties in the child similar to what Bion calls nameless dread. This incapacity works as a disorganizing force in the child who feels unsafe at the loss of violent intolerable affects (Mizen 2003). In these terms, we could postulate that the child of a traumatized parent develops an attachment similar to the disorganized attachment described by Main and Hesse (1990). The trauma in the parent functions as a disorganizing force which transforms the parent into an unpredictable adult who cannot think and feel and has no capacity for containment and empathy. This very way of responding to the child's communications is felt as disorganizing because it generates intolerable anxieties in the child. A possible attachment to this kind of object is assimilated and re-enacted.

Differentiating and ordering

We began to use Anna's past not to reconstruct, but to construct a missing link between the past events and the way they concerned her. What seemed important was not only to give words to the irrepresentable but also to create an environment in which this process could 'feel safe'. While Anna was describing her grandmother's nightmares, I began to imagine with her how her grandmother's pregnancy might have been and how her mother as a foetus might have felt, what grandmother's relationship with food was like, grandmother's potential anxieties around a baby growing inside her. This imaginative reverie fulfilled a double function. While it was helpful to the patient at an implicit level since it informed the whole way I was with her – my curiosity about her was making Anna feel that she was in the presence of a thinking, imagining 'mother' who was willing to represent in her own mind Anna's external and internal world – it also gave her permission to begin to question and reflect upon what, until then, had remained unthinkable for her. Anna began to speak of the shadow of death gravitating around grandmother. We began to wonder if her mother might have been traumatized by her own mother's nightmares, how this side of her grandmother might have contributed to creating a version of a terrifying mother in her mother when she was a child. We began to question her mother's eating disorders and emotional flatness in relation to her own mother and to Anna's grandmother's undigested trauma. Rey (1994) has written extensively about phantasies in anorexic patients, about how they avoid food for fear of devouring or being devoured by their mother due to a basic confusion between them and how food becomes confused with separation. He has also described tube-fed patients who were saved by the tube, having developed a secure attachment to it, as a predictable object. In Anna's therapy, we began to wonder how her own mother could have resorted to anorexia as a way to find an internal separation between herself and her own mother who could have been perceived by her as dangerous and unpredictable. We imagined the tube as a cold but predictable agent that was not traumatizing and did not project emotions but limited itself to fulfil its function of feeding her. We began to think of a confusion between her grandmother and mother around death and life which had been transmitted to her. Her mother had resorted to anorexia as if her identity was possible only as an alive dead state. Anna's eating disorder had a similar function.

Anna was inclined to believe that although her grandmother was alive, a part of her seemed lost. Similarly, she described her mother as if she was emotionally dead. This confusion between death and life got re-enacted in our work. Like her death-giving eating disorder, which was an attempt to get rid of the deadly, and seemed to fulfil a liberating function, coming to therapy was for Anna like eating and digesting deadly elements and this, in reality, was life-giving but felt to her death-giving. I often felt that Anna had great difficulty in digesting our work and preferred to stuff herself with my words, instead of taking them in. She would then complain about the pain that thinking was giving her; she would have headaches and was not able to listen to me. But then if we were in silence, she would be afraid of it, and ask me to talk.

At the end of a long period in therapy in which we had been dealing with these kinds of problems, I said,

> I was thinking of your grandmother's fear of seeing and talking . . . maybe your mother has learnt to live with silence, these daily silences that you have absorbed . . . now they are in you, and when you eat and steal the bread, you would like all the silences to speak, and come out, and have words and tell stories about your mother and your grandmother. But instead, there is only silence, and then you are afraid that this silence is you, and if you vomit the bread, you then vomit yourself, and then it is the end, as if you were made of silence . . . you need words . . . we need to find the words that were given dead by your grandmother to your mother and that she then gave to you. To find words for the silences takes a lot of courage.

Although these thoughts of mine were pure speculations, they were functioning as the maternal provision of the psychological matrix (Garland 1999) Anna had never received. Her mother seemed to be blind to Anna's bingeing; she seemed not to notice anything, and we began to think that as a child, she might have had to be impermeable to suffering and feelings. My curiosity and imaginative questioning created a container for the split-off experience of the grandmother and for how it might have affected her mother who needed to protect herself from the deadly. This relieved Anna of the impossible attempt to assimilate it into herself without having the containing capacity to do so.

One day, Anna seemed to have found a way of expressing how it felt to her to be a child growing up with an emotionally flat and mentally absent mother. She said, 'When I was a child I always had to adapt. I had to be quick'. Although I was not pushing her to follow my reverie and mental excursions, the frequency of our meetings was in some way having a similar effect on her. I thought that she had transferred onto me and the work we were doing together a feeling similar to the one experienced in childhood. So I said,

> There was no time for baby Anna to grow slowly into a big Anna. . . . Now, with me, you can hopefully protest when it seems to you that I push you to

be quick and hopefully you can say to me what you could not say to your mother: 'Slowly, I need more time!'

Later I added, 'Would it be possible to think that when you vomit, you vomit your anger for not having had the possibility of going slowly?' I was trying to differentiate between what she felt she had to absorb but was inimical to her self because, although it had been transmitted to her and indirectly influenced her, it had nothing directly to do with her, and what was an intrinsic part of her, and needed to be integrated.

Around this period Anna began to plan a journey to Auschwitz. Going there was not only part of her desire to put words onto the deadly silences she was now beginning to recognize and name but also a way of hoping to find parts of her that, confused with parts of her grandmother, she might find where she thought her grandmother had lost them. One of these lost 'parts' was her capacity to cry, which she felt she had never had. She did not remember having ever seen her mother or grandmother cry. We were able to see how Anna was beginning to differentiate between her own unprocessed emotions and feelings, and those of her mother and grandmother, that had been passed on to her and had been mixed up with her own in a chaotic and undifferentiated way. The split-off experience of the grandmother had become a sort of bizarre object (Bion 1967) made up of undifferentiated fused mind and body parts. Anna was hoping to find in Auschwitz her grandmother's lost human predictability, that once refound, would have worked as the missing link that would re-establish a hypothetical lost order. Anna's mother's experiences of being partly mothered by this bizarre object represented an early developmental catastrophe for baby Anna, which had affected her primary self in the way Faimberg describes in her book *The Telescoping of Generations* (2005). Anna was confronted with a traumatic chaos of bodily and emotional events so that no distinction existed between body and mind, me and not-me, and Anna's sense of agency could not unfold. Anna's ego was not an agent, and it was this which needed attention. Anna spoke of feeling guilty for not having taken the pain away, and, with this in mind, we began to understand her eating bread as a reparative gesture – a desire to absorb what was in fact too inimical to her mother and her own self, and then to eject it, magically.

Two years later, after a lot of internal and external order had been made, including the visit to Auschwitz, Anna could say, 'Now for example, when the eating disorder kicks in, it is different from before. Before I was blank. Now your voice is there. Your voice is silent but is there. It is observing me'. 'How?', I asked. She replied, 'It is looking at me but not in a judgemental way and it doesn't make me feel guilty. Your voice is simply looking at me and what I do'. I responded,

> My voice can look at you vomiting and is alive, and sees it, but is silent. My silent voice is different from all the silences that you are vomiting because it is a voice, while the silences that you have inside are words and feelings which do not have a voice. I look at you vomiting all the badness that your

grandmother could not digest, at all the confusion that your mother could not understand, and I am silent because we need to hear the words that are inside you, they need to be heard.

For Anna the irrepresentability, the negative, the non-representation was this I, this me, this little child, once foetus, later baby who felt confused with the abandoned and lost child in grandmother and mother. It was this 'I' which needed to be discovered. Attention seemed to function as a catalyst: my capacity to tolerate the deadly, look at it and stay put, was connecting Anna with her capacity to recognize, order and name the deadly while tolerating the underlying anxieties. My capacity to stay above the deadly, describe it in a language which would contain it but open it to life was helping Anna to begin to integrate experiences and link them in a coherent and meaningful way into herself while she was beginning to discover that she was this 'I'.

It was only when Anna could begin to discover real feelings in herself, among which were also feelings of love and compassion for her mother, grandmother and herself that she began to feel more alive. Above all, there was a terrible feeling of loss that needed to be tolerated, the feeling of all that she had missed through the traumatic inter-generational history into which she had been born. Finally crying, Anna could say, 'I am crying because I cannot go back, and can only go forward, and everything has really happened. I am crying because I would like to go and visit my grandmother and interview her, but she does not want to hear any of this'.

Now that Anna had found the words and a story to tell about herself, it seemed that nobody wanted to hear it. At least she had found a way to separate from the past, a way of forgetting it, while her mother and grandmother could never remember it because they had never forgotten it.

Second clinical case: Misha

Laub (2012) postulates that the inter-generational trauma has an equally traumatic value, independently of the transmitter, be it the maternal or the paternal line. I will now present some clinical material of my work with a male patient for whom the transmitter of trauma was in the paternal line. Although the devastating consequence of the transmission seems to support Laub's proposition, I will return to this point later, where I will give some thought to a possible fundamental distinction which needs to be made when thinking of the transmission of trauma and its transmitters.

Misha's grandfather was in the White Army, fighting against the Bolsheviks. He managed to escape to Turkey after the defeat and later moved to another European country. There he married a woman of Russian origin and had a son. He never spoke about his experience, but one memory was transmitted: that he had seen some of his fellow soldiers being literally castrated by the Bolsheviks. When World War II started, he was called to fight against Russia. Because of his loyalty towards 'Mother Russia', he hid with his son for four years, until the end of the war.

Misha's father

Misha's father subsequently became an active communist. In the 1950s, he travelled a few times to Russia, and because he was suspected of espionage, he was unable to carry out any sort of profession. Although a university graduate, he had no choice but to work as a harbour porter. He married very late and spent his life being angry and resentful. Misha remembers his father living in constant fear of the telephone being tapped and of being followed. Together with his own father, Misha's father must have experienced the Revolution as a real exclusion and rejection by his siblings, as being taken away from his mother Russia. Grandfather felt 'castrated' in his capacity to adapt to a new country, learn the language and live a normal life there. The loss of his country coincided with the loss of his identity and sense of agency. The external traumatic event had important resonance in the internal world of Misha's grandfather, let alone in his capacity to digest and make sense of such brutality. Misha remembered his grandfather's mistrust in goodness and how his father had invested all his energy in the impossible task of regaining what his father had lost: identity and integrity in his son's eye. Misha's father grew up under this show: he had tried to repossess his father's lost 'potency' and sense of agency by becoming a communist himself, but unfortunately, his hopes were unmet. His lifelong search was undermined by a black hole which resolved in a traumatic way with the end of the Soviet era and a total loss of identity on his side.

Misha

Misha spent his life in fear that the secret about his father would be revealed. He moved to London 20 years after the end of the Soviet Union, in order to feel free from the pressure he felt he was experiencing in his country. His fears were given fresh airing every time someone asked him personal questions. Misha grew up with the unspoken conviction that there was no hope for him. He was given the unconscious message that his life was very precarious. He found himself living with the conviction that his potency, identity and sense of agency were fake and could be taken away as soon as people would find out his father's past, which for him was still a present. This past was Misha's only internal truth, which covered an irrepresentability that was equated with his own vulnerability and fragility. For him, his father's past and his secret and his own vulnerability and fragility were one and the same thing. Misha did not have the capacity to challenge his conviction and was absolutely sure that if people found out about his father, he would have a breakdown. To survive this fear, Misha changed country and sought help.

Repossessing the lost potency

It took a few months in his analysis before Misha was able to disclose his complex past. At the beginning of our work, I became aware of his particular way of approaching any kind of problem. He would begin by telling me that he was experiencing difficulties in finding a solution for a particular problem at work for example. He would then be silent and cut off. If I asked him where he was, he would say 'In the past'.

With difficulty and perseverance over a certain period of time, I managed to bring him to externalize his thoughts and to share them with me. I finally began to understand what he meant. He used to go back to his childhood and look at every problem he had had. He would then attack himself for not having resolved each of them in a better or different way. These ruminations would go on and on, but they would always end up with the same conclusion, which was that if he had resolved the 'first problem' (the first problem he was ever faced with in his life) in the right way, he would now not have to face the very problem he was facing, and it was all due to wrong decisions made in the past that he had to face problems in the present.

These ruminations would occupy us for session after session until one day I asked where he had learnt to go back to problems of the past in order to solve problems of the future. It was then that Misha began to tell me about remembering his father and grandfather spending hours and hours together, talking about the past, revising their moves, their errors and attacking each other for their choices and faults. Very slowly, Misha was able to tell me in detail their pasts, their sufferings and their lives.

Eventually in one session, one of the many sessions in which there were long silences, I asked him, as I used to ask, what he was thinking. 'I am thinking about the past', he said. 'And what do you find today in the past?', I asked, as usual. 'My errors, what I could have done better', he answered, as usual. As usual, my countertransference response was a feeling of hopelessness. Again I felt useless, in front of a too difficult problem. Unexpectedly, in that session, a new image seemed to emerge in my mind. I began to visualize Misha's rumination as a sort of washing machine in which he was trying to clean a stain that could not be washed. I imagined that to get rid of the stain, he needed a new washing powder, not the one he used to wash with. I then imagined that in the washing machine there were his grandfather's fellow soldiers' uniforms, stained with blood. I imagined that the uniforms had been washed so many times that the fabric was about to disintegrate, but not the stain that was still visible.

This sequence of images propelled me to begin to put together a few thoughts in my mind, and, finally I was then able to say,

> Maybe you are finding only something known, which is what your father and grandfather used to do, castrating each other of a future. You too, by going back to the past and hating the you that you were in the past, are castrating yourself of a possibility of having a future. The present problem needs a present solution, a potency-giving present solution, not a lost chance to find a better solution for a lost past problem.

Although slightly bizarre, my reverie was the beginning of me repossessing some of my capacity for ordering and thinking since, in Misha's presence, I would often feel 'castrated' of my mind, incapacitated and unable to think.

While I was beginning to counteract the feeling of helplessness, at least in my mind, through the images that were emerging that I was trying to use in my interpretations, Misha's very entrenched 'coping strategy' seemed unperturbed by our conversations. The only thing that seemed to change was my capacity to stay alive and be curious about him and to withstand the attacks that his deadly ruminations seemed to have on me. Misha was not always responsive to my questions, and often I was left alone in the session to go on imagining, while he was occupied with his 'washing machine' strategy. Until one year later, when the following dialogue occurred:

AC: What are you thinking today?
M: About the past.
AC: And what do you find today in the past?
M: That I have a lot to do before I can think about the future.
AC: What do you mean?
M: Maybe . . . I wish I could change the past.
AC: Do you think that this is what your father and grandfather were hoping to be able to do?
M: They were angry.
AC: And what about you? Are you also angry that you have a problem now?
M: Yes. I think I am.
AC: So is it possible to think that when you are angry now, you go back to the past because you do not know what to do with your anger when you are angry now?
M: Yes . . . I think I want to go back to a time in which I have not been angry, a long time ago, before I was ever angry.
AC: A before time . . . and maybe you hope to go back to this before time every time you have a problem in the present and it makes you feel vulnerable. . . . Perhaps this is what your grandfather was trying to tell your father, that he had lived in that time before the war, and your father was angry because his own father could not protect him from the trauma of the war, and all the losses.
M: A time before . . . maybe when I was in my mother's womb I was in peace . . . and I was not angry . . . maybe I would like to go back there . . . maybe my mistake was to be born.

The chaos and the anxieties that Misha had absorbed from childhood were beginning to become thinkable. Misha's hope was to find someone who would help him to accept his vulnerability, his fragility, but at the same time enable him to believe in his future. In our work, we slowly began to identify feelings of shame and hate that had been transmitted from father to son and had been adsorbed and re-enacted. Those feelings were transmitted to him in the form of a belief that there was no hope for him to develop a sense of agency from which to make an attempt at mastering his future. The desire to move out of the past and equally the desire to believe in the future had been experienced as life threatening. He had been made to believe that in order to have a future, one would have had to be strong and perfect. We were able to 'translate' this idea of strength and perfection into an unrealistic state of being where feelings of shame, fear and hate do not exist. Fragility and vulnerability had, for Misha, the same meaning as loss of sense of identity and agency.

It was only after a lot of work that Misha began to have a more realistic view of his father as a vulnerable and angry man who had been fighting all his life against a sense of shame he had inherited from his own father and had passed on to his son. Misha was able to see how in all this his father was a strong man who had also paid personally for his choices. Misha began to see himself as European, as a way to include into his personal history the lives of his father and grandfather but also as a way of differentiating from them and setting for himself a different path separate from theirs:

M: When I now look at my father, I feel that he is a strong man. He is stronger than me. He still feels Russian; I feel European.

AC: Now that you can separate from your father and look at him as he is, you can see that he has made some choices, while you have made other choices. You are different from him. Perhaps you can even be proud of your father, the same way he seems to be proud of you.

M: Yes.

AC: And maybe one day you will be able to remember the story of your grandfather and father feeling proud about them, about their difficulties and their suffering.

M: This I don't know. Maybe I will tell this story to my children, if I ever marry, one day.

This was the first time that Misha was able to give himself the possibility of playing with the thought that he might also one day be able to marry, have a family and a real future. Misha's case illustrates very well how the lost life before the trauma can become equated in the internal world with loss of goodness and hope (Laub 2012; Gerson 2009; Garland 1999). While Misha's grandfather could not reintegrate the traumatic event into his self but had put defence mechanisms in place to avoid contact with it, Misha was finally able to understand and transform the sense of hate and shame that had been passed on to him and differentiate it from his own shame and hate: a new way of thinking about himself could finally emerge.

The deadly and its transmission in the maternal and the paternal line: a working hypothesis

Although it is the fact that there is trauma that matters (Laub 2012), I would nevertheless like to give some thought to some possible basic differences that might occur according to whether the transmitters of trauma are in the maternal or in the paternal line.

I am referring here in particular to the fact that close contact with the maternal unconscious during gestation might have a paramount importance in the transmission, already affecting the foetus during gestation. Instead of differentiating between maternal and paternal lines, it might be more helpful to try to trace back with each patient the extent to which the trauma might have affected the maternal unconscious during gestation, as it is possible to postulate that much deeper layers of the psyche of the foetus could be affected if the transmitted trauma interferes with the maternal unconscious during the pregnancy.

If mother's mind is already inhabited by trauma (her own or her husband's) during gestation, her incapacity to differentiate will work as a shadow under which the foetus will be developing. Authors like Rey (1994) and Raphael-Leff (1993) have given particular attention to the relevance of early psychic development to pregnancy, to inhibition of mourning, arriving at calling the womb a Pandora's box (the studies of Piontelli (1992) vividly illustrate this point). Fraiberg (1980) and Faimberg (2005) have shown clearly in their work that where there is no representation there can be no separation, only identification. If the maternal unconscious is inhabited by ghosts and void (her own or her husband's), she will not be able to transmit to her infant an internal sense of security and a version of herself as a mother who can protect her child from her own, her husband's and her child's destructive phantasy (Perelberg 1997, p. 24). The more protected the foetus is from the deadly and the void in his development, the more likely it is that he will gradually be able to build his sense of identity and of agency. The earlier the foetus or the infant has been exposed to what has been unthinkable and unrepresentable in the parents, the greater the damage on the unfolding primary self. The analyst working with patients who are affected by transgenerational trauma is required not only to relate to the chaotic mass, to tolerate the unknown, to free associate with the horror and vacuum in which the patient exists but also to imagine how the patient's life might have been from the beginning. This will be of help in creating a container for the undifferentiated, in which a shape can be given to what could not be perceived or represented.

Conclusion

In this chapter, I have tried to define trauma and made some hypotheses about its transmission, which I have understood as the transmission of disorganizing deadly ghosts and mental void. I have tried to postulate a possible way of working with the third generation by creating 'three generational interpretations' as a way to contain and describe the vicissitudes of trauma across the generations. I have described how the deadly third (Gerson 2009) and the mental void work as antimatrices and how I have tried to create a matrix in which to contain the deadly and the mental void of the three generations.

By differentiating them from each other, I have tried to contain the psychic wholeness of each of them in separate but interrelating ways. I have tried to create a language for and with the patient, which contains the deadly, but also works as an opening to life. I hope to have shown how the analyst has to connect with the patient's void in such a way as to give voice and life to what seems to be unrepresentable and has no expression. It is the analyst's responsibility to help the patient to find a language for the irrepresentable. This language is the language through which deintegration and reintegration can start anew – a language that is able to create some space for the third-ness described by Britton, a lively space for reflection and meaning (Britton 2004).

I hope to have been able to show that this language begins with attention. With attention and courage, the analyst can approach the deadly and the mental void to which the patient has created an attachment. It was precisely because of lack of attention that these patients felt themselves to be living in an undifferentiated timeless world, the world of trauma. The patient needs to be able to transfer the deadly on to the analyst in the hope that he or she can stay put and find a way of managing it. I hope to have shown that the earlier the patient has been confronted in their development with a deadly third, the deeper the influence on their unfolding self will be, with devastating consequences.

Angela Connolly suggested that in working with inter-generational transmission of trauma, reconstruction is important (2011, p. 607). Meredith-Owen in his paper on Jung's shadow addressed how it is possible to work around the trauma in an impressive and magnificent way without being able to penetrate the trauma, but by creating a sense of self working 'around the blank impress' (Meredith-Owen 2011, p. 688). In this chapter, I have taken a different view. I have spoken about construction, different from reconstruction, as a way of penetrating the blank and creating a canvas which connects the 'blank impress' to the rest of the fabric of the self.

This canvas is a patch, but it does not emerge from hallucination; it is the difficult and skilful darn of a patient mender. The choice of threads springs as much as possible out of the internal and external reality of the patient. The patch gives life to what in this chapter I have called the 'deadly'. For the first patient I presented in this chapter, the deadly meant a confused mixture between trauma and herself. By vomiting, Anna was hoping to get rid of something inimical to herself which seemed to her to be her Self. For the second patient, the deadly was the future, as if there had been a past before the past in which he would have felt protected from a deadly future. Perhaps we can postulate that Anna's experience of the deadly was operating from the beginning of her life, while for Misha there was still a place, maybe in the womb, in which he 'remembered' having felt safe. Both their enactments were enmeshed with the transmitted traumas of their parents. Both my patients could begin to forget the deadly as soon as they began to know about it. Only then could they begin to remember it because they were beyond it.

Acknowledgement

This is an edited version of a paper that was presented at the *Journal of Analytical Psychology* May 2011 International Conference in St. Petersburg entitled The Ancestors in Personal, Professional and Social History.

Note

1 First published in *Journal of Analytical Psychology*, 57, 5, November 2012.

References

Auerhahn, N., & Laub, D. (1984). 'Annihilation and restoration: post-traumatic memory as pathway and obstacle to recovery'. *International Review of Psychoanalysis*, 11, 327–44.

Baranger, M., Baranger, W., & Mom, J. (1988). 'The infantile psychic trauma from us to Freud. Pure trauma, retroactivity and reconstruction'. *International Journal of Psycho-Analysis*, 69, 113–28.

Bion, W. (1962). *Learning from Experience*. London: Heinemann.

———. (1967). *Second Thoughts*. London: Heinemann.

Bolognini, S. (2011). *Secret Passages*. London and New York: Routledge.

Botella, C., & Botella, S. (2005). *The Work of Figurability*. London and New York: Routledge.

Britton, R. (2004). 'Subjectivity, objectivity, and triangular space'. *Psychoanalytic Quarterly*, 73, 47–62.

Brown, L. (2011). *Intersubjective Processes and the Unconscious*. London and New York: Routledge.

Connolly, A. (2011). 'Healing the wounds of our fathers: intergenerational trauma, memory, symbolization and narrative'. *Journal of Analytical Psychology*, 56, 5, 607–26.

Faimberg, H. (2005). *The Telescoping of Generations: Listening to the Narcissistic Links between Generations*. London and New York: Routledge.

Ferro, A. (2010). *Avoiding Emotions, Living Emotions*. London and New York: Routledge.

Fraiberg, S. (1980). 'Ghosts in the nursery: a psychoanalytic approach to the problem of impaired infant-mother relationships'. *Clinical Studies in Infant Mental Health*. The First Year of Life. Tavistock Publication, 164–96.

Garland, C. (1999). *Understanding Trauma*. London: Karnac Books and Tavistock Clinic Series.

Gerson, S. (2009). 'When the third is dead. Memory, mourning and witnessing in the aftermath of the Holocaust'. *International Journal of Psychoanalysis*, 90, 6, 1341–57.

Green, A. (1986). *On Private Madness*. London: Hogarth.

Knox, J. (2011). *Self-agency in Psychotherapy: Attachment, Autonomy and Intimacy*. London and New York: W.W. Norton.

Laub, D. (2012). 'Traumatic shutdown of narrative and symbolization: a death instinct derivative?' In *Lost in Transmission*, ed. G. Fromm. London: Karnac Books.

Laub, D., & Podell, D. (1995). 'Art and trauma'. *International Journal of Psycho-Analysis*, 74, 287–302.

Main, M., & Hesse, E. (1990). 'Parents' unresolved traumatic experiences are related to infant disorganized status'. In *Attachment in the Pre-school Years: Theory, Research and Intervention*, eds. D. Greenburg et al. Chicago: University of Chicago Press.

Meredith-Owen, W. (2011). 'Jung's shadow: negation and narcissism of the Self'. *Journal of Analytical Psychology*, 56, 5, 674–91.

Mizen, R. (2003). 'A contribution towards an analytic theory of violence'. *Journal of Analytical Psychology*, 48, 3, 285–305.

Moore, Y. (2009). 'Thoughts on representation in therapy of Holocaust survivors'. *International Journal of Psychoanalysis*, 90, 6, 1373–91.

Perelberg, R.J. (1997). 'Introduction to Part I'. In *Female Experience*, eds. J. Raphael-Leff & R. J. Perelberg. London: Routledge.

Piontelli, A. (1992). *From Fetus to Child*. London: Routledge.

Poland, W. (2000). 'The analyst's witnessing and otherness'. *Journal of the American Psychoanalytic Association*, 48, 17–34.

Raphael-Leff, J. (1993). *Pregnancy. The Inside Story*. London: Karnac Books.

Rey, H. (1994). *Universals of Psychoanalysis in The Treatment of Psychotic and Borderline States*. London: Free Association Books.

Chapter 5

From affect to feelings and thoughts

From abuse to care and understanding[1]

Introduction

Panksepp (1998) understands affect as a medium, a disposition, a way of being in the world: conversely an absence of affect would amount to a disengagement from the world. So 'affect' could be described as a potential for object relation, 'feelings' as the capacity to be in object relation. This chapter attempts to illustrate the difficult journey from affect to feelings, and the role that containment has to play in it. McGilchrist (2009, p. 184) describes this journey as follows, 'Affect is the irreducible core of experience, it is the heart of our being, and reason emanates from that central core of the affect, in an attempt to limit and direct it'. Neuroscience helps us to frame our human experience: this chapter would like to show what it means to live it.

Jung wrote 'Psychic Conflicts of a Child' in 1913, four years after Freud's 'Little Hans' (Freud 1909). He was following Freud's suggestion to explore infantile neurosis in children. While Freud was more interested in the conflict between instinct, the outside world and the ego, Jung seemed more interested in the development of thinking per se. He postulated that the desire for knowledge is inborn in humans and that the seeking of solutions for psychic conflicts strengthens the ego and the development of the capacity to think. Jung described the quest of little Anna (his 4-year-old daughter) who had suddenly become obsessed with a curiosity about volcanoes to find out the truth about her mother's pregnancy. Jung was interested in thinking about how the desire for knowledge unfolds: what blocks it, what stimulates it and how a child takes responsibility for it. Jung guided little Anna in her quest, respecting her alacrity and scientific interest, describing how she sublimated her neurotic nocturnal fears into knowledge. Phantasy about sexuality, pregnancy, unconscious fears of losing her parents' love and of being abandoned, as well as angry feelings towards her pregnant mother, lay beneath her burgeoning interests. This preoccupation with volcanoes represented the way Anna managed her anxieties through flight from an emotional experience. This is similar to what Green (1986, p. 160) calls 'an extensive intellectual activity which re-establishes the wounded narcissistic omnipotence, and is support for a

DOI: 10.4324/9781003268536-6

phantasy of auto-satisfaction'. But she did recover from it. Once she was ready to know, and the truth was told to her, her nocturnal fears disappeared, and she regained her serenity.

For some time, Anna treated the volcano as a substitute for something else she was afraid of experiencing: her anger and hostility towards her mother and her newly born baby brother. Because there were other minds there – her mother's and her father's – who were helping her to digest and understand herself, a learning experience that could impart meaning had been able to take place, Anna could abandon her interest in the volcano and digest the truth about her parents' sexual intercourse, her emotional reaction to it and the birth of her little brother. Jung seems to say that at the end of her search, little Anna was able to cope with her reality, had achieved a stronger ego and could manage the complexity of her feelings towards her newborn brother and her parents. To paraphrase McGilchrist, the core of the affect could be contained and channelled. An experience of hostility from which little Anna had been trying to escape because of its explosive nature could now be faced, managed, understood and integrated.

Matte Blanco (1975), in his book *The Unconscious as Infinite Sets*, puts forward the notion that the magnitude of affect is a function of the balance between symmetrical and asymmetrical experience. Matte Blanco's framework offers a new way of theorizing about affect (Carvalho 2013, p. 46): as symmetrically inclined unconscious affect is potentially infinite, a limited space with boundaries – that is, an asymmetrical finite universe in which feelings could have a particular place – seems to offer protection from such potential overwhelmingness. Bion's notion of containment (Bion 1962), as Bion pointed out (Bion-Talamo in Rayner 1995, p. 150), can be understood as the function that translates infinite affect into finite feelings. In this chapter, I explore what it might mean to live at the mercy of raw affect and what it takes for ordinary object relations to unfold. Drawing on the clinical material of my work with an adolescent patient who experienced emotional neglect and abuse, I hope to show the journey that patients like mine have to undertake in order to resolve unmetabolized affect. The pressure of such affect blurs the distinction between abusive relationships that offer spurious promises of refuge and ordinary relationships which can help affect become a manageable part of daily life.

Indeed, initially such an ordinary, 'healthy' relationship may actually be experienced as itself abusive because it helps such patients establish contact with the molten lava of their own internal volcanic feelings. But through the slow transformation of affect into feelings, these patients can begin to differentiate between the impact of external neglect and abuse and the core affect of their own being. In the wake of this, they can come to recognize their vulnerability in seeking the false shelter of abusive 'love'.

The patient I am writing about did not have a mind to rely on which could help her to understand and make sense of her feelings; her long analysis finally became the transformative place where that could happen.

Theoretical consideration

According to Bion (1962), the process of containing one's own affect is possible only when a mental capacity is in place thanks to which affect, initially experienced as bodily events, can be tolerated and held as long as is necessary for it to become known and transformed into a proto-thought (or an unconscious phantasy). He calls this the capacity to transform beta into alpha (Bion 1962). The capacity to transform affect into an emotional experience that can eventually be thought about requires a mind and a body which are linked together and can work together. This is what Bion (ibid.) calls container contained, and it brings about the capacity to have an experience that can be lived and known about. Put in these terms, the intercourse between mind and body could be seen as the realization of an archetypal potential that can only be constelled when, through interaction with another, enough capacity to bear affect has been established. This comes about initially by splitting such experience into good and bad, for in its rawest form, undifferentiated affect may be experienced as an event which may be simultaneously hateful and loving. As alpha function expresses the capacity to give internal meaning to experience, this capacity to differentiate affect into different kinds of feeling is fundamental. Experiences which cannot become alpha remain beta, unable to be informed with meaning and hence nameless – 'nameless dread'. These can neither be split nor repressed; they can only be dissociated. When the psyche is unable to bear such experiences which are threatening the self, they must perforce remain unprocessed and be feared as deadly. The capacity to feel and think can only be constelled by a self that is capable of processing otherness, of recognizing the potential for a new emotion in what might be otherwise experienced as an alien threat (Ferrari & Stella 1998 [quoted in Carvalho 2009]). If this otherness is not contained, the affect associated with it becomes a persecutor against which the unity of the primary self defends itself; deintegration out of this primary self is experienced as disintegration (Fordham 1985, p. 153).

Such patients have to be helped to explore such deintegrations instead of being left afraid of being disintegrated by them. In other words, they need to be held in such a way as to be able to experience the affect as long as it is necessary for it to become embodied, humanized, meaningful. This is the prerequisite for beta to become alpha. Differentiation from unity (primary self on the one side, caregiver on the other side) can be experienced as an abusive threat from within and without of such intensity that it may destroy the self. But deintegration necessarily involves such differentiation; it means moving away from a relating that insists the other is absolutely attuned. The initial experience of such a differentiation is felt to be so threatening and violent that it is experienced as if it were abuse. The recoil from such a threat leaves these patients condemned to a life of exile from themselves in an incomprehensible world, in which they are blind to their own emergent passions and desires. Such patients can become prone to abuse, as well as to become abusive themselves. Their desire to control their object reflects their need to control their own affect: concomitantly once their objects are allowed to be free and separate, their affect is also liberated to unfold into feeling.

From affect to feelings and thoughts   79

A literature review with regard to dissociative and borderline phenomena associated with such a profile is beyond the scope of this chapter. My aim is merely to describe and reflect on one clinical example of living on the edge of object relation, where undifferentiated affect is perceived as infinite and dangerous, and fusion and control feel the only possible alternative. In the course of this, I will consider abandonment and longing as undigested affects that have never been contained and therefore threaten to flood the recipient with nameless dread. Emotionally neglected patients actually fall prey to abusive others because the abuser seems to promise a sort of 'fusion', which is seductive to these patients who see it as a protection from that differentiation which threatens to bring with it overwhelming emotions. Thus the actual abuser cannot be perceived by these patients as abusive until the moment when he fails to protect these patients from their own affect. Conversely, another who is actually helping these patients to experience emotion through containing their affect can be perceived by them as abusive. The clinical material will show how this represents a major problem in transference.

My patient's history

Mary was 15 when she started once-a-week therapy with me. I will give a brief account of her life as it was understood by her and others at the beginning of her therapy. At the end of this chapter, I will recount her revised biography, modified as it was by our work which lasted seven and half years and moved from one to two, three and four times a week.

Mary's mother was raped: Mary was the baby of this intercourse. Mary's mother soon became attached to a second man with whom she had a second child, a daughter, who was born one year after Mary's birth. Mary's mother began to suffer from depression, and the two children were repeatedly put into foster care for periods of up to a few months until their mother was able to mother them again. The relationship with this second man slowly deteriorated, and he left for another woman. Mary's mother met another man who was younger. He lived nearby and began to look after the children in the mother's absence when she was at work. He sexually abused Mary when Mary was 8. Mary only disclosed the abuse when she saw this man subsequently inviting her sister to bed with him. The two sisters were taken away from home and put into care with a new foster mother, Mrs Y. Mary's mother was denied parental rights, and so the relationship between the children and the mother slowly dwindled to an exchange of letters and telephone calls. The new foster mother was able to develop a good relationship with Mary's sister, but not with Mary. In order to help Mary overcome the difficult relationship with her mother, she told Mary to hate her mother and to forget her. At this point, Mary entered a very difficult period. She stopped eating and accused the foster mother of wanting to kill her by beating her, by banging her head on the radiator and by poisoning her food. An enquiry did not substantiate these claims. Mary was put in a children's home for girls with eating disorders where she immediately began to eat again. Two years later, she was fostered by a new family. This placement was very successful, and it was this last foster mother who referred Mary to me. Mary had been able to develop a strong bond with her new foster parents who did not have children of their own. She was very affectionate, but terribly controlling of her new foster mother. Mary had meanwhile lost touch with her biological mother and sister. The man who had abused her had been put in prison and had written a letter to Mary to apologize. By the time we started therapy, he had died.

Year one: idealization as necessity and defence

The movements of my patient's psychic development were closely paralleled by her physical movements in the room during her analysis. They constitute a sort of map – a geographical movement of psychic states – that constitute the first symbolic attempts of the patient to represent herself in relation to another and to herself.

Mary sits at my feet and holds my hand. The therapy begins; the transference is total and concrete. Mary gazes at me with an intense look of adoration, as if she knows I will save her life. Her hand is sweating, and she is distressed; she holds my hand even more tightly. Her foster mother told her that I will help her to solve her problems. At this stage, her biggest concern is to find her biological mother again. She longs to meet her, and she spends a lot of time thinking about her. Soon she will be 16, and she hopes her mother will send her a letter, a card. I do not dare to take my hand away, even though I know that it is against recommended practice, but perhaps this is 'the exception that proves the rule', so I allow her to hold my hand, as she will continue to do for the first year of therapy. Holding my hand enacts contact with the breast to which Mary needs to feel strongly attached before she can experience a satisfactory weaning. My hand is a talisman, a magical tool which will make us one, inseparable. Holding my hand makes her feel protected from an unpredictable me and an unpredictable her. In the course of the work, I come to understand the holding of my hand equates in the transference to a benevolent mother's image she is holding inside herself. Holding on to this image has always saved her life. In moments of distress, since she has been put into care, she learnt to survive by holding on to her mother's image, which protected her from nameless dread. This image, as much as my hand, was a sort of idealized maternal image, the precursor of a good object. It will only be much later that I will understand that holding on to the internal image of her mother, as well as my hand, in an almost omnipotent way was a desperate attempt to prevent the catastrophe of being at the mercy of a bad object, which like her own affect, could possess and annihilate her.

This initial phase of the therapy revolves around getting hold of my hand, holding it tightly and not wanting to let it go, a sort of re-enactment of her life. Mary begins to text me in between sessions. She wants to touch base. 'Are you there?' . . . 'See you on Tues'. The texting begins to increase, in parallel to her fears that I could die, hate her, abandon her, get rid of her. By the end of the first year of therapy, the pattern begins to change. Mary arrives furious and has a go at me, 'a week was so long'. She asks me if I am depressed, 'you are so calm', 'is everything ok?' Then she calms down, takes my hand, and holds it tighter and tighter until the end of the session when the fury returns. She is not angry with me so much as with the fact that she cannot control my hand. This hand belongs to me, and although I keep coming back without being depressed, there is nothing she can do about not having my hand or me all to herself. If she did, she would not have to wait, would not have to feel furious or afraid, feel anything at all. In the meantime, I offer to increase the frequency to twice a week, but this offer frightens her even more. She begins to fear I will abuse her by making her more and more dependent. It will take a few months of preparation until she decides to accept my offer, which feels to her, despite everything, to be a seductive move. It may make her feel special (on the one hand), but am I going to abuse her (on the other)? What are my motives? She says yes but keeps watching me. I introduce the idea that perhaps she should not hold my hand anymore. The move from one to twice a week brings the abuser Mr X into the room, and, as I wean her from my hand, I become identified with the abuser. There is a wish to be 'abused' so as to be special and not have to separate from me. In these months, she wants me to adopt her. This would be the best solution.

Years two and three: letting go of the hand-breast and the beginning of differentiation

With this increase to twice a week, Mary has begun to use the room in a different way. She arrives in a state of fury and sits far away from me in a corner. She pours out her anger at me for being a control freak. What on earth do I want from her? Why do I make her suffer so much? First, I make her attached to me only to then end the session and send her away. But why do I want to see her twice a week? Is she special? Her hope of being loved, that she is special, makes her come close to me after 20 minutes. She sits close to my chair and tries in some way to seduce me to give her my hand back. Ten minutes before the end of the session, I begin to prepare her for this whereupon she stands up and tries to convince me that I should adopt her. But then a few minutes before the end of the session, seeing that her manoeuvres have brought no results, she sits opposite me saying she will not leave the room, and she means it; so I leave the room at the end of the session, while she remains alone until she is convinced that I will not come back and all her efforts have been to no avail. This moving back and forth, close and far away from me, represents a first beginning of splitting: it is as if Mary is thinking, 'I am in control; I have lost control; I am angry at not being able to control; I feel safe because I am in control. Interestingly enough, however, I am also safe when I'm not in control because nothing awful happens after all. Alessandra sends me away but comes back'. In all this toing and froing, she begins to discover something new, my calmness and through that a new way of thinking. A desire to know herself emerges from the need to understand this situation.

Letters between sessions replace the hand-me she cannot have. In between sessions, she begins to think. She finds me confusing, and she does not understand why I don't abuse her. If I want to see her more often, it must be because I think she is special, but because I don't want to adopt her, it must mean I will end up abusing her. The abuser, Mr X, feels back in the room, chiefly when she is angry and confused, and then she sits far away from me. With the abusive Mr X, the abusive mother also comes into the room: the mother who did not protect her, who abandoned her and did not come to her rescue. Mary begins to remember and speaks about the mother who did not protect her. One day, she admits to herself that she always felt that Mr X was not ok, but she was seduced by the expectation of feeling special because she was chosen by him. This is why she allowed him to do what he did. She is able at this point to tolerate me saying that by holding my hand she was hoping to seduce me by making me feel special so that she could have me all to herself. It is around this time that foster mother Mrs Y enters the room. With Mrs Y's entrance, all possibility of thinking is obliterated. Why, why, why did she abuse her? Why did she poison her food? Why did she bang Mary's head onto the wall? Mary becomes a brick wall against which I bang my head. The fury I have to tolerate is incredible, and it is to this fury that I want to dedicate a few thoughts.

My sense of what Mary was really asking me to think about was why she had been abused and why she had allowed the abuse and not stopped it. My understanding was that her mother's abuse consisted of her incapacity to contain her child's feelings of exclusion and rejection. Consequently, by allowing Mr X to abuse her, Mary was searching for a way of looking after the unmanageable feelings that her mother had not been able to contain. When she finally lost the hope of being reunited with her mother and was put into care, her first foster mother told her to hate her mother. On a very deep level, this meant to Mary that she had to let go not only of her actual mother but also of the primordial image of the good object she had projected into her. Doing so meant the loss of any protection at all, and of being invaded by nameless dread. Hence her fantasy that her foster mother was poisoning her and exposing her to the dangerous hand of abusive beta elements. By allowing the actual abuse, she had hoped to escape the experience of the dread of the terrifying feelings she did not know how to deal with and at whose mercy she felt. By reporting what she felt to be Mrs Y's abuse, she was hoping to be saved from nameless dread, a fear compounded by the terror of her own hatred of her mother's incapacity to mediate it.

Understood in these terms, her fury was directed not so much against an object that leaves her, as against an object who exposes her to unbearable affect; in this case, the mother who left her feeling excluded and neglected, then the foster mother who stirred her hatred for her mother and, finally, the abuser who induced unbearable feelings of jealousy when he began to abuse her sister and left her behind. At the deepest levels of affect, all these experiences become linked, undifferentiated and confused, one consequence of which was my patient's accusation that her foster mother had abused her, thus deflecting her internal fear of annihilation into her. A similar muddle surrounded the delay in Mary's reporting of the actual sexual abuse, which only happened when the perpetrator turned to her sister. Mary became invaded by unbearable feelings of exclusion and jealousy that were confused with an even more primitive abuse: the unmanageable volcanic feelings of rejection that she must have felt when her mother became ill and put her into care. We will see later how the affect is attributed to the one who puts her in touch with it, even though they are not responsible. This is why she accused Mrs Y of abuse, and, as we shall see shortly, why she accused me. Slowly the picture begins to emerge of a very hurt girl who is so confused as to be in a constant panic, so much so that I suggest we increase our work to three times a week. Mary is hesitant but agrees.

Years four and five: the emergence of a third

Mary's fear of being abused reappears, but by coming three times a week, she begins to move in the room in a different way. She begins to use the couch as a sort of neutral place. She sits on the couch when she can bear being not too close or not too far away from me. She begins each session by giving me a letter she has written for me – this represents her thinking in between sessions – and while I read her letter and comment on it, she sits on the couch and from there she listens and replies to what I have to say.

It becomes clear that when she sits on the couch, she is in a relationship with me. When she sits close to me, she is either trying to control me or her feelings, but when she sits far away from me, she is desperate because she cannot control me and is hoping to abuse me in order to pre-empt any thinking or feeling. It is around this period that her biological mother sends her a card for her 18th birthday, in acknowledgement of her daughter's maturity.

Mary has to face reality and meets her mother after ten years. She has to recognize her mother's fragility and mental vulnerability. Suddenly she is confronted with real pain, but she does not know how to bear it. It is the impossibility of avoiding the pain that we have to face together that propels Mary into a psychotic episode. A few weeks after having seen her mother again, Mary is about to meet her sister whom she had not seen for six years and who was left with her foster mother Mrs Y when Mary was taken into the children's home first and then to her second foster mother. Mary is able to confess to herself that the reason she disclosed Mr X's abuse was the fact that she saw him inviting her sister to bed with him. This was unbearable to her; she had suddenly realized that she was not special, and the pain she could not bear propelled her to disclose the abuse. She had to face now her own guilt about having put herself and her sister at the mercy of social services, and the pain of feeling responsible for the loss of her mother. Having spelt out all that, she sat far away from me. She began to scream that it was all her mother's responsibility for not having protected her, for being mentally fucked up.

She was able to hear from me that she felt I was like her mother and was not able to protect her from the pain of seeing with her own eyes how many contradictory feelings she was experiencing, some belonging to the past, some belonging to the present. And that how afraid she was that the only refuge from all this would be abuse that offered the promise of shutting out all this mess.

She left the room in the middle of the session, shouting at me, saying I was like Mrs Y, I had made her come here for four years only in order to abuse her and to get pleasure out of it. She had believed in me, but I was the worst of the abusers, my way of getting pleasure was to humiliate her even more than everybody else. She went, saying she would never come back; she would kill herself. Outside it was raining, and I did not move from my chair. Ten minutes later, she came back, totally soaked. I helped her to put her coat on the chair, while she was sitting far away from me, her back against the radiator. Suddenly she began to bang her head on the radiator, saying I was abusing her, that I was banging her head on the radiator, that I was Mrs Y.

Slowly she recovered. Meanwhile, I was saying that it seemed as if the terrible pain she was feeling was coming from me, as if I was really banging her head on the radiator, as if I was really poisoning her food with my words. I said that all her life, she had run away from this pain, which seemed unbearable. I said that she had mistaken the pain for abuse, and the abuse for the pain she was running away from. I also added that her mother had not been able to protect her from this pain, and this is why she hated her mother so much, the same mother she had also always loved.

Mary left and the next session, she announced that 'the holy spirit had helped her to understand that I was right'. One might postulate that while the psychotic episode may have been an attempt to seek refuge in the infinite magnitude and complete symmetry of the unconscious (Matte Blanco 1975) – thus avoiding having to come to terms with asymmetrical consciousness and pain – the emergence of her newly acquired capacity for reflection and differentiation had led Mary to locate in the holy spirit what we might call hope. The experience of having been deeply understood, and the hope arising from that, seemed to work as a third element, a binding force, an integrator of past experiences. Although Kalsched might emphasize the 'holy spirit's' role as a 'transpersonal container in the absence of the personal one' (2013, p. 42), I read Mary's communication as more indicative of a conscious move towards differentiation between herself and her objects, and between affect and abuse, with a consequent increase of ego strength and capacity to create meaning for herself. Mary was now able to contain my words and reflect on them but did not seem to know how to name this – to her still unfamiliar – activity of her Self. What my patient was attributing to the 'holy spirit' was her own capacity to resolve psychic conflict.

Despite this, Mary's fear of pain, which I now identify as her terror of being in touch with feelings, was still unbearable. The next session, she sat very close to me on the floor, as a way of asking for protection from the feelings. Slowly she began to recover from this episode, which was bringing her in touch with her past and with the confused way in which she sought to contain emotions through abuse. Reality was knocking at the door: the meeting with her mother had made her face her mother's limitations, her own and mine. The perfect mother talisman 'hand-me' that was supposed to protect from pain was not useful to her anymore, but having to relinquish it had propelled her into a psychotic state in which there is no difference between me and not-me, between external and internal, between past and present.

It is near the end of this fourth year of our work together that her foster father died of a heart attack. At the time of this terrible loss, I suggested increasing the analysis to four times a week and moving the therapy onto the couch.

Years five and six: thinking begins, accompanied by the emergence of persecutory feelings which become gradually manageable

The increase in frequency does not affect Mary in the way it did in the past. She is not so much afraid that I will abuse her as of the feelings she has to bear, which she experiences as if they were abuse. She is now using the couch, and she spends a lot of time screaming and crying. Why did her foster father die? Why was she abused? Why all this suffering? Although there is a hysterical quality in her way of wanting to enact rather than feel the feeling – a theatrical way of suffering – it becomes clear that Mary is slowly learning to digest unbearable emotions, and she is making use of me as a container for them.

The more she is able to bear feelings, the more she is able to have a realistic relationship with people around her. She begins to build up a lasting relationship with her biological mother and sister, and she is becoming less controlling of her foster mother and of me, which means accepting our limitations and the fact that we are separate. She has to give up her wish to control us and her emotions in relation to us, her omnipotent hope I would adopt her and above all, she has to come to terms with her foster father's death. From the couch, she develops an observing eye through which she can slowly and gradually look at herself and the world around her. It is this eye which she did not have before, the same eye which Oedipus blinded in a desperate gesture to avoid recognizing the reality of his circumstances. This capacity for reflection, the missing link (Britton 1989), arises from triangulation, the ability to look on at ourselves and others. This geometrical form emerges through acknowledging the separateness of two people and allows feelings previously experienced as alien to now be accepted and integrated. The fear of being abused by feelings had brought my patient to escape suffering at all cost by collapsing such triangulation and turning to actual abuse as an alternative option. She had confused containment and abuse and was desperately muddled as to how to relate to others. While Mary had primarily been concerned to avoid suffering, she was now beginning to integrate the 'evil' feelings she had felt abused by: longing, envy, jealousy, hate, despair. She was learning that only by 'marrying them' could she be saved from real abuse and chaos. Finally, she could begin to differentiate between abuse and containment and begin to see the implication of the real abuse she had experienced. At the end of her sixth year of analysis, Mary had reached the age where she could finally access three thick files that social service had collected about her case. Her case was finally closed.

The files helped her to put order in her life from an external point of view of events, and she was then able to revisit her past with a different internal eye.

Year seven: end of analysis and emergence of the depressive position – retelling her story

While Mary was getting used to having me help her sort out her feelings and emotions, I was beginning to feel that our analytical arrangement was becoming too comfortable to her. I began to feel that she had adjusted to our work as if it was going to be infinite; therefore, I decided to introduce the idea that one day we would have to separate and that our work together would at some point end. This coincided with her wish to find a full-time job and become financially independent from her foster mother. We agreed to continue for 18 more months, and we set a date for the end of our analytical relationship.

The plan of ending her analysis led Mary to resort again to feeling abused by a me who was now fed up with her and wanted to get rid of her, like her mother who was depressed and had given her up for some months when she was a baby. It was the real terror of having a breakdown, ultimately of dying, that propelled her to offer to pay more, to increase to five, six and seven sessions a week. I had to be very firm in resisting all her attempts to convince me that she was not ready to end. For several months, I was the worst abuser ever until Mary met her first boyfriend. The desire to have a close relationship with another human who was different from me propelled her to risk falling in love. The separation from me meant not only having to accept her past and give up her desire to control emotions and others, but it also opened up possibilities of her sharing the intimacy she had experienced with me with someone else. She began to enjoy a sense of independence and of liberation from me, as well as being very sad at having to leave me.

Mary was 22 when she ended her four times a week analysis with me. She had been in a relationship with her boyfriend for six months, and she was beginning to explore her sexuality with him.

At the end of her analysis, Mary was able to revisit for us her story. Her mother was a brave but unstable young woman who had started a relationship with an irresponsible man who did not feel ready to have a baby. He wanted her to abort the child and left her abruptly. Mary's mother decided to keep this baby and, after meeting another man, she tried again to build a family with him. Unfortunately, she was too unstable, and she began to suffer from depression and her marriage ended badly with a divorce. She had nevertheless always made sure that social services would look after her children when she felt unable to do so. When Mary was seven, her mother met Mr X, an immature and perverted young man who betrayed her mother's trust. Mary's mother could not protect her children from the abuse (we had no information about her own childhood), and they were taken away from her. Mary's mother fought to get them back but understood that she was not strong enough to have a family and accepted her fate. After having disclosed the abuse, Mary became seriously ill, was depressed, and subsequently psychotic. Once her former foster mother had given her permission to hate her mother, this acted within her as a real poison. The loss of the mother she had been holding tight to in her mind propelled her into a world without meaning, towards death. Hate seemed to the 8-year-old Mary a real poison which had the power to kill her. Almost at the end of her analysis, she discovered that she had been taken to a psychiatrist by her former foster mother and had indeed been given antidepressants which Mary had mistaken for poison in her persecuted state of mind. After this she was assigned to a home and subsequently fostered by a kind and childless couple: there she could be looked after properly and experience normality. Once she had re-established contact with her mother and sister, she was able to maintain a regular relationship with them. She was able to make some reparation for the past, including the difficulty in facing the fact that she had had a better chance than them with her second foster family, as this couple looked after her not only emotionally but also financially in a generous way. She was able to forgive Mr X and Mrs Y, to mourn the death of her foster father and allow her foster mother to be free to have a new life after her husband's death. Mary is now in a relationship with a suitable young man and works in a nursery as a teacher. She has moved out of her foster mother's flat and now lives on her own.

Ultimately, Mary was able to work through the negative transference and resolve her analysis. The capacity to accept the limitations and imperfections of her analyst helped Mary to develop a way of managing her affect and find a place for anger and aggression in her personal development, as much as for love and fondness. This was substantially different from her initial presumptions about love (control) and hate (deadly affect).

Conclusion

In this chapter, I hope to have shown that it is possible to think of abuse not only in terms of the relationship between the caregiver and the infant but also in terms of the relationship that an infant experiences between their mind and body. The infant who is failed will not learn how to contain and hold the pressure of affect: a rudimentary alpha function cannot be constellated in the mind. Although an archetypal guiding force (nature) accompanies the infant in this task, it is necessary for the infant to be held and contained (nurture) by a caregiver who can help the infant experience the pressure of affect without its gathering lethal intensity. When the mind can accept what the body is forcing into it, the affect can be experienced and thought about. This was not the case for Mary who could not learn how to feel and, for fear of being abused by affect, looked for ways to escape her 'destiny'. While some people try to escape the abusive impact of overpowering affect by a compulsive continuing repetition of abuse, Mary had the courage to seek an analysis.

I hope to have shown that separation and loss are as necessary for development as attunement and holding. These alternate, and the maturation of the person consists in allowing this process to evolve without controlling it. As this unfolds, it becomes possible to separate from 'the first object of desire' (Britton 1989, p. 100) and look for subsequent objects of desire, as my patient has been able to do.

The capacity to bear affect is a lifelong journey which begins at birth and needs to be negotiated again and again over time, at each stage of life. If it has never been constellated, its negative will constitute the individual's being. Having never been contained, this 'negative' will be repeatedly experienced as 'raping, abusing and scaring' the patient, as well as anyone with whom they become involved. Abuse might feel seductive to these patients as it promises protection from such painful feelings which threaten, initially, to be made even more intrusive and persecutory by the differentiation within containment offered by the analytic relationship.

Note

1 First published in *Journal of Analytical Psychology*, 59, 1, January 2014.

References

Bion, W.R. (1962). *Learning from Experience*. London: Heinemann.
Britton, R. (1989). 'The missing link: parental sexuality in the Oedipus Complex'. In *The Oedipus Complex Today*, ed. J. Steiner. London: Karnac Books.
Carvalho, R. (2009). 'Doing the splits between the Tavi and the SAP'. Unpublished.
———. (2013). 'A vindication of Jung's unconscious and its archetypal expression: Jung, Bion and Matte Blanco'. In *Transformation. Jung's Legacy and Clinical Work Today*, eds. A. Cavalli, L. Hawkins, & M. Stevens. London: Karnac Books.
Ferrari, A.B., & Stella, A. (1998). *L'alba del pensiero*. Rome: Borla.
Fordham, M. (1985). *Explorations into the Self*. London: Academic Press.
Freud, S. (1909). 'Analysis of a phobia in a five-year-old boy'. *SE* 3.
Green, A. (1986). 'The dead mother'. In *On Private Madness*. London: Hogarth.
Jung, C.G. (1913). 'Psychic conflict in a child'. In *The Development of Personality*. CW 17. London: Routledge & Kegan Paul.
Kalsched, D. (2013). *Trauma and the Soul*. London and New York: Routledge.
Matte Blanco, I. (1975). *The Unconscious as Infinite Sets*. London: Duckworth.
McGilchrist, I. (2009). *The Master and his Emissary*. New Haven and London: Yale Press.
Panksepp, J. (1998). *Affective Neuroscience. The Foundations of Human and Animal Emotions*. Oxford: Oxford University Press.
Rayner, E. (1995). *Unconscious Logic*. London and New York: Routledge.

Chapter 6

Clinging, gripping, holding, containment

Reflections on a survival reflex and the development of a capacity to separate[1]

Introduction

Before birth, the infant lives inside a mother's space. After birth, a mother creates with her body (her arms, her breast, her warmth and attention) a near-uterine state for her infant. It could be called the marsupial space (Rey 1994), a space of transition between the total dependence in the womb and the increasing independence of separate existence. For the first few months of extra-uterine life, the infant's physical space is largely the same as the mother's physical space. As the baby grows and develops in terms of mobility and independence, he gradually emerges from the 'pouch' of mother's orbit, and his personal space becomes increasingly defined by his relationship with the general space of the wider world. As this happens, the infant's internal space begins to be formed (an 'internal world' containing psychic 'internal objects'), together with a sense of a 'core self' (Stern 1985), which we could also call the personality of the infant with his own sense of identity. This internal space is first experienced very concretely, as sensations for example, until later the growing infant is capable of creating mental and emotional representations of the external world inside. These representations are in essence what the term 'internal object' means. In time, they evolve into representations of a more complex nature.

In this chapter, I would like to explore how the notion of external and internal space is constructed in relation to the mother and to the infant's sense of identity during the first months of extra-uterine life, and how the relation between space, other and sense of identity can become distorted. I argue that it is very important for our clinical practice in relation to early attachment issues to understand this process of construction. The foetus in the womb, the infant in the marsupial space and the adult in general space: it is in these transitions that the personality structure finds its foundation. If this process is disrupted, new experiences in life do not help to create new psychic structures. Instead, the experiences are forced into inadequate structures.

The infant in the marsupial space

Odgen (2008) describes the relationship of mother to infant in the very first months of life as 'the autistic-contiguous mode', characterized by the sensory

DOI: 10.4324/9781003268536-7

experiences of the infant in relation to his mother. According to Ogden, the infant needs to touch and to be touched by his mother in order to apprehend himself. Bick (1964, p. 484) postulates that skin and mouth sensations are the prerequisites for the acquisition and representation of 'an ego', the personality of that infant with his own sense of identity. Held in mother's arms while connecting with her smell, voice, gaze, and heartbeat (Jakobi 2013) with her nipple in his mouth, the infant lives through and learns about different bodily sensations. Referring to the behaviours of infants during the sensory motor preverbal stage of development, Rey warns that if something goes wrong in this phase, in later years, it might result in a breakdown of the perception of a 'sense of me' (Rey 1994, p. 34). Rey suggests that in this early phase, the relation me-another is not sufficiently differentiated for the infant to distinguish between the loss of the object and the loss of a sense of himself. Although the infant is relating to an object from the beginning of life (Ferenczi [1924] was the first to postulate this), the capacity to perceive this object as separate is still rudimentary and interconnected with his developing sense of self: the self is intertwined with the object as a self-object (Fordham 1976, p. 13), just as in physical terms the infant simply cannot survive without the care of the mother. The presence of the body of another who holds the body of the baby is paramount. The body of this other is not merely flesh, but has some specific intelligence, and provides an accurate understanding of the baby's needs. Winnicott expresses this when he says 'The mother places the actual breast just where the infant is ready to create it and at the right moment' (Winnicott 1958, p. 238). Fordham (1976, 1985a) has also stressed the importance of there being ample opportunities for such illusion in early infancy, and the danger of a disastrous impingement from a baby becoming prematurely aware of the bodily separateness between himself and his mother. The empathic psycho-physical reciprocity at first fosters the illusion of 'identity' (Fordham 1976, 1985a), but gradually, the infant acclimatizes to the bit-by-bit tolerance of separateness. While the uterus gives to the foetus a total experience of connection, in the marsupial space a different vital active link between mother and infant has to be found and is re-establish again and again. This link provides the basis for the consolidation of a sense of being oneself that exists over time, in space with or without another. Without mother's presence, an infant might feel as though he is disintegrating, falling apart and dying (Fordham 1985a). However, in the 'pouch' of the marsupial space, perhaps as a result of physically taking in milk, mother's voice, smell and look (a physical inside which finds its psychological correlate in an emerging internal world), a differentiation between external and internal takes place. The experience and the memory of being held by the mother's body and mind – perhaps retained first as a physical imprint of a basic experience of self that is held and understood and then as an internal representation in the infant's developing internal world – will help and sustain the growing infant as he is faced with new sensations and new situations when his mother is not in his space. In other words, the experience of being held will become progressively internalized. The capacity to internalize a good experience and the capacity to identify with it, is crucial to the self's capacity to cohere and integrate new experiences into what we call an ego (Fordham 1985a).

Illustration from infant observation

With the following vignette from the observation of a 22-month-old girl, I hope to be able to show what I have tried to describe in the abstract terms of metapsychology. Little Lia is seen here, as I postulate, trying to internalize in a physical-psychological way a good image of herself at a moment when it seems lost to her. We will see how she differentiates between internal and external. Faced with a difficult new situation, she seems to lose her sense of herself. I would like to focus on what she does in order to re-find the lost sense of herself: Her mother calls Lia and asks her to help mother with a puzzle. Lia goes to mother and does the puzzle very quickly: there are five pieces, she succeeds in putting four pieces together, but the fifth doesn't fit. Lia becomes very agitated, cries, stands up, falls, bangs her head, looks outside the window and seems lost. She then goes to her father who is coming into the room, saying, '1,2,3,4,5,9,9,9,10'. She comes back, sees her ballerina outfit, puts it on with her father's help and starts dancing. Her father puts a record on, and they both dance. Mother gets a Polaroid camera and takes a picture of Lia. As soon as the picture is developed, Mother shows it to Lia who looks at herself, opens her mouth and tries to swallow the image of herself on the picture (the child literally tried to eat her image off the photo, not the whole photo). After that Lia has a look at the puzzle. She goes straight to the piece she couldn't place before, picks it up and is now able to put it in the right way.

In this vignette, Lia seems to be reconnecting in a primitive physical way to a good experience of herself. She 'eats' the Lia who was having a good experience and we see that after this, she has regained the self-confidence that was briefly lost to her. We might speculate that she needs to take inside herself, to swallow, the 'Lia who is looked at with love' (by mother, taking the photo). Lia seems to connect with a previous internalized experience of taking in something good. This previous experience must already be 'inside'. I suggest that this concept of inside begins to be formed by the infant taking in mother's milk, her voice, her look. The experience of something going inside must be responsible for the beginning of differentiation between inside and outside. By eating the good image of herself, Lia seems able to identify with a good mother who is feeding her with something good. In the transition between feeling capable and losing that sense of a capable self, Lia searches for something to grip onto. By connecting with this something in a meaningful way, 'swallowing it, taking in inside', she can let go of her grip. In this process, Lia seems to have achieved some capacity for symbolizing: she is not eating food in order to make herself feel well, for example, but she eats in pretend a lovely representation of herself, that she is already familiar with. This good image of herself from inside can sustain and help her to integrate a new situation, linking a new experience to an old one. In this way, Lia is strengthening her ego and her identity.

Imre Hermann and his clinging reflex

While Bick, Bion, Winnicott, Tustin (1972, 1981) and Ogden have stressed the importance of the active role of the mother in creating the marsupial space by holding and providing a container for the psycho-physical needs of their babies, a forgotten Hungarian analyst, Imre Hermann, has studied the active participation of small infants in this process, calling their input 'the clinging reflex' (1936, p. 349). Hermann postulated an instinct for clinging and an opposite instinct for 'going in search'. The urge to wander, to go in search, is somewhere between clinging and the capacity to separate: a break in the primary maternal bond may lead to a desire to wander, which has an aspect of desire for discovery, yet ultimately is an exploration towards re-finding the lost mother. The capacity to separate was seen by Hermann as a third instinct, a reaction formation against the clinging instinct, an attempt of the infant to gain mastery over the loss of the primordial mother-infant relations. It is beyond the scope of this chapter to give justice to Hermann's ideas. Nevertheless clinging, separating, going in search are important aspects of development. They belong to a hierarchical organization of development (Fordham 1976, pp. 84–6) in which the inner and outer worlds are slowly distinguished and differentiated while a sense of being oneself remains consistent in the absence of the mother. This is the transition from an infant who relates to a primordial mother by clinging and gripping onto her while she holds him, to an infant who can let go of her as he takes in the experience of being held. This infant is then capable of re-finding her, or aspects of her, tolerating both intimacy and separation without his basic sense of self being at risk.

Bowlby (1958) in his paper 'The Nature of the Child's Tie to His Mother', referred to Hermann as follows:

> Hermann (1933, 1936) has noted that infant apes spend the early weeks of their lives clinging to their mother's bodies, and also that there are many clasping and grasping movements to be seen in human babies, especially when they are sucking or feel threatened. As a result of these observations, Hermann postulated a primary component instinct in human beings, an instinct to cling. (p. 356)

Hermann saw the remains of the clinging instinct of primates as present in humans in the form of a reflex, and he understood the Moro (startle) reflex as such, as well as the heat orientation reflex. Hermann was reluctant to regard this as an object relationship; he saw it as a survival reflex. Alice Balint (1939) and Michael Balint (1937) expressed their indebtedness to Hermann and went further than he did. They postulated active tendencies in infants to relate to their caregivers. They called it an archaic, egotistic way of loving, its main characteristic being the lack of any appreciation of the mother's separateness. This form of object relation is not linked to any of the erotogenic zones, but it is something of its own (Spitz 1954). They called it 'primary object love' (Balint, M. 1937, p. 90 ff., 1939,

p. 110). Bowlby was influenced by Hermann, the Balints and Spitz in his formulation of what he then called 'primary object clinging' (1958, p. 371), a mixture of Hermann's clinging reflex, Balint's concept of primary object love and Spitz's idea of survival attachment.

This 'primary object clinging' is indicative of an innate preconception of an archetypal mother, a mother who is not yet known as a complex being, but whose presence is expected prior to any experiences of the actual mother by the infant; it is to this mother that infants cling in the marsupial space. The infant clings with his senses to this primitive version of the mother, while she with her eyes, smell, nipples, skin, voice and attention works as a magnet that repeatedly gives the infant the opportunity of feeling integrated. Bick's (1964) idea, that mother's body and mind give a sense of integration to her infant, finds in Hermann (1936) its companion. The infant opens up to his mother; finding her allows him to let go and integrate this new experience inside. The infant is changed by his experience. Little Lia, to paraphrase Hermann, was 'going in search' of something to grip onto, as she did not seem to have enough sense of integration when she was faced with a new difficulty. Her mother offered her a photo. After having 'taken in' the photo (or an experience of herself on the photo), Lia could let go of mother and photo and go back to her task, this time successfully. When the infant has managed to take something good inside himself, he can survive for some time away from mother's space: it is from inside that he can find the resources to overcome obstacles. Lia seemed to have acquired a sense of cohesion, an inside in relation to an outside, the 'pouch' of a self within herself. In order to continue to move out of the marsupial space, she needed to 'feed' this 'pouch' with another nourishing experience which would sustain her in yet another difficult task. Her mother was holding her appropriately in this transition.

I would now like to present some vignettes from two different infant observations to show how two different babies react when they separate physically from their mothers after a meaningful interaction. Both babies are between 1- and 2-months-old. The capacity of each infant's mother to separate after a meaningful interaction is very different, and I would like to focus on the infant's reaction at the end of a powerful 'moment of holding and clinging' between the two. While one baby is able to separate and integrate the experience, the other baby cannot and seems to stay clung to the experience, or rather onto a substitute version of the experience of the mother, which is closer to the realm of the imaginary or archetypal. I suggest that while one baby feels held by the introjected experience, the other continues to grip and hold onto something for fear of not surviving the separation.

I will then discuss the observations in relation to Hermann's hypothesis of a clinging reflex in the infant and how a capacity to separate from the primordial mother, or the primary object clinging, can be achieved. I suggest that the creation and acquisition of an internal 'pouch' is what one would call 'the prerequisite for the capacity to symbolize'.

Vignettes from infant observations

Baby Ae

Mother puts her baby, 65-days-old, to the breast. Baby Ae starts gulping hungrily, like a thirsty person downing a glass of water, in big, noisy gulps. I can hear her noisy sucking and see her head bobbing up and down as she sucks vigorously. After a few minutes Mother says that Baby is falling asleep and is trying to decide what to do: to fall asleep or to continue sucking. Usually, she goes on sucking in her sleep or falls asleep with the nipple in her mouth. Baby remains in this state until it is almost time for me to go. Suddenly she wakes up. Mother is leaning over her and talking to her playfully, and Baby responds with a wide-open mouth, smiling, joy streaming from her eyes and laughing without any sound. I am amazed by the connecting gaze that holds the two of them in a very private communication. It feels like the 'tension of a magnet'. It is as if all that exists in this moment is the two of them, nothing outside this gaze matters; time has frozen for a moment. It feels very powerful and hypnotizing, a gaze connection that can happen only between mother and baby. It looks as if each of them can see who the other is very well, and they love what they are seeing. 'She always looks like that', Mother says. Baby then closes her eyes, and slowly Mother puts her in the bouncer. Baby seems calm and relaxed, allows Mother to put her down without protesting, and Mother takes me to the door.

The observer can describe very well how Baby Ae is magnetically attracted: the description of the observer seems to stress the capacity of mother and infant to be united in a relationship in which both attract each other in a way that links them together, creating a powerful connection. Mother's gaze is powerfully attracting her infant's eyes which cling to mother's eyes. Mother is responding to her baby with a matching intensity of gaze. Their desire to penetrate each other's eyes suggests that the baby has already acquired a primitive notion of internal space. With this, I suggest that the baby seems to know that there is something inside mother, as if she wanted to go inside her with her look. Mother must be experienced as a three-dimensional object by this infant, not merely as a two-dimensional entity onto which she can cling. The intensity of the empathic holding onto each other seems to be nourishing for the baby, who then can let go and rest, leaving the mother fascinated by the 'love' that her baby is expressing for her. This moment of meeting (Stern 1998) seems to help mother and baby to separate for a little while because each of them is holding onto the experience inside. Baby Ae seems to show this when she looks away from mother, 'reintegrating' (Fordham 1985a) the experience with her. This is what Bion calls 'digesting an experience' (Bion 1962). Although I am speculating here, for an internal space to emerge, I would suggest that letting go of a good experience is necessary. The internal space is the result of gripping onto a primordial mother while being held by her, having a good experience with her that makes the infant feel integrated, letting go of the mother, taking in the experience and transforming it into a symbolic representation of a self who can survive over time and space during separation from the primordial mother. The repetition of this process in different situations seems to be responsible for the acquisition of a more sophisticated internal representation of oneself and other in space over time.

Baby Bee

The previous observation can be contrasted with the following observation of Baby Bee. Baby Bee (35-days-old) is breastfeeding quietly. Then she takes her mouth away from the breast, and I see her opening her eyes widely. After some uncertainty, her eyes focus on her mother's face. Baby's gaze seems more controlled and steady now, as she looks up at her mother. Without looking at her baby, Mother says that the 'boob' is much more important than the bottle. It is a lot more than just food, it offers her baby warmth and Mum's smell. She continues by saying that it is a mistake for women not to breastfeed.

Baby then takes her eyes away from her mother's face and looks around for a few seconds before she closes her eyes, ready to fall asleep. Mother does not want Baby to fall asleep. 'It is a struggle', says Mother, 'I have to push her to be awake a bit longer and eat, otherwise, she falls asleep, and then she will be up again in a few minutes'. Mother does not let her baby go to sleep. Baby makes a movement towards Mother's face with her hand. 'Don't scratch me', says Mother. Then Baby Bee opens her mouth widely, but she is nowhere near the breast. It seems Mother is a bit puzzled as to what this means, but Baby keeps opening and opening her mouth; then she looks at her mother and then just turns her face away from her. She looks around until, finally, she locks her gaze on a distant mirror. It is too far and too high for her to see anything reflected in it except for a pool of light. I follow the baby's gaze and notice that the mirror is the brightest spot on the wall.

From the observation, it seems that the mother of this baby is not able to 'meet' her baby. The baby seems to feel unheld by her mother; she clings to the light reflected in the mirror, as she does not seem able to get an adequate grip on her mother's eyes and mind. I suggest that Baby Bee, to protect herself from a fear of disintegration, 'goes in search' of another surface that can give her an experience similar to what she might be expecting from the primary object clinging. We could postulate that the light in the mirror has some quality of mother's gaze. Nevertheless, the mirror is two-dimensional, and we will see how this will impact on the hierarchical organization of the development of this baby.

A week later, something similar happens: again today, Mother decides to put her baby to sleep as soon as the baby falls asleep at the breast. Mother takes the baby from the breast and puts her in her cot. Baby seems to be quiet, but she soon becomes restless. She starts making small noises of struggle; she lifts her legs, makes pushing movements and lifts her arms up and down. She then starts moving her eyes and her head until, eventually, she focuses her eyes on the window from which daylight is coming into the room. This seems to calm her. Again, in the previous vignette, the gripping and holding situation is abruptly and prematurely broken. Baby Bee suddenly woke up in the cot and, unable to find the breast or mother's eyes, went in search of the light coming from the window with her eyes. This vignette seems to suggest that the experience with her mother at the breast was not nourishing, as Baby Bee is not able to find a representation of herself inside herself who can survive without gripping onto a surface in the absence of her mother. It is possible to postulate that this infant is afraid of disintegrating if left alone. She needs a sort of transitional surface, which has some connotations of primary object clinging.

The phone rang, and mother picked up the phone in another room: Baby abandoned her focus on the window and turned her head towards the door from where her mother's voice was coming. Baby now turned half her body towards the door and kept her head turned in the direction of the mother's voice. Hearing her mother speaking on the phone seemed to calm her. She was no longer restless, and slowly she fell deeply asleep for the 20 minutes until the end of the observation. It seems difficult for Baby Bee to be able to relax, hold onto a good experience inside herself and make use of it when separate from her mother. We can postulate that Baby Bee needs more maternal holding, and in the absence of her mother, she grips onto something external, which seems to provide some sort of substitute for the experience of being held by her mother. The mirror and the window might provide the infant with light, something of the experience of mother's eyes, as well as a place to focus on, which can give the infant a sense of integration after having lost mother's holding function outside and inside.

Baby Bee 68 days old

Mother has guests in the house, and suddenly says to her baby, 'I will try to put you to sleep'. She takes her to the bedroom and places her on a soft mat where there are toys hanging over her head. Mother says that Baby really likes these toys, they catch her attention. Mother then leaves the room, and the baby is left to be entertained with the toys over her head. She looks at them mesmerized, with her eyes wide open. She throws her hand abruptly far out and grabs the zebra toy. This seems to be an accident, but as soon as she has the zebra in her hand, she grabs onto it tightly and squeezes and moves the toy energetically. Her eyes and head are turned in the opposite direction where another zebra is hanging. Baby's full attention is directed toward that zebra. I am sitting close to her, but she is so absorbed with the toys that she is oblivious of me. Her left arm holding the zebra is moving up and down, pulling and shaking it. She seems to be intrigued by the toys, but I don't sense that she is particularly happy or excited to be left alone with them. She makes noises with her mouth and sticks her tongue in and out all the time. She is restless; she moves her arms and legs, and at one point, she spits out some of her food.

Baby Bee's difficulty in digesting the feed seems to show that this baby has not yet fully achieved a sense of internal space in which food and experiences can be digested. This baby has not yet fully found a way to grip solidly enough onto her mother, and her mother does not match her need to be held for long enough. Baby Bee goes desperately in search of alternative experiences, as she does not seem to have a good enough physical experience in the marsupial space that she can then internalize.

It is noteworthy that Baby Bee resorts to objects that in Mother's absence seem to provide some substitute for the experience of being held. Holding onto the zebra might be a way of bypassing the emotional turmoil she is in and clinging onto a good version of herself feeling held by mother.

At 11 months, this baby is still incapable of standing and sitting upright. To move in space as a separate being, an infant has to relinquish the reflex response of clinging onto external objects. I suggest that this is possible only if the infant has internalized a representation of himself that has been sustained over time in different situations. This includes his capacity to be angry and hateful of mother's coming and going.

Baby Bee sees a balloon and wants to get to it. She cannot move very far. She struggles. She takes the dummy which is attached to her clothes and puts it in her mouth. She is not complaining and seems determined to get to the balloon. She tries to move forward but can only move on the same spot. Her knees are flat, so are her arms. She tries to turn on her back. She makes a semi-turn but does not manage to turn completely. I would suggest that Baby Bee's capacity to move independently is inhibited by her fear of experiencing catastrophic rupture whenever something (including mother's impatience) intrudes on her relationship with her mother. To foster the illusion of continuity of an adhesive relationship with her mother, and to protect herself from unmanageable bodily events that have no name, Baby Bee has found in clinging onto objects via her eyes, hands, ears or whole body a way of surviving the real separation from her mother. Baby Bee does not seem to have been able to internalize a version of herself capable of feeling integrated when she is alone. When she loses her object, she immediately goes in search of another one to cling to. She is incapable of sustaining herself when separate. I would suggest that the development of a sense of three-dimensionality results from introjections of meaningful moments with a mother who is able to hold the infant physically and emotionally over time in space. The fact that Baby Bee is not able to stand up on her own at 11 months seems to suggest that she has not yet introjected a version of herself with an internal space. She behaves as if she were two-dimensional, like the objects she clings onto; they help her in the transition from being held by mother to being without her. These objects do not have a mind and do not provide any understanding of her needs; they mirror her experience with her mother.

We might describe the whole process in the following way: first, the baby clings onto a mother who has an inside and is nourished by the interaction with her as this mother is capable of meeting him. If an experience of being held has not been good enough, at separation, the infant 'loses' his mother instead of being able to let go of the experience. A representation of himself being held by her cannot become internalized because the experience has not been nourishing. The baby feels empty inside and resorts to gripping onto a version of his mother in the hope of finding some internal nourishment: the capacity to internalize and to symbolize seem to be interrelated and to be linked to a mother with an inside who can hold her baby while he is developing this inside for himself. With this development comes an ability to represent himself as capable of surviving in her absence.

Fordham (1985b) has described this kind of experience, when an infant is not held long enough while having an interaction with his caregiver, as an 'abandonment'. To avoid the sensation of abandonment, of being ripped apart from mother, the infant reacts by clinging onto something (goes in search of an alternative object to cling onto) as if to preserve an internal illusion of the mother holding him, and of him holding onto her. Thus, the movement of the infant is a survival movement, and it is attached to a phantasy of unity. This phantasy is defending the infant from feelings of disintegration.

Hermann's 'clinging' reflex underpins Winnicott's 'transitional object'

Winnicott (1953, 1958) introduced the concepts of transitional object and transitional experience in relation to the mother-infant bond. I would suggest that transitional objects embody all the components of 'mothering'. They are a first concrete representation of the good feeling of being held by mother. They can be clung to, enabling the child to have a phantasized bond with the mother when she gradually separates for increasingly longer periods of time. The transitional object is important at the time of going to sleep and as a defence against anxiety, for example, when the infant re-finds in the soft rug the softness of being in mother's arms. At a later stage of development, the child no longer needs the transitional object. He is able to make a distinction between 'me' and 'not-me', and to keep inside and outside apart and yet interrelated. It is possible to postulate that transitional objects are the precursors of a capacity to symbolize, in a phase between having internalized the experience and still holding onto it in a concrete way. I would suggest that Imre Hermann's concept of the clinging reflex as a transitional movement is the developmental precursor of what Winnicott calls a transitional object. It validates Bick's and Ogden's hypotheses that the infant needs to be held by another while showing that before the infant is capable of representing to himself the bond with his mother through an object that can be held onto in moments of transition, he seeks to remain linked to her in a physical way using his sensory motor apparatus. Bowlby (1958, p. 368) refers to an instinct to cling to the tree that is present in apes, stemming from the reflex of baby apes to cling to their mothers' fur. Using a vignette from my work with an adolescent patient, I would like to show how clinging can be a pre-transitional gesture that keeps infant and mother linked in space.

For this patient, it has always been very important to be seen and be smiled at by others. This was also happening at the end of each session with me. After we were able to do a great deal of work from which we could identify the reason for that, at the end of the last session of the week I said, 'I understand why you are telling me this because when people smile at you, it gives you great satisfaction'. On Monday three days later, the patient came back telling me that after

Thursday's session she 'had fallen in a tunnel, there was no one to hold her, and it had taken her the whole weekend to re-emerge from her state'. She was afraid of dying, and the reason for this was that, when I had said that seeing people smiling at her gives her great satisfaction, I had pushed her to see it, and by seeing it, she had let go of her grip . . . this had made her fall into the tunnel. Later we were able to think more about this tunnel, but for now, she could only describe her terror of falling forever, of dying and, worst of all, the sensation that there was nothing and no one that could help her.

Nevertheless, we were able to see together in later sessions that this experience, precipitated by me, was reconnecting her to a past experience of having felt dropped by her mother. Like me over the weekend, her mother had left her when she was a few months old. Although my patient had felt as if she was falling forever in a tunnel, she had not only been able to survive the event she was confronted with at the weekend but also tell me about her experience. Together we could reflect on the fact that there was an aspect of her who could observe, feel and tell me about it. What the patient seemed to have lost over the weekend, was the experience of herself connected with another. This loss felt to the patient as if she were about to lose her whole self. To put this another way, we could say that my patient was still gripped onto a very early experience of being seen by the smiling eyes of her mother and that she needed to come back to this experience every time she separated. Because my patient had so abruptly lost her mother's gaze, and this loss had never been mourned and properly acknowledged, she had remained gripped onto mother's smile (in others) as a way to protect herself from being in touch with the feeling of falling into nothingness that she must have felt when she was an infant and had lost her mother. By remaining gripped onto the eyes of others, my patient had held onto a very precarious sense of self. It was as if she could only exist if seen by another. This clinging on was a survival mechanism. It did not allow my patient to strengthen her own sense of being a separate person, capable of moving and developing in space. When she was finally able to let go of her grip, my patient experienced a mini breakdown which could be recovered from because of all the work we had done before. My patient was able to emerge from the tunnel by imagining taking herself in her own arms. At first, she found it difficult, it seemed to her that all her limbs could not be contained in her arms, but slowly she got used to the image and was able to re-discover a lost sense of balance. She could do this because, in her work with me, she had internalized a good experience in which she had been contained and held. This experience allowed her to let go of the old necessity to grip onto the gaze of others. Gripping onto a gaze was useful as a transition: it represented an experience that was good, but it could not be relinquished because it had not yet been symbolized and introjected.

Discussion

The importance of being held by mother's minded body is paramount. Infants learn that in their mother's arms, it is possible to be tolerated during many different states of their own being, and it is possible to tolerate difficult experiences within themselves. I suggest that separation from this holding and containing mother can successfully be achieved as the growing child digests the good experience with her. The nourishing experience provides him with a sense of balance and a centre from which he begins to move in space alone. While mothers work hard at holding and containing their infant's body in different situations, babies hold actively onto their mother's body using their sensory motor system. By letting go of each experience, they set the foundation for the beginnings of independence.

For Piaget (1936), action, motor activity, is the first source of all manifestations of life. He suggested that it precedes and controls perception and sensation. It precedes thoughts. The action of clinging onto mother, or to mother's space, seems to be the first act of survival that a baby is capable of making.

Starting from this survival reflex, there is little doubt that the infant will soon wish to make part of his space the gratifying object he needs for survival and growth. His early discovery of the appearance and disappearance of the object in his space will prompt him to desire keeping the good object as part of himself or of his good space as a concrete experience. The frustration of not being always able to keep the good experience in his space will increase the desire for the mother to be in his absolute possession (Rey 1994).

Gripping on as a transitional movement represents the experience of having found the capacity to cling to the primary object. Holding on in this way may enable the infant to remain connected with the good experience in his space. If this experience has not been sufficient, then when it is lost, as was the case for my patient, the transitional movement cannot be relinquished, with all the consequences I have discussed earlier.

While Baby Ae was able to separate from her mother and hold onto a good experience inside herself, Baby Bee needed to go in search of, and grip onto, objects in order to manage every separation from her mother. By clinging on in this way, Baby Bee was reconnecting with the sensation of being held by her mother or by bits of the mother, and this was helping her with the transitions between being in mother's space and a fear of annihilation that she might have felt away from mother's space.

The little vignette from my work illustrates an experience of abandonment and shows how my patient clung onto a good experience in mother's space every time a difficult separation was approaching. She had no internal representation of how to survive a separation from her mother. The analytic work seems to have provided her with a good experience of being held: when she could let go of an old defence, she found within herself the capacity for psychic survival. An internal representation of herself holding herself could emerge, and she could look at, even explore, what until then had to be avoided. An early construct had remained unlinked with words or representations and was triggered autonomously and repetitively. The transitional movement protects the infant from feeling that his personality may disintegrate and provides him with a sense of safety.

Clinical implications

I would now like to focus briefly on patients who suffer from anxieties that antedate 'splitting' (Bick 1964, 1986; Fordham 1985a). These anxieties concern the integrity of the body and its skin boundaries. Tustin (1972, 1981) has described the terror of losing parts of the mouth, of falling, liquefying or of losing body contents. She suggests that these sensations are precipitated by a traumatic realization of bodily separateness at a stage of development where being together with the primary object may be experienced as forming a unity. If there is no internalized representation of being held and contained, a mother may be experienced as unable to contain the bodily sensations of the infant. While the differentiation between internal and external remains unclear, the infant may confuse sensations, emotions, his own skin boundaries and those of his mother. Since mother and infant are scarcely differentiated, it seems that the damage brought about by traumatic bodily separation happens to both the child and his mother, in the infant's perception. Using the evidence of clinical material from my work with a child and an adult patient, I suggest that the defences generated by such experiences of traumatic separation are directed towards re-establishing the continuity of the bounded sensory surface upon which the integrity of the self rests. Such defences may be what Fordham (1985a) called 'defences of the self' (pp. 152–61).

Hermann's clinging, or gripping, reflex represents a movement towards survival. It is a movement that (according to Piaget, cited earlier) precedes sensation, perception and thought. As such, it is imprinted in the implicit memory, and it is to this automatic movement that patients resort in order to escape from terrible feelings of dissolution. If the experiences and feelings that underpin the clinging are not investigated and transformed, clinging may become an addictive behaviour, a malevolent attachment that works against development, based on a delusion. I will illustrate this with two further examples.

Olympos: clinging to the illusion of being all wrapped up with mother

Olympos, an autistic child, did not want to relate. Relating (it takes two to relate) to him meant destruction. He perceived any attempts I made at relating as a destruction of his boundaries. If I looked at him or talked to him, he would attack me mercilessly in order to repossess the parts of himself that he felt I had taken away from him. After his attacks, he would end up on the floor, floppy, unable to move. It took some time for me to understand that what was going on between us was the re-enactment of a primitive attachment that went back to the marsupial space. My 'relating' felt to him like 'separating' him from the survival mother onto whom he was (in phantasy) gripped. By attacking me, he was trying to repossess her and the bit of himself that felt lost to him with her. My presence felt like an impingement into their unity. His incapacity to move, floppy and paralyzed on the floor, represented the implicit memory of his tragic separation from the mother of the marsupial space that he experienced as a ripping away of his surface. To defend from this impingement, Olympos decided to spend the time of his sessions hidden in the toilet close to my consulting room. From outside, very slowly, nonverbally at first, I began to connect with him and he with me. The wall between us seemed to protect him from the fear that I would destroy his boundaries, as if he needed some concrete 'real' reassurance that there was a skin which would hold him and keep him together when we met and parted. This process took more or less a year until he finally dared to re-enter the room with his body upright, gently testing the 'being together' in the same room. For Olympos to mourn and let go of a phantasy of being held and protected by a version of his mother that he had gotten to know in the marsupial space (he had become suddenly autistic when he was a few months old) seemed impossible. Letting go of his illusory clinging onto her seemed to fill him with a fear of becoming totally helpless and floppy, as he showed when for a moment, he allowed himself to be like that. He lost his capacity to move in space over time and behaved as if he did not have either muscles or bones. In some way, he was showing that he did not have inside himself any sense of being held, from which he could move in space.

Alice: clinging to a phantasy of being at the breast

Alice reacted to separation by being overwhelmed with terrifying anxieties, as of dissolving into gas, no longer knowing where her body ended. She was enormously preoccupied with her own bodily boundaries. She would periodically react by binge eating until she put on a huge amount of weight. During these periods, she was bulimic. Binge eating would calm her anxieties and relieve her of the fear of disintegration. Once she had regained a sense of balance, she would become anorexic, would stop eating and then lose an enormous amount of weight. It was only after a few years of working together that we could understand that every time she tried to relate (and lose weight), she would re-enact the loss of her grip on the idealized mother who held her at the breast. She would choose a man who rejected her, and then, overwhelmed by terrifying anxieties, she would go back to her bingeing practice.

Alice did not seem to have a representation of herself separating from the breast and surviving the separation. She would reconnect with old sensations of bodily dissolution and disintegration. To overcome these experiences, she would try, like little Lia, to reconnect to a good experience of feeling held at the breast, but in a much more concrete way. So she would begin to eat ad infinitum in order to cling onto a satisfactory experience at the breast that she did not know how to separate from. Attempts to separate from this illusion made her feel as if she had no boundaries and was unable to live as an individual. Bingeing and sucking the breast were equated at a very unconscious level, just as separation was equated with her fear of dissolution into gas.

Conclusion

Early identity with the mother, which may stem from the instinctual pull towards possessing something so beautiful and of paramount importance for survival, must be relinquished for separation and individuation to take place. What cannot be internalized, symbolized and then relinquished externally becomes an imprint, an enduring permanent relationship of identity with the mother in the unconscious. This is then the primary attachment schema.

I have suggested that the model of the infant clinging onto the mother in the marsupial space represents a primary element in the structure of personality. Experiences of traumatic rupture may interfere with the process of gradual internalization of the sense of a 'me' who clings onto and is held in the maternal space. I have provided some illustrations of how analytic understanding can enhance a possible 'transformation' and the development of a capacity to let go of the instinct to cling as the patient becomes more able to symbolize.

Patients who are attached to a way of perceiving themselves and others formed in a very early phase of life are incapable of relating (as whole people with an independent mind and body) to others, with their independent minds and bodies.

While gripping onto mother's body is a survival reflex for babies, remaining gripped to her in phantasy can become a delusion that works against development. This can stop a person from making use of the human help that we try to offer to each other in our lives.

Acknowledgements

I would like to thank my students, Zara Genova and Katerina Serafidou, for having given me permission to use some vignettes of their infant observations.

Note

1 First published in *Journal of Analytical Psychology*, 59, 4, August 2014.

References

Balint, A. (1939). 'Love for the mother and mother love'. (English translation, 1949). *International Journal of Psychoanalysis*, 30, 251–59.
Balint, M. (1937). 'Early developmental states of the ego. Primary object love'. (English Translation, 1949). *International Journal of Psychoanalysis*, 30, 265–73.
Bick, E. (1964). 'Notes on infant observation in psycho-analytic training'. *International Journal of Psychoanalysis*, 45, 558–66.
———. (1986). 'The experience of the skin in early object relations'. *International Journal of Psychoanalysis*, 49, 484–86.
Bion, W. (1962). *Learning from Experience*. London: Heinemann.
Bowlby, J. (1958). 'The nature of the child's tie to his mother'. *International Journal of Psychoanalysis*, 39, 350–73.

Ferenczi, S. (1924). *Thalassa*. London: Karnac, 1989.
Fordham, M. (1976). *The Self and Autism*. London: William Heinemann Medical Books Ltd.
———. (1985a). *Explorations into the Self*. London: Academic Press.
———. (1985b). 'Abandonment in Infancy'. *Chiron*, 1–21.
Hermann, I. (1933). 'Zum Triebleben der Primaten'. *Imago*, 19, 113–25.
———. (1936). 'Sich-Anklammern Auf-Suche-Gehen'. *Internationale Zeitschrift fuer Psychoanalyse*, 22, 349–70.
Jakobi, S. (2013). 'The pulse at the Centre of being'. (Talk presented at the 11th International Conference of the Journal of Analytical Psychology, Boston).
Odgen, T. (2008). 'Working analytically with autistic-contiguous aspects of experience'. In *Autism in Childhood and Autistic Features in Adults*, ed. K. Barrows. London: Karnac, 222–46.
Piaget, J. (1936). *La Naissance de l'Intelligence chez l'Enfant. The Origin of Intelligence of the Child*. New York: Routledge, 1953.
Rey, H. (1994). *Universals of Psychoanalysis in the Treatment of Psychotic and Borderline States*. Ed. J. Magagna. London: Free Association Books.
Spitz, R. (1954). 'Genese des premieres relations objectales'. *Revue Francaise de Psychoanalyse*, 18, 479–575.
Stern, D. (1985). *The Interpersonal World of the Infant*. London: Karnac Books.
———. (1998). 'Non-interpretative mechanisms in psychoanalytic therapy: the something more than interpretation'. *International Journal of Psychoanalysis*, 79, 903–21.
Tustin, F. (1972). *Autism and Childhood Psychoses*. London: Hogarth Press.
———. (1981). *Autistic States in Children*. London: Routledge.
Winnicott, D.W. (1953). 'Transitional object and transitional phenomena'. *International Journal of Psychoanalysis*, 34, 1–9.
———. (1958). *Collected Papers. Through Paediatrics to Psychoanalysis*. London: Tavistock.

Chapter 7

From not knowing to knowing

On early infantile trauma involving separation[1]

One of the main reasons that brought Jung to separate from Freud was Freud's belief that infantile experience is paramount and profoundly influences the person that each of us becomes. Jung felt this approach was deterministic and convinced that there must be more (Jung 1961; Kerr 1994; McGuire 1974), he plunged into the scholarly study of our written heritage: philosophy, physics and metaphysics, anthropology, astrology and mythology. In his search for this unknown 'more', Bion's O (1970), Jung sought guidance from the experience of those who had lived before. By finding other ways of understanding the psyche, he hoped to prove that Freud was wrong.

Ironically, separating from Freud was problematic for Jung precisely because it evoked his own unknown and unresolved infantile trauma of separation. Writers including Winnicott (1964), Jackson (1963), Satinover (1985), Fordham (1985), Feldman (1992) and Meredith-Owen (2011a, 2011b) have discussed the mental crisis Jung suffered as a result, elaborating on this early trauma and how it informed his personality, and how analytical psychology is founded on Jung's attempt to make sense of what he was experiencing and his internal working through.

Liber Novus, The Red Book (2009) is the testimony of how Jung was able to emerge from his mental crisis, out of the darkness of his unconscious to be reborn alone, without the help of a mother. Instead, he created a matrix for himself using the written heritage he studied. In *The Red Book*, he constructed a boundary around this unknown past experience and found a way to deal with the beta elements provoked by his traumatic separation from Freud. Yet, despite his capacity to heal himself and to create an entire psychology based on explorations into his self, it is possible that Jung did not understand the infantile origins of his trauma.

Vestiges of experiences that have not been contained and mediated by the maternal matrix are not available to explicit memory (Mancia 2007). They are stored in implicit memory, so have emotional impact but no meaning. Unlike the repressed unconscious posited by Freud, these primitive memories have never been represented mentally and, therefore, cannot be expressed. They affect the personality because they inhabit a 'non-existent' desert of the mind, which has no name. These memories emerge only as acting out, as symptoms that need a

DOI: 10.4324/9781003268536-8

semantic significance. Emotional events in the present reconnect us with suppressed emotional events in the past in such a way that past and present become inseparable, conflated.

His break with Freud brought Jung into contact with an earlier traumatic experience of separation that had been suppressed (to use Green's 1998 formulation). By containing it, he was able to explore it, and this contributed to a growing sense of self (Jung 1961). Some of Jung's legacy to us is represented by his clinical and theoretical research into these areas of the individual's primal protomental experience and its relationship with reality.

In this chapter, I use a clinical case to look at early infantile trauma involving separation. My aim is to think about technique and how to work with patients who present an ego that has varying degrees of maturity and strength but contains a split-off part, a fragment or pocket with associated non-ego contents. Particular attention is paid to the need to create a maternal matrix (what Botella and Botella (2005) call figurability) in which the patient's early trauma can be recovered and the split-off part can be integrated. Even with a considerable level of ego development, it is a constant threat to stability to have such an unintegrated primitive area in the personality. Relating to one specific case, I focus on the rigidity of those areas, and on the difficulty of spotting them in analysis. Progress in analytical theory and technique must be sought at the frontier of analysis, in the difficulties that might seem impossible to overcome. This frontier is a 'no man's land', open to progress as well as to failures. This is the zone of the unrealized trauma (Bion's Caesura, 1977). A psychic trauma becomes known when it is recognized as such by the analyst and/or by the patient. It acquires full significance when both realize this (Baranger, Baranger, & Mom 2009).

When dealing with pockets of preverbal areas, one finds an absence of representability; instead, there are subjective states of feelings and body sensations with phantasies attached, which have never been tested in reality, confusion between subject and object and symbols expressed in a very concrete way. Although Jung had little to say about these problems, much of his work was concerned with them (Jackson 1963). In his search for 'more', Jung did find O, the truth, although he could not understand it in the way we can now think about it. Nevertheless, he lived it and experienced the phenomena that represented it. Experience precedes knowing about it.

At the end of the chapter, I come back to Jung and this quest. I pay particular attention to the problem of knowing, Bion's K, with the aim of showing that in order to stay open to Jung's dictum 'there must be more', to stay open to O, we must challenge our knowledge again and again and accept that what seemed known to us (K) can suddenly turn out to be a belief, a false certainty. This realization is possible only if we allow ourselves to be touched by O, by the truth, and experience its phenomena. The challenge of O reframes our knowledge (K) anew, allowing us to grow and develop. In a sort of parallel process, both patient and analyst are faced with this difficult exercise. The challenge consists in being open to experience, in breaking and repairing theory in the struggle to evolve.

Understanding can be only in transformations in O, which then must be understood. In this respect, Jung created a precedent.

A few thoughts on early infantile trauma involving separation

In his paper 'Abandonment in Infancy' (1985), Fordham made an important distinction between separation and infantile trauma involving early separation, which he called abandonment (1985, p. 21). According to Fordham, abandonment is a traumatic experience and differs from other forms of separation in which sadness, pining and grief are experienced. In abandonment, there is no internalized image of a mother who can physically hold and mentally contain her infant because the actual mother has left her infant without her mediating and containing function. Experiences that have not been mediated by the mother, for which no maternal matrix has been provided, are split off, dissociated and not integrated into the rest of the personality. They are known only implicitly, and so affect the rest of the personality in the form of symptoms, or through acting out. As somatic delusion-illusion, preverbal bodily events that have never become word, they trap the person and prevent development and growth. The problem in analysis is how to create a container in which the terrifying somatic event can emerge so that a matrix can be provided, and, with it, meaning.

In the following case material, I present the problem of patients who have employed early defences against abandonment and the difficulties for both patient and analyst in their quest to transform 'O' into 'K'.

Clinical presentation

The patient 'lost' her mother when she was a few months old. While her mother was ill (present, but absent for her infant), she was brought up by another member of the family, who looked after her in a rigid and strict way. My patient was not conscious of this trauma, as she became very attached to the maternal substitute, who loved her but created for her a container similar to a psychic straitjacket. This took the form of strict rules that the infant had to follow: no sucking, sleeping on command, potty on command, weaned at 4 months and fed with a spoon on command. This maternal substitute could be viewed as emotionally abusive, but she provided a strong container for the patient's infant self. Like an iron box, it held the infant together, preventing her from breakdown after the traumatic loss of her absent-but-present mother.

The patient is a well-adapted woman who has been successful professionally. She came to analysis because she felt she was approaching a mid-life crisis and had lost a sense of direction. She had always felt that life was a fight that had to be endured, and her description of this fight had the intense quality of something in her internal world that had to be understood. Only in retrospect did it become clear that this patient had created around herself a strong defence, and she was operating in life like a soldier who would attack any problem, external or internal. Her 'credo' was that she had to be good, and everything that was in the way had to be annihilated, including emotions, feelings and thoughts that could be considered by her as 'bad'. Her understanding of the world was black and white, and while she was operating (sic) for the world to become white, she was totally unconscious of this and had no means of knowing herself or others in a more realistic way. In her mind, it was a matter of willpower.

First dream of the patient:

> *I was riding a bicycle. This seemed to be my task, just going on and on pedalling, every push on the pedal felt difficult and heavy, only at some point I realize that I was pulling a rickshaw, which was attached to the bicycle. I understood that it had always been there. I looked back, and in it was another me, in a comatose state. She woke up, had a look around and passed out. I realized I had to keep pedalling and pedalling. I became aware that I had always taken this other me with me.*

Through the image of the dream, we began to think of a split-off part of her that was traumatized. This part was carried around by another part of her, and a lot of energy was employed in this difficult exercise. We began to think that our difficult task in analysis was to get to know the split-off and traumatized part in relation to her early history and in relation to herself.

First break: separation and hallucinations

Freud described the splitting of the ego as passive, an ego subjected to a traumatic event allows itself to be split. For Klein, trauma splits the ego, and while one part remains in contact with reality, the other part, and the object attached to it, stops developing. According to Fordham, it is not the ego that splits, but two different experiences that remain separate because they are irreconcilable. These are linked with two experiences of the object to which the self was relating. Although the self has the capacity to link experiences (ego bits), some ego bits can remain unintegrated. Following Fordham's hypothesis, I began to think of my patient as having had two experiences of herself in relation to her object: these two experiences seemed to be linked in a way that had to be understood, and while one was positive and growth-promoting, the other seemed to be unthinkable and dreadful. The dream seemed to be showing in a powerful way that the patient had not been able to integrate these two experiences into herself. Something had made her feel totally helpless, and a helplessness that had no name emerged in this image of an ill, comatose part of the personality which could not sustain contact with reality and had no way of expressing itself. The challenge of the work was to create a boundary around this something that had no name. The dream represented the first attempt of her psyche to find meaning for something unknown that needed understanding.

The dream was an image of an experience of total loss and helplessness that had to be introjected but never understood. Confirmation of this became apparent in her relationship with me in the sessions. I began to have two experiences of my patient on the couch: a very alive woman, energetic and full of interest, and one who would suddenly become silent and lost. Although she was alert in these lost moments, she could not free associate; she was 'blank'. If asked what she was thinking, she would reply, 'Nothing, I am only waiting for you to tell me what to do'. Slowly, we began to understand that she would put herself on hold and wait for instructions. In the first part of the analysis, it was difficult to know what might have provoked these moments, which did not seem to be connected with anything. When she became blank, she had two experiences of the analyst, first as the lost mother, and then as the maternal substitute who would rescue her.

I began to relate to the patient's blankness as to her early trauma. The lost mother was somewhere present in the analysis, but then the patient lost the analyst and related to her as to a substitute mother/analyst who would tell her what to do and think. I began to imagine that the blanks represented an experience so confusing that it would re-traumatize the patient again and again. The trauma had happened so early that it had no form, only confusion, confused and confusing nameless dread. There was no way of expressing it. I began to imagine that the part of the personality linked to that experience of early loss was still attached to the self but had lost all hope of being found. Perhaps the rigid rules of the maternal substitute, like the rigid rules of the analysis to which the patient had committed eagerly, provided a container for the patient's past experience. Because of anxieties and confusion, the part of her personality that lived alienated at the edge of the self had not developed the ability to create the symbolic structures by which we face absence and loss. Nevertheless, in analysis, the repetition of an early experience could be observed, and some understanding could begin to take place.

I began to understand her silences – at the beginning of the week, in the middle of a session, or during the last session of the week – as a re-enactment of her early trauma: the straitjacket of the analysis was holding her together, but the loss of her mother was re-enacted again and again without the possibility of understanding it. In blank moments, the patient was motionless; at times, she felt cold and would cover herself with a blanket. Sometimes, her stomach would produce noises. It took a long time for us to understand their meaning, and I will return to this. I began to postulate in myself that the blank moments were attached to the rest of the session by feelings that at that point we did not know about. As the rickshaw was attached to the bicycle by a link, these unknown feelings were the link between two experiences of my patient in relation to her objects. We did not yet know about them, as my patient did not seem to feel anything.

When the first summer break arrived, I was curious to see if the blanks could be accessed or if we had come close to them in some ways. With the break, the straitjacket of the analysis would be lost, and I wondered if the loss might reconnect my patient with the experience of the abandonment. The patient experienced this first break as a catastrophe. She hallucinated my presence, and these hallucinations, although very frightening and confusing, helped her to survive.

Some thoughts

It took some time for us to understand that the hallucinations were not serving the purpose of reconnecting the patient with me or her analysis, they were simply helping her to keep away from the split-off part of her personality. While the separation could have helped her to contact something of that early experience, by hallucinating my presence, she was defending again and in a more manic way against the terror of the early experience. By keeping me with her all the time, the patient had not separated from me, as if the summer break had not taken place. It was possible to make a first hypothesis according to which the lost object (the primitive mother) had not been represented internally. By fusing with an experience of the lost object, my patient was telling me that it was possible to think of her early experience with the lost mother as having been very ambivalent. She seemed not to have been able to create a good and a bad image of the lost mother but only to identify with an idealized aspect, the love-giving mother. During the break, she was desperately trying to identify with this aspect of her mother in relation to me in order to protect herself from her mother as the aggressor, the lost mother. This powerful and terrifying aspect of her mother was still unknown to us and had no representation in her mind.

We began to think of the mini breakdown she experienced during the summer as a way to keep away from a catastrophic childhood experience in which she had not been held or contained, mentally or physically. Idealizing was a defence against a terrifying experience that had to be avoided at all costs. The straitjacket of the mother substitute and the analysis could now be thought about as the rickshaw containing an unknown experience which had to become known.

After the first summer break

After the break, the patient began to complain about feeling confused. This confusion had the quality of a primitive confusion, a product of her earliest relationship in which the search for clear and differentiating answers was not adequately met. It is possible to postulate that, when the primary self of my patient was hit by reality with the loss of the mother, a 'patch' (the phantasy of fusion) was produced, which protected the self from the impact of unbearable reality. Her initial dream gained a new meaning: it was as if the whole self of my patient was moved by the phantasy of reunion, the capable part of the patient, with the traumatized helpless part attached, was moving through life with the unconscious hope of re-finding the lost mother of infancy. Perhaps my patient had spent all her life hoping to be reunited with the lost idealized object, and this hope gave her the motivation to move on in life. The patient had transferred this hope onto me, and, indeed, she had been able to reunite with an aspect of me during the break, but it was the idealized me, while the me who had left her was blanked out.

During the break, the 'comatose' part was abandoned again. I had become the mother substitute who had taken the mother from the infant. In order to survive the loss, the patient hallucinated the lost mother-me and survived the break in the same way she must have survived the maternal abandonment. We can see that the summer break was a lost opportunity for mourning. The repetition of a past experience was the only way the patient was able to cope with a situation in the present that was linked with a past experience. The repetition was also a defence against an experience that could not be recovered. In identification with the abandoning mother-me, the patient was re-abandoning herself, as she preferred to be fused with an idealized me, leaving in the rickshaw a dead-alive part of herself.

The question remained as to which experience of the object the comatose part was relating to? Also, what were the feelings that were linking the two experiences of the object? There seemed to be no representation of them. 'In parallel to the symbiotic relationship with the idealized object, there is always a symbiotic relationship with the dead alive object' (Baranger 2009, p. 215). In the unknown content of the split-off part was a terrible experience of the object and of herself, and knowing it created a terrible confusion in my patient. This confusion was one way of understanding the link between the two experiences of my patient and her mother. Secondary splitting and idealization were employed in the struggle against a primitive and unbearable confusion. This confusion had to be tolerated in our work for the two experiences to become closer and known.

Encouraging my patient to think about the break, to tell me how she felt, to clarify the content of her hallucinations, was a way of getting her to look at it as a real event, in which I had not been with her. By showing her that I did not know what had happened to her, I encouraged her to think about it, to test her desire to deny something real that troubled her, which she did not want to know about. By attempting to ignore the hallucinations, she was keeping the comatose part of herself in a dead-alive state. As if repeating the abandonment of her mother, and in identification with her, she was leaving the other part of herself to deal with a lost object that was constantly re-traumatizing her. It was extremely difficult to keep in my mind the part of her that needed to be attended to, but which my patient disregarded with considerable nonchalance.

After the second summer break

When we resumed work after the second summer break, my patient said 'no' to me. She did not want to come back to her analysis. For a long time, she kept saying 'no' to me. It was difficult to understand which experience she was refusing. Was it a 'no' to possible depressive feelings due to the break and the experienced cruelty of the mother-me? Or was it a 'no' to the substitute mother-me who was asking her to enter again the straitjacket of the analysis? Although terribly painful and difficult to deal with, this 'no' was the beginning of a breakdown (sic) of an unthinkable past experience that needed to be understood.

While the patient was silent and uncooperative on the couch, I began to hope that I could become someone else, not a better mother, not a better maternal substitute, but a thinking object that could provide a matrix for the terrible experience which until then had never been understood.

It was at this point that I began to think of the hallucination as a form of protection, an early form of relationship that was known but which, like the womb, needed to be mourned. Then she had had another early experience, one that had not been fully known, which was difficult to represent and understand. Looked at in this way, her 'no' could have a new meaning. It could be understood as a 'no' to any other experience of me but the idealized one, to her fear of having to come to terms with an unrepresentable reality, to her rage with me for forcing her to look at the status of things and, possibly, as a 'no' to mourning the womb-like relationship she wanted to have with me. Her 'no' also meant having to accept a relationship to the blank experience.

While the patient was beginning to separate from the maternal substitute by saying 'no' to me, she was also expressing the unresolved feelings that were connecting the two experiences of her mother. From the beginning of the analysis, these feelings were expressed in the form of sounds produced by her stomach. As she became more in touch with the feeling of confusion, these stomach sounds gradually diminished, and, finally, they disappeared.

The two experiences of the same object and herself, linked together, could now begin to be analyzable. Slowly, it became possible to bring them closer in relation to her early experiences and to me. The idealized object and the dead-alive object were now the same in their two manifestations, as well as the good-person aspect of the patient and her dead-like other aspect that needed to be understood. Bringing these two aspects closer was creating a great deal of confusion. This confusion was in some way a confirmation that the loss had happened at an early stage in which clear differentiation had not taken place.

Some thoughts and further developments

I began to understand the two images of my patient with their mirror-objects as having their origin in early states of primitive identity between infant and mother.

In Fordham's language, the adoring baby adoring an adoring mother in parallel to a dead-like baby mirroring a dead-like mother could be understood as two archetypal experiences. Subject and object could not be differentiated because of lack of containment. The experience and its representation were identical, and symbolization was not possible. Re-enactment was the only way to symbolize and transform what could not be digested and understood. In Kleinian language, the infant part of the patient had introjected but not assimilated both aspects of the mother and identified with them. With her 'no', the patient was rebelling against the lost idealized mother, the maternal substitute, the old known way of relating.

According to Klein, if the ego bit rebels against the experience, the object attached to the experience also rebels. It was likely that the semi-dead-like aspect of the object would now become a persecutor and that I would become that aspect of the object in the transference. For this part of the ego, the infant and her experience of that aspect of her mother were still undifferentiated. By describing to my patient what I thought was happening, I hoped to create a matrix for understanding, for representability and differentiation. This understanding might provide an antidote to her fear of a persecuting me, which like the dead-like mother would be a persecuting experience that my patient had to avoid at all cost. Perhaps she was afraid of falling to pieces if she were forced to reconnect with that early experience.

For Klein, the fear of disintegration is mitigated by the introjection of the ideal breast and identification with it. This protects the infant from the knowledge of a persecutory breast, which becomes a superego that persecutes the ego bit. The rickshaw, like the iron box of the maternal substitute that had saved her from disintegration during that early experience, was now trapping my patient in such a way that she could not move on.

The patient's infant part was maintained in a near-death situation to avoid feelings of needs, rejection and helplessness. It was to avoid those feeling that my patient was rebelling against her analysis and me. By rebelling, her dead-like part was waking up, and, in an omnipotent way, she was denying our work, her dependence on me, possible depressive feelings, rage and hate: a survival defence against helplessness. Her insistence on wanting to leave me had a psychotic quality. For Bion, the psychotic is what has not become a thought but has remained an allergy to the frustration of an absence. This was the blank that my patient and I were hoping to transform into a feeling and a thought.

The early relationship of my patient with the mother was broken by the trauma of her absence. In that absence, there was a no-thought, an emptiness that was held together by a second skin, an armour, the iron box of the maternal substitute. I was hoping to find in the archaeology of her mind a 'tooth, one mandible, and reconstruct a whole personality from this fragment' (Green 1998, p. 659). This fragment, possibly her feeling of confusion and the sounds of her stomach, was the first link between the two experiences of the mother that my patient had been unable to know about.

Inside the rickshaw

The patient's stomach sounds needed particular attention. Instead of becoming alive, something would be evacuated through her intestine. It is possible that these sounds were a defence against devastating emotions. Her 'no' was a last desperate attempt to control emotions that were attached to the experience of the lost mother. Now that she was becoming separate from the idealized object-me, and I was becoming a persecutor, the unresolved feelings attached to the experience of the loss of the idealized mother were becoming free and could no longer be controlled.

The difficulty in the analysis was to help the patient to feel all these feelings in such a way that when the phantasy attached to the persecutor became known, or a partial representation of it, the feelings attached to that experience would feel less persecuting because they were known, and the patient had learnt to feel them. Encouraging the patient to stay in touch with these feelings was difficult because they were frightening her. She had no experience of being physically held when she had powerful bodily feelings that felt as if they were fragmenting her. She had been abandoned to them.

Second part of analysis

In the second part of her analysis, my patient began to feel something she did not know about, which evoked panic in her. By now, although reluctant, she seemed determined to understand herself, and a different relationship between us could emerge. It seemed that my curiosity and attention to her had stimulated a similar interest in herself. Her 'no' to me slowly unfolded into a 'yes' to herself, and then into 'I want to know more about myself'. The panic was evoked by a long known and suppressed sensation that we identified as a feeling of utter helplessness.

This coincided with our understanding of a recurrent dream in which she was in bed, paralyzed. Understanding the dream was perhaps the second element in the difficult construction of a representation of the experience of the lost mother. Although my patient's conscious self was very ambivalent about the analysis, her unconscious seemed willing to cooperate by providing elements that were paramount in our work of constructing a matrix of figurability (Botella & Botella 2005). It was deeply moving for my patient to identify the feelings of total helplessness that the dream described. A once unbearable bodily event now had a name and could begin to be known and thought about.

My patient had been contained by the womb and had adapted to her mother's care after birth, but, with the premature loss of her mother, she was trapped in the iron box of the strict rules of the maternal substitute. This new container had become a prison from which my patient could not escape. By putting a name to this old, unknown bodily sensation, we were able to transform it into a thought. Helplessness could be understood and felt.

The experience of rejection for my patient had been so profound that she maintained the near-death situation to avoid the feelings connected to it. Instead, the experience seemed to be encapsulated in a terrible sense of helplessness that she had converted into a sort of religion. This was her destiny.

In order to know more about her lost capacity to form a representation of the lost object and its mirror image of the lost baby, we needed to find ways of exploring the delusional aspect of the absent mother mirrored by the abandoned baby. As we did with the hallucination related to the idealized object, we needed to connect with a delusional representation of the loss in the negative.

By allowing me to become a companion to explore with her the persecutory feelings that inhabited the void, helplessness, shame and fear, the patient was moving away from experiencing me in the transference as identical to her experiences. I was becoming the provider of the maternal matrix that she needed. Once separate, I was available to investigate, question and think about what had not seemed knowable to her. In this process, her suppressed feelings could become felt, known experiences.

Slowly, the terror of abandonment could be explored again and again with all the feelings attached to it. My patient could develop and connect with a third position from which she was able to observe, feel and think. From this position, the patient could begin to separate from the lost object and finally begin to dream something about the unknown experience. With this, symbolization could begin.

Coming closer to the delusional aspect of the suppressed experience and its possible representation

Around this time, my patient dreamt that she was in a room with a terrifying presence. In the dream, she thought it was probably the devil. We were beginning to connect to the experience of the lost mother and the feelings that were connecting her with that experience of the mother. A few months later, a second dream brought us closer to that experience.

> *I am at the hairdresser. He not only cuts my hair; he also asks me to talk freely and express my thoughts. I do this but then admit to myself that I was communicating with the devil. The devil was a sort of friend who would help me, but also a terrifying agent.*

This dream gave rise to many memories: my patient's childhood fear of the devil, her terror of the dark and finally an association with the film *Rosemary's Baby*.

Slowly, she began to trust that the good hairdresser/me could create order in her head, transforming beta elements into thoughts. An image was becoming available to her, and words could be found to describe something that until then had remained unthinkable. Only by accepting the devil as a container could the content of a terrifying experience become known and thinkable. Was this unwanted baby a devil? Was this why she was abandoned? Or, worse, was this baby the daughter of the devil itself?

While this dilemma remained unthinkable, my patient had spent her life wanting to punish herself or aspiring to saintliness to eliminate the devil part of herself and/or feeling damned by birth as a daughter of the devil and without hope of salvation. There seemed no way for her to escape this destiny, trapped in the iron box of her infancy.

Now that we were slowly able to make meaning, and some possibility of understanding could emerge, the capacity to create a phantasy could be recovered. This meant that bodily events could be linked with images that had been lost, and the ego could find again the lost sense of fit between mind and body. Finally, we understood the two aspects of her symbolic experience of the devil:

a) The hateful abandoned child is abandoned by a horrified mother.
b) This child can only hide what it fears is its devilish nature, in terror of finding out that her nature cannot be transformed.

This unconscious dilemma had been trapping my patient: she could not escape her nature, but, if her nature were discovered, she would be punished and abandoned again and again.

Now we could understand her profound fear of relating to others, her fear of being rejected, and, with it, the fear of meeting the real self she could not escape. In parallel, we were able to understand her fear of meeting the devil in the other. The constant terror of this made her feel she had to be very good, but also to punish herself for desiring freedom, which would have damned her if she had attained it.

The phantasy of the devil was a very primitive way of representing the terrible experience of hate and loss, and it was necessary to transform this first delusional representation of her experience into one closer to the truth, to reality as it is. This primitive defence against early loss could be relinquished when something that had remained unknown could be recovered and reintegrated. Finally, the feelings connecting my patient with that early experience could be felt in relation to others without their delusional components. By integrating a suppressed experience, my patient was reaching a level of separateness that is the foundation for the capacity to experience wholeness and passions.

Conclusion

The potential for wholeness and a sense of self resides in primal emotional experiences: they are true. These primitive experiences need to be understood (K). This understanding brings us closer to 'O', reality as it is, and our unique relationship with it. The attempt to experience reality, and our capacity to know about it, needs to meet with adequate conditions in order for us to develop an evolved sense of being. This includes a capacity for mental growth and a development towards integration of experiences. The fluctuation between states of disjunction and wholeness is a lifelong task, which includes the capacity to separate from primitive phantasies and identification with aspects of the parents, to bear affects and to transform them into emotions, feelings and thoughts. When an experience cannot be represented, it can only be enacted: indigestible facts (beta) cannot be understood and transformed. This represents an obstacle to the growing sense of self, to K and to O.

In the difficult task of sustaining patients in their search for self, the analyst must find ways of becoming a sort of auxiliary conscious and unconscious ego, able to perform for the patient what has gone amiss, such as the capacity to create meaning between mind and body, and to (re)find the ego's sense of fit between mind and body (Garland 1998). For my patient, this has meant being able to name previously unnameable primitive experiences that belonged to the past but were active in the present and to find a different way of knowing herself in relation to them as they are. In our work together, in our investigation of O, we have been able to come closer to beta and to O.

As I have broken down theories and put them together again, I have tried to make sense in myself and for my patient of her unknown experience, which she has now understood in a different way. I have used the patient's past as a beta element that had to find new meaning in the present. This transformation brought integration of a split-off emotional experience of the past that was always present and, although unknown, was connecting all her emotional experiences in such a way that present and past were confused.

I have tried to construct a matrix around an infantile experience. Using free association, the theory of child development and observation of the patient's capacity to relate to me, I have formulated with the patient a way of making sense of her past experience and transforming it into something new. Preverbal bodily events that had remained somatic delusions could now become known. The grip of bodily events and of their resulting delusional-illusional states could be relinquished. In this chapter, I have shown how somatic delusions could become feelings and thoughts. Two different primitive emotional experiences of my patient in relation to others could be put together, and the feelings attached to them could be felt and understood in relation to her experiences.

My clinical approach is similar to Jung's, keeping open to 'O'. I have tried to link my reverie to the childhood experience of my patient, relating to it from a personal, individual point of view. I found archetypes of the collective unconscious and personal unconscious phantasies. Jung sought something 'more', and I have tried to show that this more – in Bion's language, beta and O, the ongoing search for meaning (K) – requires elaborating on emotions and an analyst who is very much in touch with feelings. It is primal emotional truth that we need to reach: every emotional experience in the present reconnects us with those in the past. The past obscures the present, and past emotional experiences must be integrated in order to understand the present.

Like Jung after his break with Freud, my patient and I encountered suppressed events that were hidden but present and which were trapping her. Understanding and transforming them freed my patient from imprisonment. We approached the unknown past with courage and curiosity and were able to transform beta and O into K. This transformation has helped my patient, like Jung (1961), to achieve a sense of wholeness and of self. Our work brought us closer to the real thing, to O.

Note

1 First published in *Transformation. Jung's Legacy and Clinical Work Today*, eds. A. Cavalli, L. Hawkins, M. Stevns (London: Karnac, 2014). Republished by Routledge, New York, 2018.

References

Baranger, M., Baranger, W., & Mom, J.M. (2009). 'The infantile psychic trauma, from us to Freud: Pure trauma, retroactivity and reconstruction'. In *The Work of Confluence*, eds. M. Baranger & W. Baranger. London: Karnac.

Baranger, W. (2009). 'The dead alive'. In *The Work of Confluence*, eds. M. Baranger & W. Baranger. London: Karnac.

Bion, W.R. (1970). *Attention and Interpretation*. London: Tavistock.

———. (1977). *Two Papers: The Grid and Caesura*. London: Karnac, 1984.

Botella, C., & Botella, S. (2005). *The Work of Figurability*. London: Routledge.

Feldman, B. (1992). 'Jung's infancy and childhood'. *Journal of Analytical Psychology*, 37, 255–74.

Fordham, M. (1985). 'Abandonment in infancy'. *Chiron*, 3–21.

Garland, C. (1998). *Understanding Trauma*. London: Karnac.

Green, A. (1998). 'The primordial mind and the work of the negative'. *International Journal of Psychoanalysis*, 79, 649–66.

Jackson, M. (1963). 'Symbol formation and the delusional transference'. *Journal of Analytical Psychology*, 8, 145–59.

Jung, C.G. (1961). 'After the break with Freud'. In *Memories, Dreams, Reflections*, ed. A. Jaffe. New York: Random House.

———. (2009). *The Red Book*. New York: Norton.

Kerr, J. (1994). *A Most Dangerous Method*. London: Sinclair-Stevenson.

Mancia, M. (2007). *Feeling the Words*. London: Routledge.

McGuire, W. (ed.) (1974). *The Freud/Jung Letters: The Correspondence between Sigmund Freud and C.G. Jung*. Trans. R. Manheim & R.F.C. Hull. Princeton, NJ: Princeton University Press.

Meredith-Owen, W. (2011a). 'Winnicott on Jung: destruction, creativity and the unrepressed unconscious'. *Journal of Analytical Psychology*, 56, 56–75.

———. (2011b). 'Jung's Shadow: negation and narcissism of the self'. *Journal of Analytical Psychology*, 56, 674–91.

Satinover, J. (1985). 'At the mercy of another: abandonment and restitution in psychotic character'. *Chiron*, 47–86.

Winnicott, D.W. (1964). 'Memories, dreams, reflections by C.G. Jung'. *International Journal of Psychoanalysis*, 45, 450–55.

Chapter 8

Giving voice to psychic pain

The British-Mexican connection, on the vicissitudes of creating a home for street children[1]

In psychodynamic thinking, the concept of containment is a basic one. It starts in infancy when the mother contains her baby in her womb and allows, together with her husband, a place in their minds to develop so that their infant can be thought about. It is from their minds that father and mother monitor their infant's physical and psychological growth. It is thanks to this experience that the infant will discover that he too can develop the awareness of being a person with a mind from which he can contain his feelings, his emotions and his thoughts (Winnicott 1965, pp. 35–55).

There are many children who have never been able to develop a mind as such; indeed, to have parents able to bring up their children with their psychological needs in mind is a great privilege. Unfortunately, there are children for whom physical well-being is already a luxury. For these children, survival is a priority, as there is no adult there to care for them physically, let alone emotionally.

There are countries in which the state overcomes this kind of problem by setting up social interventions to offer children protection and to compensate for what parents might fail to provide, but there are other countries in which the state is socially and economically not organized to offer an alternative solution; issues like 'protection' of the child's survival are left to private organizations, such as the church, non-governmental organizations (NGOs) or single individuals. Although this chapter will deal with the practical effects of this problem, a discussion of its implications is beyond the scope of this work. In particular, I will describe my work in a Mexican city and how an NGO working with street children has been able to move from offering protection and ensuring survival to the children they are working with, to help children to develop minds of their own. In this, they try to provide something that for the normal development of children is expected.

From protection to containment

In the 1970s, a Brazilian Catholic priest, Paulo Freire, developed what he called the 'Theory of Liberation.' In his book, he postulated a theory of liberation for the poor that would allow them to develop socially and economically (Freire 2000). He saw the lack of education as the main reason for chronic poverty.

DOI: 10.4324/9781003268536-9

His teaching inspired many people all over the world to become more active and to teach writing and reading to those who were ignorant and poor. In the late 1970s, a group of six intellectuals in a large town in Mexico, inspired by Freire's theory, decided to act by building a home for street children and adolescents. Their aim was to offer 'survival and protection' to the children, a home, food and education. They soon realized how difficult it was to convince street children to come and live in the home. Street children do not trust adults, as they know from experience that adults might be keen on exploiting them in order to sell their organs or to use them for drug dealing or prostitution. In time they developed what they called Operación Amistad (Operation Friendship), a complex and skilful way of befriending street children with the aim of offering them to come and live in the home they had just built.

Developments

In 1998, a member of that group which had meanwhile become an NGO, Fundación JUCONI (Junto Con Los Niños, which means together with the children), came to London and asked the Tavistock Clinic for help. It had become clear to the workers of the NGO (who, according to the Mexican educational system, call themselves educators, as they are not social workers or therapists) that a physical shelter, schooling, and food were not sufficient for the successful rescue of the children. Paul Freire's theory revealed itself to be insufficient. In 1999, Gianna Williams began to travel to that Mexican city in order to work as a consultant for the NGO. Williams is a former Jungian analyst who, after training in Zürich, came to London and did the child and adolescent training at the Tavistock Clinic. She worked closely with Michael Fordham introducing the method of infant observation at the Society of Analytical Psychology. She is now a very influential psychoanalyst and member of the International Psychoanalytical Association in London. Williams has written about her work with JUCONI (Williams 2008, pp. 253–266).

Without using any jargon but discussing in the group every educator's experience of each child, the interactions the educators observed, including the relationships the children were establishing among themselves, Williams started sharing with the group a psychoanalytic way of thinking: an interest in making links and, most of all, a curiosity in attempting to give meaning to psychic pain and in recognizing defences against it. Williams also introduced Bion's idea that what is perceived as an attack may be a communication; indeed, many children would run away during their stay in the children's home (Bion 1959, pp. 308–15). This teaching helped the educators better tolerate their often-painful work; in fact, the turnover of staff in JUCONI is very limited. Gradually, the educators began to observe the children with a different eye and listen with a different ear.

Williams introduced the educators to the idea of a therapeutic intervention called Special Time (ST), which was tried out for the first time by Shirley Hoxter in the '70s in a family centre in London (Hoxter 1981).

ST is a regular weekly slot of 45 minutes of total attention offered to a child by an adult (one-to-one) in the same place and at the same time. The central skills of ST are observing, listening and asking very few questions. Children can make whatever use they like of their 45 minutes. Every child has a box with some material in it, pens, sheets of papers, etc., and a calendar with all the dates in which his ST will take place.

This method proved very useful to the educators, who were beginning to discover how important total attention, curiosity and a non-judgemental attitude can be in the relationships they were creating with the children seen for ST. Seven educators began to offer this kind of intervention to the children living in the home.

In 2007, Gianna Williams asked me to help her supervise the educators who were offering ST and subsequently to take over for her. This was the starting point of my contribution; I began to supervise via email and Skype each session that the educators were sending me in written form. In 2008, I travelled for the first time to Mexico to meet the educators and see the children's home. ST were increasing in frequency, and help was needed. Spanish-speaking, qualified child psychotherapists were approached in order to meet the needs of our supervisees.

Special time

A model was created in which each ST lasted one year, from February to the end of January of the following year. Children who wished to have a second, third or fourth go had to put themselves on a waiting list to start the next round of ST with the first educator available. This system conformed to the need of the children's home to avoid too strong a transference to one particular educator over a long period of time and to encourage a transference to the children's home itself with the educators as part of the institution. Another advantage of this method was to avoid a too-close rivalry between the children over one possible favourite educator. Every child would have to adapt to another person at each round and learn to relate to each of them in a different but similar way as they all were adhering to the rules of ST. In a parallel process, the educators were faced with a similar reality. At each round, they would have to change supervisor and adapt to a new way of supervising, receiving comments written in a different style. This was possible because they too, like the children, were relating to what Williams had represented for them, a new way of thinking – all of us supervisors were representing that new way of thinking.

While at each round of ST, the children were able to represent to themselves a more coherent history of their pasts and have more realistic views about their futures, the educators were learning to bear more pain, to witness and suffer for their children in a way that just a few years previously did not seem possible. From their 'protective arms', (the house) the educators began to offer the children a mental space within which emotions, feelings and thoughts could be contained.

Our team of supervisors was holding and reflecting this space in London through modern means of communication: the Internet, emails and Skype.

This work was becoming so interesting that by 2011, I decided to liaise with the Tavistock Clinic and create a Tavistock Certificate for the educators who had never had therapy themselves and had no training in psychodynamic work. I felt that the experience with the children and the capacity to learn from the supervised work needed some form of recognition and 'protection'. A one-year course, Understanding Communications with Children, Special Time, was created by me, and the Tavistock Clinic recognized it as a certificate. The manager of JUCONI met us in London to discuss the actual feasibility of the course, and in 2013, the course started. We were by then six supervisors.

Nine educators have now completed this course. The aim of the course has been to consolidate the educators' knowledge, offer more structured theoretical background through teaching in situ and, essentially, to continue the work of supervision in written form – the educators email us the session, and we treat it as a document which has to be commented on sentence by sentence.

Running away, being found

I will now discuss what have been the biggest challenges that the children and adolescents have created for ST and how they have been overcome.

Street children have learnt to run away. Running away becomes an internal working model, powerfully described by Symington (Symington 1985, pp. 481–87) as a way of approaching life, or a repetition compulsion, as Williams (Williams 1997, pp. 25–31) puts it. From the pain of having been excluded from the love of their parents (by having been abandoned by parents who go to prison, disappear, go to work in the United States, simply leave the child with an old grandmother who has no means or start a new life somewhere else with another partner), the children have learnt to cope by running away. Running away represents attachment to an idealized parent that 'will be found' (an antidote against difficulties that is based on despair, an idealized form of manic hope). For these children, realistic hope is too dangerous, as it means giving up the fairy tale of re-finding the lost parents and accepting the reality they live in. Only this recognition will put the child and adolescent in the position of assessing what is 'good enough' and give up unrealistic dreams of blissfulness. Running away becomes a perverse way of thinking, when things don't go well, one runs away. Many of these children manically hope to reunite with their parents forever and reject what the good but limited home has to offer. Remaining attached to idealization makes them denigrate and run away from what they have, unable to value what is really possible. I will now show how this state of mind impacts on ST and how it might slowly shift through the work in progress with the educator.

Christian (17 years old) ran away a few weeks after his admission to the children's home. One educator was allocated to him for his ST, but after already missing two sessions, Christian ran away with another child from the home. He stole a motorcycle, a month later was found stealing food at the market and was taken by

Giving voice to psychic pain   123

the police and put in prison. For certain reasons, he was put in an ordinary prison with adult prisoners. While JUCONI was working at getting Christian back to the home, an arrangement with the prison was made whereby Christian's ST would continue, and his educator would go every week to visit him in prison, the same day of the week, at the same time.

E: Christian, I am here to offer to continue your ST, but we need to agree on some points.
C: I don't need to think about it though. I'll come anyway.
E: How come you are so decided? In the home, you never came to your ST.
C: Because I understood that I did the wrong thing; I should not have left the home like that. You certainly know why I am here. . . . I stole, stole a few things, then I stole a motorcycle, I bought some drugs, and so on until they caught me at the market . . . and brought me here.
E: It is indeed a very difficult situation.
C: I am using here the security plan JUCONI taught me at the children's home; in case of danger do not react, ask for help. But I am not able to control myself. Look here (he shows me a big wound on his arm), yesterday they put me in isolation. Two guys were trying to take my food away from me, and I could not control myself, so I reacted, and one cut me.

While at the beginning Christian seems to want to impress his educator with his 'maturity', we will see how difficult it was for him to give up his belief that he can count only on himself, and he cannot trust anyone.

Since that initial meeting a few months before, Christian did not attend his ST in the prison. His educator used to hear that Christian was in isolation and could not see him. Despite his good intention, Christian was, in some way, still on the run. By session 25, his educator was told by the police guard that today Christian was there, but he was 'crazy, impossible to reach, unworkable'.

> I walked towards Christian; the policeman said, 'Don't let this man in; this bloke will punch him'. I kept walking and came up to Christian. I asked the policeman to leave us alone. He did not move. I asked for privacy, and he locked the door. Christian held his arms stretched out; he was crying, but with what seemed to me a gesture of extraordinary courage, he walked towards me. Before I could lift my arms, I understood that he wanted to embrace me. I embraced him too, and although he was still crying, I realized he was slowly calming down. He then sat down, and I asked him where he wanted me to sit. He pointed at the chair opposite him. I took his box out of my bag and put it between us. Still crying, Christian opened his box and took out a small notebook that was inside. He began to write something on it. When he finished, he looked at me; I saw that he was not crying anymore. He made a movement towards me, so I sat down on the floor. Christian took out everything that was in his box, including his calendar with all the dates of his ST. He marked today's date as if it was a very special date. In this moment, something

powerful happened. It was as if I too became aware of Christian's ST, and I felt as if the supervision, the course, the reading had really changed me. I felt much more intelligent, more experienced; I understood everything, including my own feelings, my emotions and my capacity to understand expanded.

The work of supervision had consisted of offering constant encouragement to the educator to continue to go regularly to the meetings and survive Christian's absences. The work done in supervision was a work of real hope, as we had no assurance that Christian would decide to take up his ST. It was not coming from a place of despair, nor of manic hope; only the tenacity of real hope – and this time we both were rewarded – brought educator and adolescent to meet in a powerful way. Some defences shifted, and the acceptance of reality brought them both to recognize each other's importance and to integrate past, present and future. From that session onwards, working together became really possible, and, when eight months later Christian could come back to the home, a big shift had happened in him.

I will now present another vignette from the ST of another child, Ramón (14 years old), who had run away with Christian and was found a few days later trying to steal a car. His sessions could continue in the children's prison he was put in for six months. His educator would go for every session of ST to the children's prison to give Ramón his session. In this session, we see how painful the work of acceptance can be for these children and how difficult it is to bear 'reality' without idealization or denigration. While Christian was 'idealizing' his capacity to survive on his own, even in the cruellest prison, Ramón reacts by denigrating his family; this is a powerful defence against the pain of having been abandoned. We can see that for both children it is possible to abandon their defences only when they realize that they are held in mind (the educator does not forget them), and this is in itself a very powerful therapeutic tool in the development of a capacity to think. Experiencing another mind that can think about them has such a powerful impact on them – omnipotence and deprivation find a powerful antidote.

R: I have many brothers, and my favourite one is called 'fart'. There is another one called 'caca'. Well, no; 'caca' is my sister. Then I have another brother who is called 'slag', and another one called 'swine'. He began to laugh until he repeated, 'Yes, yes', and repeated all the names of his brothers and sister.

E: I have never heard people with such names. . . . It must be very painful for them to have to carry such names . . . these are names used to insult people, not to call them.

R: Ha ha, 'caca', 'fart', 'slag' . . . I have another one who is called 'diarrhoea', another called 'rubbish', another called "louse', another one called 'pubic hair'.

E: I did not know you had so many brothers, and with such names . . . you seem to be the only one with an ordinary name.

R: It is our mother who gave us these names. . . . There are more: 'caw', 'poop', 'stupid'. [And he went on and on. At the end, there were more than 20 brothers with such insulting names.]

E: I am amazed that at least to you your mother gave an ordinary name.
R: It is all my mother's fault; her name is 'cerda' (female pig = slut) . . . yes she is called 'la cerda' . . . ha ha ha ha ha . . . and do you know why she is called 'la cerda'? Because she is a female pig! [And then imitating a pig he moved around saying,] 'Yes, she is a pig and so are all my brothers and sisters'.

In fact, Ramón's mother was found by the NGO and alerted about her child's state. JUCONI's policy is to try to find the parents of street children and, if possible, establish a relationship between them and the child. In this case, JUCONI had tried to connect with her, but she did not want to know anything about Ramón, as if Ramón had never been her own child.

Later in the session, we continued:

E: It must have been very painful that she did not come at all.
R: No, it does not matter; I did not want to see her anyway. Do you think I want to mingle with a female pig (slut)? Not at all, not at all.

We can see how painful it is for Ramón to know that he is not in his mother's mind and how he transforms the pain of being the only one among her children that has been rejected by her. In his next session, Ramón asked his educator if other children in the home were asking about him, if his photo was still there. Now let us see a vignette from the next session:

R: Is my photo still there?
E: Yes, it is.
R: It might be at the bottom of the panel.
E: Yes, it is.
R: So, the new children who have come to live in the house might ask, 'Who is this child whose photo is at the bottom?' The educators will answer, 'This is Ramón, a child who ran away and is now in the children's prison'.
E: Do you think that this is what they are saying?
R: Yes. And when I come back, I will tell them, 'Look, I am back again; don't run away, it is no good'.

In order to survive, Ramón needs to destroy his own mother (and his brothers and sister) with whom he cannot imagine being happy and close, and instead imagine that he will manage alone to survive the prison and come back to the children's home like a hero, as is depicted in the following:

R: I know that when I come back to the home everybody will be waiting for me. Those who already know me will say [his face lifted], 'Welcome back, Ramón!' All the educators will be there, telling me, 'Welcome back, Ramón, darling; this is your home!' And I will begin to smile at everybody, and I will say, 'Thank you, thank you'. And I will kiss everybody [he was making faces as if he were rehearsing the event], and the new children will say, 'Ah, this is Ramón, but he does not look like the photo; how come?' And the educators will answer, 'Well, he has spent a few months in the children's prison; he has grown, matured. He has suffered a lot'.

E: It seems to me that you have been thinking a lot about your re-admission.
R: Yes, everybody will be happy to see me again.

On the other hand, we can see how the concept of a mind with space for him is really occupying Ramón's mind, and how, while reflecting about his experiences, he is beginning to develop a mind of his own.

A few sessions later (five months into his ST), Ramón begins to discuss his death with his educator, and he seems very preoccupied about being remembered then. This persistent thought will be the red thread of the second part of his ST. Ramón is really trying to make sense of what it means not to be in anybody's mind, to be abolished; only death comes close in his mind to what his experience has been. It will take many more rounds of ST for Ramón to be able to have a better sense of this in relation to his mother, himself, and others. Nevertheless, three sessions before the end of his first round of ST, when he is back in the home and has to separate from his educator, he begins to talk about the terrible pain of not living with his family.

Double deprivation and omnipotence as a defence against survival anxiety

Children who are deprived of parents who can look after them physically and mentally tend to develop strong defences against the pain of having been deprived of what is archetypally expected. Survival anxieties give rise to omnipotence, the child becomes the invincible hero, and to double deprivation, the child tends to reject what he has and goes in search of something that in his mind is better and promises total happiness. These children cling on to an internal object that promises them blissfulness. Equipped with these defences, they become impermeable to fear, invincible and without needs. When these defences begin to crack, the mental pain the educators and children have to bear is very heavy, and the work of supervision becomes, for the educator, an important refuge and nourishment.

Esteban

I will now present a brief résumé of four years of ST with a child called Esteban. My aim is to show how, from omnipotence and double deprivation, Esteban was able to begin to talk about mental pain, fear and anxiety.

Esteban was 8 when his old grandmother died, and for some reason, he was brought to the children's home by a neighbour who had heard of JUCONI. Esteban has never been a proper street child, but his life was a life of neglect, abuse and extreme poverty. His mother left his father when Esteban was 1. She left with her three older children because her husband was an alcoholic and hit her regularly. She decided not to take Esteban with her because he was too small, and perhaps she left him with his father out of guilt; at least he could have one child to look after. Shortly afterwards, his father brought home woman after woman, until Esteban was 5, and the next woman stayed for two years. During these two years, he was sexually molested by her, and his father went to prison for stealing from a shop. Esteban went to live with his grandmother who was extremely poor and eventually died one year later. He went to school from the age of 6, but by the time he was moved to the children's home, he could barely read and write.

Four years of special time in a few words

In the first round of ST, Esteban used to masturbate – possibly a sort of 'sexualized thumb-sucking'. In this way, he did not need to relate, and he was locked in his own world, soothing himself. Only slowly did Esteban begin to play with toys, and, by the end of his second year of ST, he enjoyed playing with a penguin who 'lived on his own in the north pole'. In this way, Esteban was showing how he used to survive emotions and make himself impermeable to suffering and pain. Close to the end of the second year of his stay in the children's home, his father agreed to see him, and Esteban began to meet his father in prison regularly on a monthly basis, accompanied by an educator. This reality, together with the life in the home, broke down the penguin attitude of Esteban, and a chaotic picture of his internal world emerged in the sessions of ST; La Parca (a dressed skeleton worshipped in Mexico as a deity) began to fill his sessions together with policemen, doctors, the spider man, children, criminals and teddy bears in constant and endless fights of destruction.

In his third round of ST, Esteban was allocated a male educator (in years one and two he had two different female educators), and he began to spend most of the time playing football in the sessions. His aggressiveness, rage and desire to compete and win were contained in fighting with his educator who remained stronger than him and was able to contain Esteban's emotions in a physical way. It was towards the end of the third year of ST that Esteban began to show some fear of his own deepest emotions; he acquired the habit of going to the toilet during meaningful moments in the session, spending some time there. It was when his educator began to address these 'mini-running-away attempts' that Esteban could begin to talk about his life, his father, his memories of the past and his great fears of the future. At the end of his third round of ST, Esteban was 11 years old. He took a break from ST and resumed with the fourth year when he was 13. His educator, in her detailed session reports, observed and interacted with a child who had changed a lot: a young adolescent full of fears and anxieties about his future, including his fear of becoming an alcoholic like his father; his difficulty in imagining a future outside the children's home; his desire to reunite with his father once he came out of prison. By the end of that year, Esteban had developed a more coherent sense of himself in the world. Naturally, the work offered to the children in the children's home helps enormously with their psycho-physical development; all the more, the attention encountered during ST offers the child a space in which their internal world emerges, is given particular attention and subsequently finds expression and meaning.

It is a powerful experience to see that although these children have not known what we would call 'a normal upbringing, they can develop what is normal and to be expected in a human being: a capacity to feel and suffer, to think about themselves and others in a coherent way.

Trauma and repetition of trauma

It is not always possible to reconstruct the past of these children. Sometimes there is no one who remembers it. We know that humans tend to repeat their traumas in unconscious enactments and that these repetitions have two sides; on the one hand, the trauma serves as a basic experience around which our deepest experiences of identity are formed, and on the other, repeating a trauma might have some value in trying to understand and order it. It is beyond the scope of this chapter to go into the details of this problem; nevertheless, in the following story, I would like to show another way of understanding 'running away' as a repetition of a trauma that has happened but cannot be remembered (Cavalli 2012, pp. 597–612).

One day, Alberto disappeared. He had lived in the children's home for a few years, had had three rounds of ST and was well adjusted in his development. Alberto was now 17, had learnt a practical skill and was in the process of looking for an apprenticeship. He could live in the children's home for another two years. The educators of the home were puzzled by his disappearing one day, and it was only after many months that Alberto was found. The story he told was the following:

One day he found a job as a builder for a man who took him in his car and showed him what he had to do. This man left Alberto in a region of the province far away from the city. Alberto did not feel able to run away because he found himself 'lost', incapable of orientating himself. He stayed there and worked for the man who did not pay him and brought him little to eat.

It was only when he was found by JUCONI in extraordinary circumstances, and after he had recovered from what had been a sort of kidnapping, that Alberto could emerge from a sort of dissociation, suddenly remembering what it was like when his parents had left him with a neighbour before they disappeared. He was 5. They never came back. Eventually, he ran away and later went to live in the children's home. He had lost his memory of that event. In his subsequent ST (his fourth round), Alberto was able to reconnect with that lost memory, and the past experience could be reintegrated into his life history and worked through.

Separation

Separation is the most difficult aspect of ST. Children and educators are afraid of suffering separation; it has been a very complex task in supervision to guide educators in preparing the children well for the end of their STs. The fact that there are so many rounds of ST for each child facilitates the experience of separation, and its re-working brings about old conflicts and memories, as well as new insights for the children, educators, and supervisors.

On my first visit to Mexico, I did some observations of the children in the home. In particular, one child drew my attention. I did my observation in the classroom the children used for their homework. Normally, there is an educator to supervise them and help them with their questions. I observed that every time the educator had to leave the room for some reason (get a pen, call another educator, etc.), this child would lie down on the floor in the foetal position, and as soon as the educator came back, the child would stand up again, able to continue with his task. In one hour, the educator had to leave the room at least six times, and inevitably the child would lie on the floor and then stand up. In my mind, trying to make sense of my observations, I thought that the educator represented the spine of the child, and without his presence, the child would collapse like a baby, unable to hold himself up. I found it very interesting to see the child jump up again as soon as the educator came back, as if his presence helped the child to find the external support he had not yet developed internally. The comings and goings of the educator were working as mini-separations and mini-re-encounters, which, for the child, were so helpful. For most of the children, leaving means 'abandonment'. The separation from each round of ST at the end of each year helps the child to integrate endings and new beginnings and serves the purpose of learning what ordinary children know – that a good separation is when the child has internalized the presence of his parents and can survive without them. The fact that ST is taking place in the children's home allows the child to separate from it while still being held by the home that offers containment in the transition from one round of ST to the next.

The institution as a family

In this chapter, I have tried to show how much work has been necessary for a home for street children to act as the 'parental couple' in order to offer what for other children is ordinary. The NGO, the fundraisers, the educators, and our team of supervisors, including Gianna Williams' input, have acted as the 'parental couple'. We have offered our cultural tradition (psychodynamic) as a link between the maternal and paternal functions of the home. This link has created a space for growth. As happens in families, children leave and go to create their own families; by now the oldest children of the children's home have left, but they approach JUCONI asking for help in the upbringing of their own children. JUCONI is setting up different kinds of interventions with preventive work in mind. At the same time, those educators who have completed our course are now beginning to teach educators of other institutions how to set up Special Time, and I, using the Mexican experience, am setting up a similar certificate for psychologists working with children in Russia.

I would like to thank Sandra Cortés-Iniesta and José Francisco Meregalli for allowing me to use some vignettes from their Special Time case material.

Note

1 First published in: *From Tradition to Innovation: Jungian Analysts Working in Different Cultural Settings*, eds. C. Crowther & J. Wiener (New Orleans: Spring Journal Books, 2015). Republished as: *Jungian Analysts Working across Cultures: From Tradition to Innovation*, eds. C. Crowther & J. Wiener (London and New York: Routledge, 2021).

References

Bion, W.R. (1959). 'Attacks on linking'. *International Journal of Psychoanalysis*, 40, 5–6, 308–15.
Cavalli, A. (2012). 'Transgenerational transmission of indigestible facts: From trauma, deadly ghosts, and mental voids to meaning-making interpretations', *Journal of Analytical Psychology*, 57, 5, 597–612.
Freire, P. (2000). *The Pedagogy of the Oppressed*, trans. Myra Bergman Ramos. New York: Continuum.
Hoxter, S. (1981). *The Old Lady Who Lived in a Shoe*. London: Tavistock.
Symington, N. (1985). 'The survival function of primitive omnipotence'. *International Journal of Psychoanalysis*, 66, 4, 481–87.
Williams, G. (2008). 'Work discussion seminars with the staff of a children's home for street children in Puebla, Mexico'. In: Rustin, M. & Bradley, J. (eds). *Work Discussion: Learning from Reflective Practice in Work with Children and Families*. London: Karnac, 253–66.
Williams, G. (1997). 'Thinking and learning in deprived children'. In: *Internal Landscapes and Foreign Bodies: Eating Disorders and Other Pathologies*. London, Duckworth & Co. 25–31.
Winnicott, D.W. (1965). 'The theory of parent-infant relationship'. In: *The Maturational Process and the Facilitating Environment*. Madison, CT: International University Press. 35–55.

Chapter 9

Identification – obstacle to individuation, or

On how to become 'me'[1]

Introduction

In this chapter, I would like to illustrate the problem of identification with aspects of a lost object as a defence against traumatic loss. I will link, using clinical material, the defensive use of identification to the blocking and breakdown of the process of individuation. I would like to put across the thought that the capacity to mourn is directly linked with the process of individuation, as individuation is connected with the capacity of the mind to process separation and mourn what is lost.

Central to Jungian psychology is individuation, the process by which individual beings are formed and differentiated. In particular, individuation is the development of the psychological individual, 'the development of consciousness out of the original state of identity' (Jung 1913, para 762). Jung's view was that the process of individuation was possible because of an inner source, some sort of internal organizing principle 'intrinsic part of the self, containing unconscious nodal points which behaved in characteristic ways' (Astor 1995, p. 140). Later, Fordham added a developmental feature to this internal organizing principle of the psyche by describing how the primary self would unfold, and how internal objects were formed on an archetypal basis through deintegration and reintegration (Fordham 1976). Both Jung and Fordham described individuation as a process of separation: from states of unconsciousness, from experiences that needed to be reintegrated and accommodated internally. They both saw the dynamic of the self as intrinsic to the process of development, responsible for maturation. So in Jung's model, identification with others, or aspects of others, finds relatively little place; it has tended to be regarded as a sort of 'unconscious imitation' (Astor 1995, p. 230), 'a process by which a person fuses or confuses his own identity with someone else's' (Gordon 1978, p. 27).

This is very different from the Freudian understanding of the psyche where there is an absence of an internal source other than the superego, which is formed by identifications with both parents (Freud 1921, p. 105). Freud's model is based on a psyche which evolves by means of a series of identifications with external whole or part objects, and the personality is constructed by the process of

DOI: 10.4324/9781003268536-10

incorporation (Bott Spillius et al. 2000, p. 364), identification (ibid., p. 361) and introjection (ibid., p. 375).

Jung understood identification as having 'always a purpose, namely to obtain an advantage, to push aside an obstacle, or to solve a problem the way another individual would' (Jung 1913, para. 440–41). The significance of this difference contributed to Freud and Jung going their separate ways in 1912 (Astor 1995, p. 140).

Jung wrote,

> Identification can be beneficial so long as the individual cannot get his own way. But when a better possibility presents itself, identification shows its morbid character by becoming just a hindrance as it was an unconscious help and support before. It now has a dissociative effect, splitting the individual into two mutually estranged personalities.
>
> (Jung 1913, para. 440–41)

Jung did not elaborate on the process of mourning he had to undergo in order to free himself from Freud's influence, he simply documented it. If we study Jung's accounts of his development in *Memories, Dreams, Reflections* and *The Red Book*, there can be no doubt that he was much more concerned with the effects of the archetypes (Fordham 1995, p. 212) than with the subject of grief and mourning. Jung emerged out of the process of separation and 'de-identification' from Freud with a stronger ego. This experience contributed to his own process of individuation.

I would like to explore the problem of separation in a particular situation – namely, when the ego is not developed enough to process loss, pain and grief. I have discussed elsewhere (Cavalli 2011) how, for the sake of psychic survival, the infant's self might recur to autistic defences to overcome pain and loss. In that case, the internal organizing principle of the self is shut down, the primary self defends from unbearable psychic pain. Fordham called this 'defence of the self' (Fordham 1976). In this chapter, I will show how identification with the lost object (in Jungian terms, as fusion and confusion) might offer to the self another solution to avoid pain and loss and how Jung's approach can be of help in understanding the defensive structure of identification against separation.

My work with a 3-year-old boy will provide some clinical material to illustrate this. The boy in question lost contact with his mother for some time when he was 9 months old. His mind was as yet inadequate to reintegrate the experience of loss, and he was unable to process the pull of the affects that he had to face. The intrinsic dynamic property of the self was brought to a standstill: instead, he resorted to identifying (fuse and confuse) himself with aspects of the lost mother. This defence protected him from having to come to terms with pre-oedipal and oedipal contents, as well as from the pain of weaning.

Brief history

Alef[2] was just 3 when he came to see me. His once-a-week therapy lasted 15 months, from October to the December of the year after. During that period, I saw the parents on a monthly basis for the first five months; subsequently, I saw them once a term. After the end of Alef's therapy, in the following two years, I saw him once a term. This was part of a review programme the parents had agreed to once Alef's therapy ended. I was concerned about consolidation, as I felt the parents had insisted on ending Alef's therapy before the 18 months I had hoped to reach with him. Alef's mother had developed cancer when Alef was 9 months old. She was still breastfeeding then. Following the diagnosis, her breasts 'were chopped off' (as she told me in the initial meeting), and when she came home after the operation and a few days spent in hospital, Alef did not recognize her. Later she lost all her hair, but 'Alef did not seem to notice'. Later, Alef became very clinging and wanted to be with Mummy all the time. He was never toilet trained.

Presenting problems

Alef was isolated at nursery and reacted by hitting other children if they came close to him. He did not want to be with his father and wanted to sleep with his mother so that his father ended up sleeping in Alef's bed. The greatest challenge was that he did not pooh normally according to his age. He had been on Movicol (prescribed by his General Practitioner [GP]) since he was 11 months old. When he was put on the pot, he would scream. The parents got used to him poohing in his pants, and as his pooh had almost the consistency of pee, drops of pooh would fall out of his anus. Though Alef's mother tolerated the fact that he 'could not be toilet trained', his father did not. He felt increasingly impatient and totally impotent. Alef had started nursery a few weeks before coming to see me, and the fact that his poohing habits did not agree with the nursery's policy had propelled the parents to seek help. On the other hand, Alef seemed to have developed an incredible ability in his speech: his language was very advanced; he spoke very well grammatically and syntactically as if he was a much older boy. The real problem was that his speech was full of nonsense as if he was an adolescent trying to be an adult: we could call this an example of nonsensical 'pseudo-maturity' (Meltzer & Harris 2011).

First session

Alef arrived with his mother and a big teddy inside his coat. He was a tiny boy and something in his look seemed mad. He did not quite seem either like a boy or a girl; he looked simply tiny, and mad. As soon as he saw me, he began to scream, but it was a scream of terror, panic – really intolerable. My neighbours arrived running, and when they saw that Alef was in his mother's arms, they left surprised.

For the first session, I saw child and mother together, and Alef calmed down eventually and finally introduced his teddy: teddy was called 'Chubby'. He told me that she was a female teddy, and he was going to marry her. He then spent the whole session on his mother's lap talking to Chubby in Pinguinese, as he told me, a language that he and she spoke fluently and nobody else understood.

He then came down from his mother's lap, sat on the floor and I guessed that he had the impulse to pooh, but he just sat down and masturbated by rubbing his anus on the floor. He was disconnected from us, lost in his own pleasure and fantasy. He did not wear a nappy and later a pooh smell overtook the room. His mother checked his underwear, and I saw a few drops of liquid pooh on his pants. She changed him as if nothing had happened, while she continued talking to me.

Some thoughts

Alef's scream was a powerful communication. Perhaps he hoped that I could understand his terror. Perhaps he was using me right from the beginning as a container-to-be-found for the overwhelming terror of his madness. In the session, I had the impression that he was telling me about his confusion, that he was trying to communicate to me what was upsetting him. Naturally, he did not know if I could understand him, and perhaps he was used to not being understood. Nevertheless, whatever I had been able to absorb from him left me with the following provisional hypothesis: there is a horizontal split in him – namely, that 'in the head', he is an omnipotent boy who can mesmerize people with his linguistic skills, while in 'the rest of his body', he presumes (via his bottom) to be a 'mummy with breasts', dripping milk. Thus his pooh is idealized and this makes this tiny boy feel important. In addition, he has a twin, a female twin that functions as a projection of himself, and only she can understand him. But these splits leave no space for the tiny boy who cannot now continue his journey of individuation and indeed perhaps he hopes to have made this tiny boy invisible.

I find myself curious about his early identification with the breast and want to explore in my assessment of him the attributes of the breast he is identified with.

Second session

Alef comes screaming in terror, but this time I take him in my arms and bring him inside the consulting room gently, asking his mother to wait in the waiting room. Alef hits me; I say that he is right to hit me because I am making him come and see me, and he does not want to see Alessandra because Alessandra is forcing him to do things he does not want to do, hear or listen to.

He says: 'My mother is going to die; my father is going to die, and I will die young'.

To this I say: 'Yes, Alef is going to die, but before he dies, he has something important to achieve, which is that he needs to become a proper boy of 3 years of age, who goes to nursery and has friends'. Alef hits me, then he hits Chubby, then he hits me again. I say, 'It is not clear whom are you hitting? Mummy, Daddy, Alessandra or yourself?'

He looks at me and says: 'Now you are going to die'. 'I don't look dead, even if you want to kill me', I answer.

Alef then kills Chubby. Looking at her with hatred he says: 'Now Chubby is dead'. But then Chubby becomes alive again, and he says in a manic way, 'This is another Chubby, I have made another Chubby alive'. He then sucks Chubby's nose as if it was a nipple.

I reply: 'You have just killed Chubby and me, and in the room with you, there is now another Chubby and another Alessandra. When you were 9 months old your Mum got ill, and when she came back, you thought it was another mother. Just the same as with Chubby and me today'.

Alef takes a brick from the box and throws it at me as if it was Chubby throwing it from Chubby's nose.

I say: 'Now Chubby's nose is throwing bricks. Before, you were feeding from it. Chubby has two noses, a lovely one and a murderous one'. At this point, Alef takes a brick in his hand and throws it at me.

'So, there are also two Alefs, one who likes Alessandra and one who wants to kill her', I say. 'What did you say? Could you say it again?' he answers. I repeat and he listens. We then play with the bricks until the end of the session in a calm way.

Some further thoughts

Holding firmly in my mind to the dynamic of the self and its intrinsic property, I felt that what I had observed was confirming my initial hypothesis – namely, that Alef was defending against growing up by identifying with aspects of his prematurely lost mother. After this session, it became possible to postulate that Alef's identification with his mother's nipples is complex. While in the first session he seemed to be telling me about his identification with a milk-giving nipple (his bottom), in this second session, he is showing me that he seems to have identified with another nipple, one which is murderous. It is also possible to postulate that the pain of losing his mother when she got ill and disappeared for some time had made him feel that his mother's nipples were dangerous, as if the terrible pain of disappointment he was feeling was coming out of the nipple and killing him. This is maybe why he threw the brick at me from Chubby's nose first. It was as if it was a way of repeating the drama in his mind of his confusing relationship with his mother's nipples. In his confusion, Alef must have identified with the murderous nipple, as well as the milk-giving one, thus assuming that he too could have in himself both aspects of the nipple of his mother.

I began to feel clearer about the confusion in which this boy was living. In order for Alef to achieve sanity, the analytic process would have to involve a proper weaning. This seemed a very complex venture, as the first weaning he needed was not from his mother's breasts but from his way of dealing with their loss.

Alef needed to be weaned off his 'bottom-mummy-milk'. In the work with him I chose to interpret this, always departing from his state of identification with his mother: by naming what was confused, I was hoping to begin to differentiate and separate for him. His massive defence against the lost mother and her breasts had propelled Alef to merge and confuse himself with Mummy, and his relationship with Chubby was in some way a visible expression of this experience, one way of showing how confused he felt with his objects. What was needed was for his own hatred to be recognized rather than remain split off and enacted.

From February until Easter

After consultation with his parents, we decided that Daddy should put Alef on the potty every day and wait until Alef had done some pooh. Father undertook to do this, and two months into therapy, Alef produced a solid pooh in his potty. Meanwhile, he had stopped screaming when he saw me. I wondered whether his identification with his mother's milk might be lessening, now that his father was becoming more involved in his life, obliging him to use the pot. But for my part, I began to feel a terrible disgust for this child in the sessions. But at least I was totally aware of my hatred and disgust for him, and I noticed in two different sessions that as soon as I was in touch with these feelings, Alef would attack me with a pointed object: a pencil, a pen. I felt encouraged to trust my earlier assumption that he had created two nipples with which he became totally identified: one which feeds and one which kills. Indeed Alef was so bound up in this phantasy that he was totally convinced that he could kill and at the same time produce wonderful pooh-milk as well. Nevertheless, the more he began to pooh normally, the more he was finding himself reduced to a normal boy, far from being magical or omnipotent. But while the magic of the milk-pooh was decreasing, we had to deal in the sessions with a murderous Alef: the more he was separated from his omnipotent identification with the milk-giving nipple the more the killing and murderous Alef was coming to the fore.

It is around this time that Alef began to play with a yellow string he found in his box. Session after session he took the string in his hands. He made a great number of knots, asking me to undo them again and again. While I was busy undoing them, I began to say, 'The string is like the connection between Alessandra and Alef'. I observed Alef 'losing' himself in the string, feeling a powerful sense that he and the string were merged. Accordingly, I said that he seemed so entangled in the string, that I was wondering if he was now confused with the string, and he did not know anymore who was Alef and who was the string. I said that the connection between Alessandra and Alef must feel strange to him, as if the connection involves all of him, and he cannot imagine a string link between us in our minds. During this period, I felt in one session a terrible physical confusion between him and me. I was able to observe myself feeling confused, having a real sense of physical merging, not knowing anymore if I was me or I was him. This confusion lifted slowly, and although difficult to bear, at least this countertransference allowed me to feel more secure about my supposition about Alef's confused state. In order to avoid any sort of gap (threatening total separation), Alef had resorted to projecting himself totally into his mother (another) like a hermit crab. His intention was not so much to control or destroy as to merge with a total identification in order to survive. I thought that he was asking me to understand what he had done, using me as a container for his confusion, repeating with me the kind of relationship he had found inside himself with the lost mother of his infancy.

One day after having played again with the yellow string, he did a drawing of me. I was yellow, like the colour of the string, and in that moment, I felt again terribly confused with Alef, as if I was both a bit of him and a bit of myself. I said, 'Oh, Alessandra is so confused with the string. We need to unknot the string so that Alef can feel Alef, Alessandra can feel Alessandra and the string remains between us and connects us when we are not together'.

It was in this session though that I felt for the first time that the confusion was beginning to become more mental than bodily, and the string had come to represent the first 'concrete thought' that was possible for him, about a confusion that could not only be represented in this way but also, perhaps, be undone through this means. Two sessions before my Easter break, Alef made a movement in the session which made me think that he needed to pooh. This was new because, although on some occasions he had managed to pooh in the pot in the morning before going to school, as a rule, he usually dripped pooh in his pants during the day.

I called his mother for her to take him to the toilet. She was tired and asked me to do so instead. I did this, saying, 'This pooh is smelly. It is good that it is not in your pants but in the safe loo', and Alef agreed.

Back in the room, he drew my face in pink on a sheet first, and then red fire all around it. He then took the sheet and attacked me in the room screaming, 'Now you are all black!' I understood this game as a symbolic equation, a first movement towards representation and symbolization. The imagined fire makes my face black in reality. Alef then took all the pencils and made them pooh in my bin (sharpening them); later he took the glue and made it drop inside my bin. To my delight, I thought that a container was emerging. Perhaps the more he was able to empty his body of pooh, the more he was able to tolerate the sensation of the empty space left, in which the beginnings of a physical and mental container could emerge.

After that, and for the first time, he took a family of ducks from his box and chose to play only Mum and baby. Probably allowing myself to be carried away by my own suppositions, I said, 'I wonder if Alef treats the pooh in his belly as if he himself was a Mummy with a baby in it, and when Alessandra says that the pooh is disgusting, he agrees, but then he wants to kill Alessandra because he thinks that Alessandra has said that babies are pooh and are smelly'.

Alef looked at me in panic and ran out of the room. He did not want to listen to me. I managed to bring him back to the room. He sat far away from me sucking Chubby's nose, with a mad look, but then came closer, and together they hit me. Alef said, 'Chubby and I are hitting you because I don't want to listen to you'.

In this session, we see clearly that my interpretation was too much for him. There is no space inside for symbolization if physical and mental space is still undifferentiated and filled with pooh.

The week after, just before the last session before my Easter break, we played with pencils poohing in the bin, and suddenly out of the blue, he screamed, 'I am not a pooh'.

Elated by his discovery I said, 'No, and you are not a Mummy with a baby inside. You are only a boy with smelly pooh inside. And next week Alessandra is not going to see you because she will go away, but she will not kill you, and you will not kill her, and she will come back, and she will be the same Alessandra as today'.

It is interesting to follow how the development of the notion of a container unfolds in his mind: from a bin into a toilet. Alef's difficulty with the pooh is a representation of the problems that have arisen in his development consequent to his mother's illness. How can he grow? Where does the pooh go? Where does his mother go with her nipples? How can he let his baby self go? And what to do with hatred and anger?

From Easter until the summer break

After Easter Alef began to come to his sessions without Chubby. His mother reported that he had not done a pooh since we last met, three weeks before. For a few sessions, he ignored me, as if I was not there, and kept writing numbers on sheets of paper, busy with himself. I tried to interpret, but he remained totally unresponsive. In my absence, he did not want to think about it. He held everything inside. He projected himself inside his version of his mother so as not to feel any separation. An old pattern for him. Eventually, he said he wanted to pee; then he came back from the toilet and asked me for paper. He wanted to continue to write numbers. I said that I will give him only three sheets. I was bored with these sessions, I said, and I did not see why he should waste all these sheets. I saw a movement of rage on his face, provoked by my answer, but he quickly recomposed himself. After having filled the three sheets with numbers, Alef continued to write numbers in the air as if I was not there.

I said, 'Alef writes numbers because he is afraid that his anger with Alessandra will come out again. I just saw it on your face a few moments ago'. After I said this, he became rigid: from his body posture, I could see that he was now holding his pooh. I said so, and he began to scream. The same scream he used to produce at the beginning of our work together.

Around this time, he became very ill, but he was still attending his sessions, coming from home by taxi, in his pyjamas; he had an infection in his tummy. He was taking a laxative and pooh was dripping so that he needed to wear nappies again. Chubby was again with him.

It was the end of May, and I said that he was looking mad, but Alessandra knew that he was not mad, he was only confused and did not dare to undo his confusion.

He threw a cushion at me, saying, 'Now you are dead'. He then killed Chubby, stamping his foot on her violently, saying, 'Chubby, now you are dead'. He then took all the pencils in his hand and threw them all over the room. He began to joke, saying that the pencils looked like drops of pooh coming out of his bottom. Because he was laughing, I said, 'I am pleased that you have recovered now. What was the matter with you then?'

'I was angry', he answered.

'Yes, and when you are angry you are so afraid and cry and scream while Alessandra would be so happy if you could simply say, Alessandra, you make me feel angry today'. The session was over, and while he was leaving he said, 'We had such a fantastic session today!'

Yet the week after Alef arrived screaming again, but this time it was in excitement. He was free of pyjamas and a nappy. He asked his mother not to tell me anything, he wanted to be the one who told me, so only when we were alone in the room did he reveal his secret:

'I did a big pooh. It looked like a stone. It came out of my bum. It was disgusting'.

'Oh, was it old pooh blocking your system?' I replied. He nodded. 'A bit like your anger last week. It came out of your system when you wanted to kill me and then you killed Chubby'.

I saw from his facial expression that he now needed to pooh and asked him if this was the case. A bit reluctantly, he nodded and went to the loo. His mother followed and he announced that a 'soft pooh' had come out. I said,

'I am pleased you are learning to be in control of your pooh and poohing feelings. Last week you were angry, but you did not kill me'.

Alef and I could now begin to think about a boy who was confused by his mother's absence and hid his anger inside his tummy, in his pooh. Out of this primary confusion he became even more confused: if anger and pooh were the same, then baby, mummy, nipples, breast and bottom, milk and pooh, me and other were interchangeable. This defence against differentiation and separation permitted him some illusion of control; at the same time, it left Alef totally lost.

After this session, his parents wrote to me saying that now that Alef was well, they were not prepared to continue to pay for his therapy. I persuaded them to continue until the end of December. I managed to convince them about the importance of consolidating.

The last session before the summer holiday, Alef came with his father. I saw a little man coming, walking side by side with his big daddy. I explained to him that we would have 15 more weeks of sessions after the holidays, and we wrote them all down in his calendar. After that Alef announced:

Alef: 'It is now hitting time'. He took a big pillow and attacked me by saying, 'I am strong!'

Alessandra: 'Yes, you are getting stronger, and you hit Alessandra because we will soon have a long break, and after that, we will have only 15 more weeks of sessions'.

Alef: 'You are dead now; dead people do not talk'.
Alessandra: 'I am dead in pretend'. I was silent for a while; then I added: 'In reality I am alive, and when you are angry with me you do not kill me, you only hit me with the cushion'.

I remained silent and he sat down. There was a moment of great intimacy and I said,

'When you were a baby, your Mum became very ill, she went to hospital, and when she came back you did not recognize her. I want to see if after the summer holiday you will recognize Alessandra'.

To this Alef said: 'Yes, I will because I am not a baby anymore!' He then drew a massive pooh, a smaller one and a tiny one. Each on a different sheet.
I said: 'When you were a tiny baby you were doing tiny poohs, now you are doing medium-size poohs, but since you were a baby, a massive rage was building inside **you**. Your Mum had gone to hospital. You became afraid of your rage, and you hid the massive rage inside your pooh. Now the old rage pooh has come out, and you can do normal-size pooh and normal-size rage when Alessandra talks about holidays'. After this Alef began to talk about being naughty in nursery.

'Yes, today Alef can be a 3½-year-old boy and behave like a 3½-year-old'. And so we parted before the holidays.

The last 15 weeks

After the holidays, Alef reported that he was sleeping in his own bed. He looked amazing, like a proper boy, wearing new shoes. He announced that Chubby was very old, and he was not interested in playing with older people, although he still enjoyed playing with his grandparents. He then announced that he would come to see me until he was 60. I reminded him that we had only 14 weeks, which would be over before his 60th birthday. He changed his mind, saying that he would come until he was 16. I refused to negotiate. We came to a mutual agreement: he would be 4 by the time we finished.

The last 13 weeks were spent with him playing with the three ducks. He was now allowing the mummy, daddy and baby ducks to be together and working out how to be in a three with them.

For his penultimate session, he arrived laughing.

Alef: 'I am laughing today'.
Alessandra: 'I see. You are not crying as you used to do at the beginning of our work'.
Alef: 'We have only one more meeting, but I have a solution. I will come whenever I feel like it'.

Alessandra: 'But Alessandra will not be able to open the door'.
Alef: 'Why?'
Alessandra: 'Because we have only one more meeting'.
Alef: 'But why only one and not a hundred?'
Alessandra: 'Because everything ends. Many things have already ended for you. You are not a baby anymore; you are not poohing in your pants; you are not sleeping with Mummy. Next week, Alessandra will end. And it is in reality, not in my imagination'.
Alef: 'I will kill you with my tongue. All my germs will kill you'.
Alessandra: 'Yet again Alef is imagining that his pointed tongue will kill Alessandra the same way he felt that his Mum's nipple was killing him when she left him and he felt so much pain inside . . . he felt he was dying . . . and he felt he was so angry and confused . . . and he tried to hide his Mummy inside his tummy. . . . And nobody did understand him. But now Alessandra is not killing him; she is just finishing her work with him, and he is only very upset because Alessandra is saying things that he does not like to hear'. Alef opened his mouth and made as if to eat my consulting room, the chair, the couch, etc.
Alessandra: 'This is also not a solution. To eat my consulting room and have me in your tummy . . . this does not work. We know it never worked, not when you tried to have your Mummy inside you when she left you and you were still a baby'. He then takes my pen and drops it on the floor.
Alessandra: 'This is also not true. Alessandra is not dropping you or binning you. She is only ending our work together. We will meet again for your last session, and in three months when Alessandra will ring Mummy, Mummy and Alef will come back to see Alessandra for a review of our work together.' He continues to drop the pencils.
Alessandra: 'Alessandra can see how upset Alef is that things are not the way he wants them. It is infuriating, and it is not fair, but that's the way it is'. Weaning was happening.

Discussion

Alef did not have an established sense of self, a sense of identity to hold onto, to help him survive the apparent loss of his mother. He did not have internalized a capacity to process emotions and think about them. The self was overwhelmed, unable to deintegrate into and reintegrate such a traumatic experience. The unbearable pain of his sudden loss must have propelled him to resort to identifying with her as a defence against his own personal infantile trauma. Possibly the very good bond he had established with his mother during the first nine months of extra-uterine life protected him from resorting to even more primitive defences of an autistic character. He must have felt that in order to remain linked to her, at least internally, when she disappeared for a few days, he had to take her inside himself (as he was trying to do to me in one of our last sessions before the ending) and confuse himself with her. It is interesting to note what kind of mother he had in mind and what kind of identification with her he resorted to, especially as these identifications happened when he had not yet developed a mind, and they were and remained expressed in primarily bodily form. One aspect was idealized (milk-giving, diffused with omnipotence), another (a mother whose nipple imparts pain that he experienced as murderous) was unacceptable and had to be hidden. Moreover, these identifications were so absolute that he was to remain totally confused and trapped in them.

So while attempting to grow up there was a very limited space for the real ego of this boy to develop, and his capacity to individuate remained squeezed between the mother-in-him, confused with his un-unfolded self. Jung wrote about the dissociative effect of identification that works at 'splitting the individual into two mutually estranged personalities' (Jung 1913, para. 441).

This quote by Jung opens up the possibility of thinking of a self with an ego that has to master the relationships with his objects, not only externally but also internally. Where identification predominates there can be no internal representation of another. In Alef's case, the intelligent boy, full of potential, was growing up in parallel and dissociated from another part of him who was behaving in identification with the milk-giving mother and her hidden murderous shadow. These appear to have been independent but co-existing selves, not linked, unintegrated.

In Bion's language (Bion 1965, 1970), Alef was confronted with 'O', in his case an experience too overwhelming and terrifying to be integrated into his self. His psyche organized itself around loss, rage, maternal care and panic (Panksepp 1998) unconsciously. His self was adapting to internal and external events in the best possible way, although this meant a standstill for his own individuation process. I found myself at this point wondering whether the material I felt I had observed in Alef was just personal to him or whether it might also draw on some archetypal aspect of the collective unconscious. In exploring this possibility, two classical papers of the wider psychoanalytic literature were drawn to my attention: 'Mourning and Melancholia' in which Freud posits the (defensive) role of identification with the lost and reproached object, due to oral incorporation, in the genesis of melancholia (Freud 1914, p. 228), and Meltzer, who in 'The Relation of Anal Masturbation to Projective Identification' elaborates on the Kleinian model (Meltzer 1966, pp. 335–42), describing precisely what I have observed in my work with Alef. My experience in this context is similar to the internal experience of Jung who, after having recorded in *The Red Book* his own personal journey, later found parallels within the wider context of religious/alchemical symbolism. I found that other psychoanalysts before me had described what I had recorded in my work with Alef.

Independently of this theoretical background, my intention in embarking on the work required with my little patient was to help this boy to connect with his mind, strengthen his capacity to feel and think and make sense of what had happened to him. Our work together enabled him to form a representation in his mind of his history, of his mother and of himself, repairing his bizarre confusion with the traumatic loss he had never been able to fully understand. From a Jung-Fordham axis, the task was to help Alef's self to reconnect with its capacity to deintegrate and reintegrate.

In the next section of this chapter, I will concentrate on the theoretical approach I have used as a platform and will elaborate on the link between abandonment and defences of the self on one side and separation, mourning and individuation on the other side. I would like to give some thought to the archetypal predisposition of the self to organize itself around what we call individuation, as well as to recur to identification with the lost object as a defence against unbearable affects.

Theoretical implications

In his seminal paper on abandonment (Fordham 1985), Fordham made an important distinction between abandonment and separation. Fordham saw abandonment as an abrupt and traumatic loss that affects the person's perception of the world. The aftermath of abandonment is confusion of emotions such as sadness, despair, shame, guilt, aggression and intensive pain. If the mind is not able to cope with such a confusion of affects, the self will resort to a massive defence mechanism in order to cope with the distressing feelings. This can be thought of as an archetypal adaptation to internal and external events that cannot be tolerated by the psyche.

On the other hand, Fordham also recognized that the capacity to symbolize was related to 'the capacity to bear the absence of an object in periods during which the valued object is lost' (Fordham 1976, p. 21). Thus the process of weaning and mourning can become a powerful antidote against such consequences of abandonment. Over the course of mourning, not only can the powerful emotions be worked through but also a capacity to represent the lost object in the mind can take place, and this can function as a reparative act (Fordham 1976, p. 21). This capacity to represent the loss, and to recreate the lost object in a symbolic way, is effectively a watershed that divides the landscape of abandonment and trauma from the realm where mourning can unfold, and separation can be borne.

When the capacity to bear the loss is not in place, the self, overwhelmed by loss and caught up in its attempt to deny it, can resort to the defences I have described in this case material: identification with the lost object. While Fordham discussed autistic defences as the most powerful and primitive defences of the self, in this chapter I have focused on the idea of another such primitive defence of the self, what I called earlier 'primitive identification with the lost object, or aspects of it'. As Fordham observed, for Jung the ego could identify with internal as well as external objects. This state of affairs is 'usually considered dangerous, and liable to result in omnipotent states' (1995, p. 64).

Alef tried to identify with the lost mother in two ways: on the one hand, he confused her breast with his bottom; on the other, he confused her capacity to have inflicted pain on him with his murderous rage about having lost her. Anna Freud (1936) described a particular kind of identification called the identification with the aggressor, which could well be understood as a person's attempt at controlling and finding mastery over a traumatic or threatening situation. In order to master and control his loss and the pain related to it, Alef reacted by identifying not only with the good lost object (the milk-giving mother) but also with the aggressor (the abandoning and pain inflicting mother), thus finding a provisional solution to cope with mental pain. He equated good and bad aspects of himself with good and bad aspects of his mother in a confused way, unable to differentiate and separate. But as these defence mechanisms became paramount, they became pathological and were crippling his development. Alef needed to be helped to dis-identify from the lost object and to create firm boundaries between himself and other whole objects. Only in this way could the trajectory of his normal development be restored and the process of individuation be allowed to take its course. Mourning becomes an essential part of individuation, as the capacity of the self to deintegrate and reintegrate is tightly linked with the capacity to open up, live through, separate and integrate experience in a symbolic way. Every new deintegration is, in Bion's (1965, 1970) terms, an encounter with 'O'. Defending against O has a crippling effect on the self which, as I have shown in this chapter, cannot then come into contact and explore unknown aspects of itself that are triggered by the event. The process of deintegration and reintegration is necessarily a painful process.

Conclusion

I hope to have demonstrated the link between identification used as a defence mechanism and unmetabolized pain and loss. To have shown how, in the absence of a capacity to bear pain and mourn loss, the self can defensively try to identify with good and bad aspects of the lost object, using identifications, as Jung understood them, as a shortcut to avoid finding authentic solutions in the self for the presenting problem. Such a state of affairs is a significant hindrance to ongoing individuation but is also rooted in the way we humans unconsciously defend against unbearable events.

I hope to have shown how deep-rooted identification can be, and how it is necessary to help patients to dis-identify from the lost object and to create a boundary between their self and the self of the lost object, working with all the affects that arise in the gap between 'me and other'.

I hope to have been able to show that the analyst needs to guide the patient in this work through all the confusion, pain, shame, guilt and murderous feelings. Only through developing the capacity to represent loss for oneself, and to recreate that which is lost in a symbolic way, can the threat of madness be left behind.

Notes

1 First published in *Journal of Analytical Psychology*, 62, 2, April 2017.
2 Aleph is the line that differentiates human territory from the divine. This line can exist only in the space of symbols. I have called this boy Alef because where separation and mourning have not taken place, symbolization cannot exist.

References

Astor, J. (1995). *Michael Fordham: Innovation in Analytical Psychology*. London and New York: Routledge.
Bion, W.R. (1965). *Transformation*. London: Heineman.
———. (1970). *Attention and Interpretation*. London: Tavistock.
Bott Spillius, E., Milton, J., Garvey, P., Couve, C., & Steiner, D. (2000). *The New Dictionary of Kleinian Thought*. London and New York: Routledge.
Cavalli, A. (2011). 'On receiving what has gone astray, on finding what has gone lost'. *Journal of Analytical Psychology*, 56, 1–13.
Fordham, M. (1976). *The Self and Autism*. London: Heineman.
———. (1985). 'Abandonment in infancy'. In *A Review of Jungian Analysis*, ed. M. Stein. Asheville: Chiron Publications.
———. (1995). *Freud, Jung, Klein, the Fenceless Field*. Ed. R. Hobdell. London and New York: Routledge.
Freud, A. (1936). *The Ego and the Mechanisms of Defence*. London: Hogarth Press.
Freud, S. (1914). 'Mourning and melancholia'. *SE*, 14.
———. (1921). 'Group psychology and the analysis of the ego'. *SE* 18.
Gordon, R. (1978). *Dying and Creating: A Search for Meaning*. (The Library of Analytical Psychology, Vol. 4). London: Karnac.
Jung, C.G. (1913). 'A contribution to the study of psychological types'. *CW* 6.
Meltzer, D. (1966). 'The relation of anal masturbation to projective identification'. *International Journal of Psycho-Analysis*, 47, 335–42.
Meltzer, D., & Harris, M. (2011). *Adolescence: Talks and Papers by Donald Meltzer and Martha Harris*. London: Karnac.
Panksepp, J. (1998). *Affective Neuroscience. The Foundation of Human and Animal Emotions*. Oxford: Oxford University Press.

Chapter 10

Noah's Ark

Technical and theoretical implications concerning the use of metaphor in the treatment of trauma[1]

Introduction

The problem in working with people who have experienced trauma is how to help them mourn what is lost – namely, life before the trauma – and accommodate and integrate the trauma in such a way that living in the future after the trauma can become thinkable, as opposed to living in a trauma which seems endless (Garland 2002). This posits two technical problems. The first refers to the construction of what really happened to the person during the traumatic event since what the person seems to remember is not always true or accurate and might be distorted (Cavalli 2014a). Sometimes the truth is unbearable, and its distortion seems to be the sole means of survival. At other times, defences against pain are put in place and the aftermath of trauma operates unconsciously and does not seem to be accessible at a conscious level. This state of affairs depends not only on the trauma itself but also on the developmental level of psychic organization that pertained when the trauma occurred, and this is the second issue I will explore in this chapter.

Some clinicians attribute the incapacity to come to terms with the lost past and mourn it to cumulative trauma (Khan 1963), implying the concept of the 'après coup' (Freud & Breuer 1895): an internal landscape in which each trauma echoes into the next one in a sort of endless set. Looking at this from a different angle, I propose that the difficulty in dealing with the [original] traumatic event might be dependent on how the psyche of the person was developmentally organized when the first traumatic event occurred, and not so much on subsequent traumas.

To clarify my thinking on these matters, I will draw on clinical material from my work with a little boy who lost his hearing when he was between 9 and 12 months old. He did not have a conscious recollection of the event but was able to construct the event and its aftermath in the consulting room with me. His still developmentally precarious internal psychic organization at the time of the trauma helped me put forward some thoughts about how trauma operates in the internal world of a person and how it is possible to work with it. Theoretical implications of these issues will also be discussed.

DOI: 10.4324/9781003268536-11

Circumscribing the traumatic event

When working with trauma, the presence of an object (the analyst) who will bear what is felt to be unbearable, not only in the present but also in the past is paramount: what is needed is an object who will go with the patient in exploration of the truth (Cavalli 2012). While the patient constructs his past in the 'here and now', it is the task of the analyst to analyze this construct. Transference and countertransference are of great help in this endeavour: they enable the analyst to feel what the patient is going through and understand how the psyche of the patient is developmentally organized. If the patient is able to integrate the trauma within his psyche, he will be equipped with an experience which strengthens his ego. Then reparation of the past, as well as of the self can take place.

It is therefore important for the analyst-patient couple to create a boundary around the traumatic event. This boundary offers a temporal and a spatial limit to an event in the life of the patient, a boundary between 'before and after' the event. This allows the patient to begin to think that it is possible to see life as a continuum, before, during and after the trauma (Garland 2002), and to integrate the trauma in space and time into their life.

Once the boundary has been created, patient and analyst can venture towards getting to know what happened in the external and internal reality of the patient by circumnavigating the crater left by the trauma. This will foster the process of rebuilding and integration. The boundary functions as a container for the split-off part of the psyche devastated by trauma. It is only when the trauma can become representable to the psyche that it can become integrated. The use of metaphors will help the psyche to reunite the realm of the senses and realm of the mind. Once the patient is able to represent for himself the trauma internally and externally, it will be possible to begin to make a connection between life before and life after the trauma.

Developmental organization of the psyche at the time of the trauma and reactivation of primitive mental structures

In my view, a well-organized psyche is a psyche able to perform two functions: one is the function that enables mind and body to work together so that somatic events can be translated into feelings and thoughts. This is the process described by Bion (1962a) as alpha function; the other is the capacity of the psyche to organize and bring together opposing aspects of reality that belong to the same experience of self or other. This is the process that Jung named the transcendent function (Jung 1916), and it is also the same process that makes possible the achievement of the depressive position (Klein 1935). No matter how developed the internal organization, this can be severely shaken by trauma. Even if real ego strength has been built up, in times of crisis, the strongest person loses some of his acquired internal strength and primitive mental ways of functioning might be reactivated. When the person affected by trauma is unable to bear the impact of loss and the internal experience of mourning cannot take place, proto-affects cannot be processed into emotions and thoughts and remain in the form of beta elements (Bion 1962a). The activation and growth of alpha elements are paralyzed, and the mind tries to control what it felt was beyond containment by using the limited means available. When mental functions are inadequate, the only means of dealing with overwhelming affects is through the body – a body that effectively has no mind to process and contain it, and which eventually leaves the body to deal with the affect on its own (Ferrari 1992). Opposite experiences belonging to the self or to the object cannot be brought together, and the person is unable to hold together experiences that seem irreconcilable although belonging to the same reality.

Bion's assumption that 'if the capacity for toleration of frustration is sufficient the "no- breast" inside becomes a thought, and an apparatus for thinking it develops' (Bion 1962b, p. 307) implies that absence is a basic condition in order to organize thinking and develop a sense of mourning. The capacity to integrate experiences into mind (Fordham 1985, p. 61) consists then in the complex capacity to translate bodily event into thoughts and, in the archetypal law of the mind, to bring and bind together opposites belonging to the same experience (Jung 1916; Klein 1935). [In this regard, Fordham links Klein's view that symbolization lies at the root of the infant's mental life, with the Jungian view of archetypal forms being present at birth which regulate the infant's behaviour and have the potential for mental representation (Fordham 1985, p. 61). However, Fordham also makes clear that this process requires a mother who holds her baby in mind: 'in a state of maternal reverie, she relates directly to her baby's protomental life and helps in the transformation of beta into alpha elements' (ibid., p. 57)]. When experiences are integrated in this way, they are representable for mind by definition (ibid.).[2]

In this chapter, I am interested in thinking about trauma that affects a psyche that has not yet developmentally reached the level of integration that Klein and Fordham link with the achievement of the depressive position. When this complex mental organization has been achieved, the person affected by trauma might in time recover his/her ability to translate bodily events into thoughts and to bring opposite aspects of experience together, although it might take some time before a sudden discontinuity in experience can be borne in mind. But what happens when these mental functions have never been activated in the mind?

It is the task of analysis to address this state of affairs, to assess what kind of solutions are put in place by the patient to cope with the traumatic event and to understand how the mind of the patient was organized developmentally at the time in which the trauma occurred. When the mind is so underdeveloped that not only can opposite experiences not be brought together but also proto-affects cannot gain shape and are not related to objects, then body operates 'on its own' to protect mind from flooding, and to secure the survival of the self. The use of one's own body in such an emergency situation would constitute a narcissistic solution

(Freud 1914). However, it is important to see such bodily activity as not only a regressive narcissistic defence against growth but also a confused manifestation of bodily turmoil and mental growth at the same time. It is a representation of how an incomprehensible experience has been shaped so far. It is the task of analysis to help the patient transform this body-mind conglomerate into differentiated digestible and representable experiences and bring together opposite aspects of reality experienced during and after the trauma.

Integrating and transcending the opposites

Bodily experiences are a meaningful starting point for mental activity. The increasing capacity of the mind to translate from bodily events to proto-thoughts improves the sense of continuity between the turmoil of the body and the capacity to make sense of what happens inside and outside the body. While this is happening, mind has at the same time to accommodate bad and good experiences, and this is not an easy task.

It was Klein (1932, p. 215) who put forward the hypothesis that binary splitting of experiences into good and bad is developmentally necessary. Idealization and omnipotence are operating at this early stage of life: bad experiences are omnipotently denied, while good experiences are idealized as a protection against fear and retaliation (Cavalli 2011). This binary way of perceiving reality is essential for healthy development as it enables the infant to take in and hold on to sufficient good experiences to allow the central core of the self, the ego (Fordham 1985, p. 60),[3] to begin to integrate the contrasting aspects of the infant's experiences, both of others and his or her own self. Klein's concept of the depressive position refers to the capacity of the mind to bring the opposites together, uniting bad and good experiences in relation to self and object. Slowly, in normal development, the more the infant has been able to integrate good experiences and to hold onto them, the more he/she will be able to integrate bad experiences into the self, coming slowly to terms with reality (Fordham 1985; Cavalli 2014b). When enough good and bad experiences are integrated, self and others can be perceived in a more realistic way as containing both good and bad aspects. This results in the strengthening of the self and the development of the ego. Through the use of language and play, the child becomes able to unify his experiences and represent world and soul via symbolic forms.

As idealization and omnipotence are steadily given up, the caregiver's independence begins to be acknowledged and accepted as mind continues to grow and develop using the body as a constant informative support. This process of integration is very painful, as the infant needs not only to bear powerful affects but also to relate to the caregiver as a person who can be loved and hated but cannot be possessed (Carvalho 2009).

For trauma to be overcome, not only does the capacity of mind and body to work together have to be in place so that bodily events can be transformed into mind but also the capacity to integrate into the self opposite aspects of an experience, which may initially feel irreconcilable. Analysis becomes the place in which life before and after the trauma can become a continuous sequence. The sequence of trauma is a particularly complex one, in which many elements are contained: identifying what was traumatic, translating bodily events into mental thoughts, mourning and bearing loss and bringing together intrinsically contrasting aspects of objects and reality.

When trauma occurs in a mind which developmentally has not yet been able to achieve such complex functioning, the work of recovery becomes more complicated, as a young mind has to deal not only with the trauma as such but also with how the trauma may have impacted on the organizational development of the mind when the trauma occurred and how the mind might therefore have remained fixated at its developmental level of functioning before the trauma occurred. Development will then be impaired because of the impinging trauma and the incapacity of the mind to integrate it into the self, leaving the self unable to continue its journey of individuation. I will now proceed with the case material to show how this can be addressed in the consulting room.

Paperino: brief history and background

Paperino was 3 when I began to see him on a once-a-week basis. His parents came to see me because Paperino was very difficult to manage. He was extremely controlling of his mother to a degree that bordered on obsessive-compulsive disorder behaviours and absolutely intolerant of any changes, welcoming his mother with terrible tantrums and majestic dismissals when she picked him up from the childminder at the end of the day. Father was kept by him in the background, as if he was an extra. When Paperino was 9–11 months old, he mysteriously lost his hearing. Nobody then understood his private tragedy. Mother was beginning to wean him then and was confronted with a restless baby who would bite her breasts, scream and was impossible to manage. This coincided with mother going back to work. Paperino's behaviour became more and more incomprehensible, something that only with hindsight could be described as utter despair; he was reacting to things with terrible tantrums, accompanied by banging his head on the floor, screaming and restlessness mania. Only when Paperino was 2 years old was the diagnosis of hearing loss made, and Paperino provided with hearing aids.

In the following year, Paperino learnt three languages, as mother and father speak two different languages, and at the childminder, he learnt to speak English. His desire to be understood was guiding him forward. Not having had a language to communicate what was happening to him had been traumatic in itself. Language must have felt to this boy a potency-giving tool. Paperino had 'lost' himself to himself during the turbulent year in which he had moved from hearing to not hearing at all while he was also losing his mother, who was going back to work fulltime. He was exposed to an absent version of his mother at a time when something terrible and inexplicable was happening to him. We might postulate that his clinginess towards his mother was an attempt to defend against unbearable psychic material (being at the mercy of the 'terrifying' version of his absent mother and unable to understand her) and against unbearable unorganized mental affect (the incapacity for his mind to make sense of what was happening to him).

Assessment: body versus mind

I decided to see child and mother together during my extended assessment. I wanted to observe how Paperino related to his mother and found it helpful for his mother to tell me their story in his presence. It took a few months for Paperino to relax; he was hyperactive, jumping up and down on the couch, at times putting himself in danger, not relating to me or to his mother. I began to think of this behaviour as the only way Paperino could let me know about a terrible experience, which had no name, but had already happened and could be expressed only in a somatic way. The behaviour Paperino was displaying in the consulting room was described as the norm by his mother. I took great care in talking to him about what he was doing, trying to relate it to something terrible that had happened to him that he did not want to think about, now with us. I said many times that he seemed terrified and did not trust that the three of us could help him understand what had happened to him. Finally, one day, he decided to sit on the floor close to me while his mother was answering my questions and revisiting the story of their trauma and its aftermath that was still present for both of them.

Paperino told me about a cartoon he loved called 'Noah's Ark'. It was the story of two ducks who had been accommodated in Noah's Ark with a number of other animals. The ark, flung at the mercy of the waves, did not offer a solid ground to the two ducks who, sliding away from each other, were lost to each other during the dramatic deluge. It was only when the flood had stopped, and the boat had regained stability that they could re-find each other. At this point, Paperino took a sheet of paper and drew the blue sea, the orange ark and the ramp, firmly placed on the ground to allow the animals to come back to land. Some aspects of his trauma were beginning to be thinkable. After having completed his drawing, Paperino lay on the couch and fell asleep. Something massive was beginning to become integrated. The metaphor of Noah's Ark was now replacing the somatic activity Paperino had been displaying so far. Some mental content could be borne in mind and integrated.

Discussion

We can postulate that Paperino is now able to translate his bodily activities into a first mental thought about his trauma. He offers us a first metaphorical representation of his personal tragedy: the loss of his mother who was weaning him by going back to work coincided with the loss of his hearing. Once he could hear again, he was able to re-find a good version of his mother, the mother that protected him before the trauma. We can assume that his clinginess means asking for protection from the dread of the return of the trauma. His attachment to this mother is 'narcissistic', as it is not directed to an object but to an omnipotent desire to control his mind from having to bear unmanageable pain. It seems that the past sessions have helped him to integrate and organize some of the mental content he was trying to cope with by using bodily activity. From being hyperactive, Paperino is now sitting down, drawing and talking to us. For now, this is all he can process.

Although we still do not know what happened to him when he was lost to his mother and to himself on Noah's Ark, we can postulate that it is contained and represented by his bodily activity. It is my job to go on exploring the missing events that have accompanied him during that time. Extended assessment: separation from mother, mind vs. body and body vs. mind. In the next session, Paperino draws for us another ark, but here the landscape is different. He draws a figure in the water who is desperately trying to get on board. Green crocodiles are attacking and biting this human, preventing him or her from getting inside the ark. As soon as I begin to investigate this figure and the crocodiles, Paperino gets rid of the drawing – he destroys it, putting the pieces of paper in the bin. In my mind, I saw this drawing as a representation of the missing bit of the puzzle, something too unmanageable for him, something disorganizing and catastrophically dreadful that could not be thought about.

I say: 'There are two arks, one in which mum and little duck lose each other and re-find each other, another one, much more complex, in which someone cannot get in and is destroyed'. While I say this, he takes two ducks from his box, puts one under the chair saying in a mischievous way: 'Hans, Gretel and Mummy. Duck pushes mummy into the oven', and he laughs. His mother is shocked, but he repeats the game a few times. I wondered to myself if the mother of Hansel and Gretel he pushes into the oven is the representation of removed psychic experiences of his relationship with his lost mother and of unorganized mental content that his mind can't think about and tries to get rid of by clinging onto his re-found mother in an omnipotent way, as if that unthinkable experience could easily be destroyed.

After this session, I felt that I had enough material to begin my individual work with him. I created a calendar for him with all the dates of our work together in the three months to come, pointing out to him the 12 weeks that his mother was going to wait for him in a separate room, while I would continue to work with him as we had done during the previous weeks. When, after a very careful preparation, the agreed date came and Paperino found himself alone in the room with me, I witnessed how frightening the unorganized mental and psychic content were to him, and how his mind refused to cope. Paperino began to bang his head on the floor, showing psychotic behaviours. He started to display some autistic stereotypic movements, screaming every time there was an impinging noise. He was terrified by the flowers in my consulting room, saying they were talking. The uncanny atmosphere that was emerging pushed me to ask his mother to re-enter the consulting room so that they could be reunited. This separation from his mother could be understood as an après coup, in which he was reliving his trauma with me in the consulting room. The current loss of his mother (from the consulting room) had put us in touch with the 'bad human' of his drawing that he had been exposed to once he had lost the 'good humans and his hearing'. Although he had told me that he did not want to have to face those contents and wanted to destroy them in the oven, I knew that was where we had to go. For now, though, I felt that he was not ready to investigate the other side of the traumatic event. I said that Mummy would continue to be in the room with us for some time. He drew a web of lines.

A: 'What is this? It looks like a web of lines.'
P: 'Yes, it is you. All around you a spider web!'
A: 'Ah, now Alessandra has been immobilized, paralyzed. She cannot say and do things that upset Paperino!'

After this, Paperino fell asleep on the couch, as if something had been understood and he could begin to reintegrate an awful experience.

Discussion

The unintegrated experience of being separated from his mother is so directly linked to his hearing loss that, for now, it seems impossible to separate these two experiences. 'No-mummy' seems to mean to him to become lost in a world that makes no sense and is so frightening, not only because it cannot be understood but because it is uncanny, dangerous and misleading, without any point of reference. Reliving this experience with me in the consulting room has helped us to understand the nature of his defences (omnipotence and control as means of survival). The unorganized mental contents that his mind cannot process are so powerful that mind deserts him, leaving the body to deal with them on its own. This gives us an insight into how terrifying his experience must have been. I can now begin to put forward in my mind a hypothesis about Paperino's dislike of his father. His father seems to represent more than anything else a threat to his omnipotent control over his mother. For now, he cannot relate to him as an object; his father's presence and his unmetabolized affect are too entangled.

The unthinkable experience has entered the consulting room with an après coup of his original trauma that catches us by surprise. Nevertheless, a slow process of integration and differentiation can hopefully now begin. Preparing to face the unknown that has already happened. For the next five months, the three of us keep working together. During these sessions, Paperino's mother began to use the time to answer her emails and work on her laptop, while Paperino spent his time playing with me. During one of these sessions, he inadvertently broke two identical cars he had in his box. They could not be mended. He spent a whole session trying to mend them. 'They are like your ears', I said. 'When you were born, they were very good ears, they were functioning well, but now they are broken and cannot be mended. Thank God the hearing aids have come to the rescue!' He looked at me with a very sad expression as if he was beginning to understand that his ears are not the cause of the catastrophe but that the catastrophe happened when his ears stopped functioning. By reconnecting with his ears, Paperino is also beginning to reconnect with his bodily self, a self with a mind that can begin to think, differentiate, process and represent. With broken ears.

The journey underneath the ark: part 1

A few weeks later, something happened while we were playing: suddenly I did not know where I was. I felt confusion and panic. Paperino talked, but I did not understand. It felt to me that he was undergoing the same experience. We were together but lost to each other. I said, 'It feels like I have lost you, I do not understand you anymore. Where are we?'

He looked at me as if he did not understand me. He then drew a half-moon. He said that inside the half-moon there was a monster, ghosts. As soon as he said this, he was in panic and ran out of the room. I stayed inside and said, 'I am putting this half-moon drawing inside your folder. Alessandra is not afraid of the monster and the ghosts that are inside the half-moon. In your folder they are safe'. As soon as I said this, he came back. He took a sheet of paper, asked for the Sellotape and sellotaped the sheet of paper over the drawing as if it was an envelope, saying. 'This is a shield!!! A shield against the ghosts!' Paperino was so pleased with his creation, and he wanted to take it home.

I reminded him of our agreement, but he insisted. I felt that what he had discovered in this session was so important that he needed the concrete proof as a reminder that he had been able to survive his fears. So, after a long discussion and reasoning, I allowed him to take the shield home. It felt to me that in that session some old defences, not useful to him anymore, had been dropped. He was telling me that he did not need his clinginess to his mother anymore but was able to discover inside himself some sort of potency in order to begin to face what was in the half-moon, now protected by the shield. Paperino with his shield was preparing for us both to go and face the monsters inside the half-moon. For now, he has told me that he is not removing them from his mind any longer. They are here, in his folder, in his and in my mind, and he is preparing to show me what they are. In a few weeks, his mother will leave the room. If he stops gripping onto his mother, he might discover some real potency inside himself that helps him face the monster and the ghosts. Maybe he now 'knows' that my mind and my thinking offer a sort of shield to the un-mentalize-able affect he did experience. My presence makes them less terrifying. His capacity to symbolize is growing. The next bit of work can now take place.

The journey underneath the ark: part 2

This time Paperino comes in easily. He opens the door which communicates with the waiting area and looks at his mother who, separated from us for the second time since we started working together, waves at him. He shuts the door and stays there for 10 minutes as if pondering about what to do. Suddenly he begins to act. He pushes my chair against the door so that no one can come in. He then goes to his box and takes out all the wild animals and one human from the family of humans. He puts all the animals in a circle, the human in the middle. Suddenly the wild animals attack the human and eat him up brutally. It is shocking to watch. We are exhausted on the floor looking at each other in deep silence. He then goes on the couch; today he needs to rest.

A: 'Ah, I say, this is the monster and the ghosts in the half-moon. I understand, it is scary!!!'

I ask him if he wants a rug, and I cover him with a rug. We stay in silence until the end of the session.

Discussion

Paperino can finally face the dreadful catastrophic affect that his body was omnipotently trying to remove from his mind. Mind was unable to process these affects and was asking body to obliterate them. Paperino is now able to begin to bear them, giving them a form. They can be understood as the psychic contents he wanted to protect his object from, sadistic attacks, the desire to destroy them for all the pain he felt they were provoking in him but also the fear that these same sadistic attacks were the origin of all his suffering. This is why he blocked the door so that his mother could not see him become affected by them. He needed a shield, a sort of assurance that he would not die, and that we would survive and give meaning to his past experience.

Now that he has been able to show me what felt terrifying, Paperino can rest and integrate an experience that can become thinkable. The metaphor of the wild animals savaging the human brings together in a very powerful way his experience on the ark: he felt lost to his objects and to his own self, torn to pieces by wild, frightening affect that felt like it was disintegrating him and all his world.

The journey underneath the ark: part 3

For the next six months, Paperino takes me at each session to a place of danger that we need to face. With a caravan which I drive, we arrive at the seaside. He needs to dive in. I help him wear an imaginary shield with which he dives into the water to face horrific animals.

At each session, he kills one of them and comes back to the caravan exhausted and frightened. I help him coming on board, offer him some tea, then cover him with a rug following his instruction. He shivers. These sessions are very moving, as we are not in pretend. He is recovering in reality something that had happened to him in reality but could not be spoken about. Often, after he has recovered from the diving, he draws for me a picture of the monsters he had to face under the water. For Paperino, drawing is very important, as if he needs to show me something real in a symbolic way. One day, after one of these journeys, he draws a robot.

A: 'Paperino is not a robot; he is a proper boy.'
P: 'With a mechanical device.'
A: 'Yes, but the mechanical device does not make him a robot; it only helps him to hear properly.'

This long period of 'diving' in his sessions ends with our second summer holiday. After the holidays, Paperino tells me about his holiday and then wants to draw.

First, he draws a heart, which then becomes a balloon. He then draws a chair, and the balloon-heart is tightened up to the chair. Then he draws a house around a chair, so there is a house and inside the house, a chair and a balloon.

A: Alessandra and Paperino have been away for four weeks, but an invisible rope has tightened them up during the break. Paperino was away, far from my house, but our rope-link made him feel safe. Now we can meet again, in my house, sitting in my chair, because we both knew that we were meeting today.

While I speak, he begins to draw a boy: face, eyes, body, bottom and a willy, a huge willy. I comment on this, and he laughs.

A: 'This boy has a huge willy. As big as his daddy, I suppose!!!'
P: 'Yes, my daddy has a big willy!'
A: 'One day when Paperino will be as big as his daddy, he will also have a big willy!'

Now that he has a 'shield', a sort of clear understanding that his ears are broken, but not his willy (which I understand as his self and his potency), we can work on a link between us, an invisible rope that not even a long break can destroy. This rope represents an understanding that absence can exist now in the mind and thinking can replace the catastrophic attacks of the wild animals which in the course of the last six months have been faced and explored.

After that session, his mother wrote to me telling me that during the night, he had a nightmare and had screamed. She went to him, and he said, 'Mammy, I had lost you; it was terrible!' The next morning he said he could hear; he did not need to put his hearing aids on. Mother cried a lot, and his parents verified that he indeed still needed his hearing aids.

Discussion

Now that Paperino can dream about having lost his mother and about having refound her in real life, he is confused, as the loss of the hearing coincided with the loss of the mother he loved. Through the work we were doing, Paperino brought to life his confusion about loss. Now the work of differentiation can start. His beloved mother has been re-found, but his hearing is lost forever. In this context, it is interesting to see how possible it is for him now to relate to his father in a different way. Father becomes a model, a potent man he wants to emulate. The capacity of his mind to bear loss, and to think, allows him to know that an absent mother is not lost, she can be re-found, and an absent mother is not necessarily abandoning him to his own destiny. He is experiencing some internal resources to cope and look after himself. He is now able to see mother and father as two separate beings, who can love and help him. He also begins to let go of his omnipotence and control, coming to terms with reality.

Differentiation and reparation

After this session, Paperino wants to fight with me. Now I am the monster he needs to face. By showing me his teeth, or his eyes full of fire, he is expecting some catastrophic reactions. Tentatively, Paperino confronts my teeth and my eyes, as if by projection they are as wild and as dangerous as he imagines his are, but slowly in the course of a few sessions, the fights become normalized. He is a normal boy, fighting with me, a normal person.

In this period, he plays again with the wild animals. The game is quite ordinary, there is nothing of the tension he expressed when he played with them for the first time. It is now all in pretend. His fear of having caused damage to himself and to his objects has now been addressed. He is not the cause of his hearing loss and of the loss of his mother. Those things happened first. His affect was secondary, as a direct consequence of those events. Paperino is sorting things out in his mind. I notice that his bodily posture has changed enormously. There is nothing rigid about him now, he is relaxed and soft, and sometimes during the session, he asks for help in a sort of ordinary way: instead of giving me instruction, we are now together. Two humans meeting and separating at each session.

Paperino is now 5½. He invents for us a new, very meaningful game. We both live on a floating 'rescue centre', a sort of boat from which we can save people who are drowning. At every radio call, by helicopter or by boat, we navigate around the ocean saving people. Paperino loves this game. I am his companion, and in each situation, we discuss what to do, how to perform. When we play, I feel that he is defence-less, as if he has gained a deep trust in me, a human being who has accompanied him on this terrifying journey. Paperino is not afraid anymore of the drowning human of his second picture. That human was confused with the terrifying monstrous affect that his mind has been able to contain, assess and digest. As much as he has been able to rescue his feelings, he is now willing to rescue imaginary people, maybe the refugees he saw on television.

In one of these sessions, he draws for us the 'rescue centre'. He draws two identical rescue rings, and by looking at his drawing, I comment 'Like the hearing aids'.

I begin to feel that our work is coming to an end. His parents agree, and we decide to give it nine months for his therapy to come to a close. Ending: the new Noah's Ark with wild animals in it (integration) After having integrated his trauma inside his mind, Paperino makes an alliance of peace with his self. He re-finds slowly the contact with his body: his eyes, his teeth, his broken ears, his heart, his mind. There he finds not only containment but a sense of potency. He also finds his vulnerability, his deafness. Now it is in the relationship with others that he needs to mediate what he has discovered about himself. With me, he has discovered trust in an object that does not know but is prepared to go on exploring. He has discovered that absence is at times more important than presence. Paperino and I prepare slowly to say bye-bye to each other. He is now a potent boy, with many friends, and a normalized relationship with his parents.

In this last period, Paperino talks to me in his sessions about events from his life, school, home, his grandparents, books he can now read, and he continues to draw. His last drawing is a big ark, stable and solid. One can see that wild animals, by now domesticated, are included. This ark is a metaphor for our work, a tribute to his courage, an expression of the sequence of his life whose meaning was missing at the beginning of our work, the link between his life before and after his trauma.

At the end of our last session, he went out of the consulting room to sit on his mother's lap for some time. I looked at them embracing each other. It was an emotional ending for all of us. Our personal and individual feelings can be accommodated inside our minds. We might imagine what this end represents for each of us.

Final remarks and conclusion

In this chapter, using clinical material, I have tried to elucidate my thoughts revolving around trauma and its vicissitudes. I have proposed to follow two different but directly linked operational lines in my work with people affected by trauma. I have shown the importance of creating a boundary around the traumatic event which needs to be identified so that a portion of life can be contained, examined and hopefully integrated. I have also explored the importance of assessing the capacity of the person to translate affect into mind and of transcending different aspects of reality. I have related this capacity to levels of developmental organization and have tried to show that when trauma affects a mind which has never been able to access this complex level of organization before the trauma, the work of integration has to contain not only the work on the trauma but also the development of the capacity of the mind to translate affects and bring the opposites together for the first time. I have shown how metaphors can be of great help in this work, and how they help the psyche bring together opposite experiences.

Using clinical material, I have given the cumulative trauma theory a different reading: trauma is what the mind cannot bear: this does not depend on the event itself but on the developmental organization of the mind when the first trauma occurred. I have shown how après coup functions in this context. I have shown the importance of using metaphors when working with trauma, as they unify aspects that seem irreconcilable. They foster the transcendent function. I have also based my work on transference and countertransference as important guiding elements. I have put a particular emphasis on the capacity of the analyst to be an exploratory object in the work of construction, someone who goes on exploring beyond what she is told. I have shown how the desire to gain potency and understanding can break real terror and fear of disintegration. I have shown that when the mind is capable of differentiation and integration, and mind and body are working together, a real capacity for love and for life in the real world can emerge.

Notes

1 First published in *Journal of Analytical Psychology*, 65, 5, November 2020.
  This chapter was not finalized at the time of Alessandra Cavalli's death on May 17, 2020. It had been accepted for publication in the *Journal for Analytical Psychology* following the Journal's peer-review process but still required some editing and revision. Nora Swan-Foster and Warren Colman have edited the chapter posthumously while maintaining Alessandra's own idiom and avoiding substantive changes or additions.
2 The original text gave only the page references for these two quotes from Fordham, which have been chosen as the most apposite to the context (in square brackets). The idea that integrated experiences are representable for mind by definition seems to mean that the capacity for representation is definitive of mind (Eds.).
3 The original text referenced page 61, but the nearest reference occurs on page 60 where Fordham refers to the process whereby 'the self grows an ego'.

References

Bion, W.R. (1962a). *Learning from Experience*. London: Heinemann.
———. (1962b). 'The psycho-analytic study of thinking'. *International Journal of Psychoanalysis*, 43, 306–10.
Carvalho, R. (2009). 'Doing the splits between the Tavistock and the Society of Analytical Psychology'. (Unpublished paper presented on 2 February 2009 at the Society of Analytical Psychology).
Cavalli, A. (2011). 'On receiving what has gone astray, on finding what has gone lost'. *Journal of Analytical Psychology*, 56, 1, 1–13.
———. (2012). 'Trans-generational transmission of indigestible facts: from trauma, deadly ghosts and mental voids to meaning-making interpretations'. *Journal of Analytical Psychology*, 57, 5, 597–614.
——— (2014a) 'From affect to feelings and thoughts: from abuse to care and understanding'. *Journal of Analytical Psychology*, 59, 1, 31–46.
———. (2014b). 'Clinging, gripping, holding, containment: reflections on a survival reflex and the development of a capacity to separate'. *Journal of Anaytical Psychology*, 59, 4, 548–65.
Ferrari, A.B. (1992). *L'Eclissi del Corpo*. Rome: Borla. Translated as *From the Eclipse of the Body to the Dawn of Thought*. London: Free Associations, 2004.
Fordham, M. (1985). *Explorations into the Self*. London. Academic Press.
Freud, S. (1914). 'On narcissism. An introduction'. *SE* 14.
Freud, S., & Breuer, J. (1895). 'Studies in hysteria'. *SE* 2.
Garland, C. (2002). *On Understanding Trauma*. London: Karnac.

Jung, C.G. (1916). 'The transcendent function'. *CW*, 8.

Khan, M.R. (1963). 'The concept of cumulative trauma'. *Psychoanalytic Study of the Child*, 18, 286–306.

Klein, M. (1932). *The Psycho-Analysis of Children*. London: Hogarth Press.

———. (1935). 'A contribution to the psychogenesis of manic depressive states'. *International Journal of Psychoanalysis*, 16, 22–48.

Chapter 11

Continuous becoming or the experience of coming into being[1]

Introduction

When the egg and the sperm meet, and the fertilized egg falls from the fallopian tube into the uterus, according to the French child analyst Françoise Dolto, an unconscious desire to be born into life and a new drive towards consciousness are actualized. The human seed is anchoring itself in the fertile 'earth' of the mother. There, everything needed for life can be found. From inside the uterus, the foetus grows attached to the mother through a link of life (the umbilical cord) that guarantees survival. The seed grows and unfolds rapidly. At three months of gestation, the foetus is capable of listening to everything outside: mother's and father's voices are recognized, noises are identified and heard. Soon the foetus begins to dance to the sounds he hears: he attunes himself to the sounds of mother's voice choosing different movements: he might move the right leg every time he hears an 'a' sound, or the left leg every time he hears on 'e' sound. This dance makes him feel connected to the mysteries of a world he does not know yet but is preparing for.

The unborn baby has a great need for connectedness! He is capable of synchronizing his heartbeat to mother's heartbeat; in this way, he begins to learn about his mother inside out: her peace of mind, her depressive states, her anxieties. Through the different frequencies of her heartbeat, the foetus begins to gain a pretty unconscious knowledge of her state of mind, of her thoughts. While he explores the world in which he lives, he slowly begins to become aware of how much the world in which he lives is linked to the world outside. Using his resources and his newly acquired knowledge based on his experience in the uterus, he might be imagining something about that other world outside: will they also dance in water like him? While inside the uterus it is very loud (heartbeat, digestion, bowel movements), he knows that in that other world outside there are many rhythms, silences, talking, moving, pausing, full of intensity, softness, loudness. The foetus unconsciously knows that he is preparing for that journey; one day he will go there, to that world he knows little about. The journey the foetus has to undergo is difficult, he has to abandon his ordered world, he has to let go and face the unknown, the chaos of the unknown. It is a tremendous step into the void.

DOI: 10.4324/9781003268536-12

'There is much more continuity between intra-uterine life and earliest infancy than the impressive caesura of the act of birth allows us to believe', says Freud. Nevertheless, in the caesura lies the secret of development, at each caesura in life we grow; we transform ourselves; we come into being; we actualize our potential; we transcend the being we were to become a bit more what we are meant to become. In the depth of the undeveloped mind of the foetus there is a preconception, an archetypal predisposition, a sort of grammar of the psyche that guides the newborn baby into chaos, into the unknown: how to move, what to search for?

A video shows that a newborn placed on mother's abdomen will create his own route to the breast, find the nipple and suckle. This stimulates the mother's milk production and sends oxytocin into the uterus, pushing out the placenta and stopping any bleeding. A series of photographs shows a newborn doing what has been dubbed 'the breast crawl'. Placed on his mother's chest, he begins to suck on his hand. Eying her nipple, he opens his mouth and lifts his body upwards. He makes stepping motions against the mother's abdomen, stimulating contractions that decrease bleeding. Mouthing the nipple, he looks towards his mother. He sucks his thumb, tasting the amniotic fluid he drank in utero. The familiar smell and taste may help guide him to the breast, which excretes a similar substance. He lifts himself up to see her and prepares to place his lips on the areola. As he gazes at his mother, he is developing a memory of her face. He opens his mouth wide to make a perfect placement, and in their mutual gaze, his mother instinctively opens her mouth in response.

Caesurae

If the birth is the first caesura in the life of the infant, I will now investigate three further caesurae that the infant has to overcome, three jumps into the unknown and chaos that he needs to allow himself to do in the next years of his life. I will use three paintings for us to picture how the journey of the infant is developing. The scope of this talk is to show that there is much more continuity between infancy and mature life than the impressive caesura of the end of infancy allows us to believe, to paraphrase Freud.

The motif of St Anne, the Virgin Mary and the Child (Figures 11.1–11.3) and the way it is depicted in the history of art seems to describe very well and in a powerful way what the scope of development in childhood is.

St. Anne represents the support of the family for the newborn baby. We can see how in the history of art this motif changes and how the relationship between baby and mother changes.

Beginning of ordering of chaos: from preverbal to verbal, from confusion to order, from unconscious to conscious

Scenario 1: A hungry baby hallucinates the breast. The attuned mother knows that her baby is hungry, and she intuitively knows what her baby needs. As a result

Figure 11.1 Masaccio. Madonna and Child with St. Anne, 1424–5 (Florence, Uffizi)

Source: Courtesy Uffizi Galleries/Gabinetto Fotografico.

of her imaginative work, the baby experiences a realization of its own hallucination (in the sense the baby knew that he was looking for something). Everything arrives in just the right way. There is a sense of fit between the baby's anticipation and its realization. This mother helps the baby to feel that chaos is tolerable.

Scenario 2: If the mother is less in tune with her baby, maybe less confident in herself, she cannot imagine what she could do, and her actions are less responsive. So she might be more mechanical, less attentive, less in tune with her baby. In this second scenario, the breast presents itself to the baby as an alien object.

While baby 1 is not afraid of the unknown, baby 2 feels threatened by the unknown and finds it much more difficult to open up to it. This scenario might become so traumatic that baby 2 might close himself to chaos and decide to stay in this very little but known environment. In this case, growth is crippled, and the seed will never come to maturation. In scenario 1, the baby feels he has created the breast. He might be thinking: 'I have created the world, or the world is responsive to me. I can transform into life what I have imagined'. Clearly, the baby does not think in this way, but events of this kind underpin creativity. Only when self-experience is reflected does the baby feel fully alive. As he praises the world, he gives voice to his own feeling-self that he feels reflected in the forms of the world, beginning with his mother's face. By doing so he transforms the world, while he is transformed. The mother's responses are like an echo.

Before birth, the infant lives inside a mother's space. After birth, a mother creates with her body (her arms, her breasts, her warmth and her attention) a near-uterine state for her infant. It could be called the marsupial space, a space of transition between the total dependence in the womb and the increasing independence of separate existence. For the first few months of extra-uterine life, the infant's physical space is largely the same as the mother's physical space. As the baby grows and develops in terms of mobility and independence, he gradually emerges from the 'pouch' of mother's orbit, and his personal space becomes increasingly defined by his relationship with the general space of the wider world. As this happens the infant's internal space begins to be formed, with a mind capable of thinking, observing, facing chaos, together with a sense of a 'core self' that we could also call the personality of the infant with his own sense of identity.

Moving away from the known marsupial space: exploring the unknown in the space between mother and infant

The physical and psychological separation between mother and infant creates a space between mother and infant and in the infant's experience, which is the rudimentary space for consciousness. The experience of separation as a painful absence is a necessary developmental aspect in the growth of consciousness. The suffering of an actual space in which the mother is absent is the necessary condition for the development of representational symbols. The first thought is the thought of an absence: no mother. There thinking begins. Creativity begins where

Figure 11.2 Leonardo da Vinci. Madonna and Child with St. Anne, 1503 (Paris, Louvre)

Source: Copyright of RMN – Grand Palais (Musée du Louvre)/René-Gabriel Ojeda.

the absence has been acknowledged. When the infant reaches the stage of recognizing the loved mother as not created by the infant but as a person in her own right, the question arises: how to survive without her? Here the problem of creativity becomes important. I will give a vignette of Lia, 2 years old.

Her mother calls Lia and asks her to help mother with a puzzle. Lia goes to mother and does the puzzle very quickly: there are five pieces, she succeeds in putting four pieces together, but the fifth doesn't fit. Lia becomes very agitated, cries, stands up, falls, bangs her head, looks outside the window and seems lost. She then sees her ballerina outfit, puts it on with her father's help and starts dancing. Her father puts a record on and they both dance. Mother gets a Polaroid camera and takes a picture of Lia. As soon as the picture is developed, mother shows it to Lia, who looks at herself, opens her mouth and tries to swallow the image of herself in the picture. After that, Lia has a look at the puzzle. She goes straight to the piece she couldn't place before, picks it up and is now able to put it in the right place.

In this vignette, Lia seems to be reconnecting in a primitive physical way to a good experience of herself. She 'eats' the Lia who was having a good experience, and we see that after this she has regained the self-confidence that she has briefly lost. We might speculate that she needs to take inside herself, to swallow an image of herself who is loved. Lia seems to connect with a previous internalized experience of taking in something good. This previous experience must already be 'inside'. This concept of inside begins to be formed by the infant taking in mother's milk, her voice, her look. The experience of something going inside must be responsible for the beginning of differentiation between inside and outside. By eating the good image of herself, Lia seems able to identify with a good mother who is feeding her something good. In the transition between feeling capable and losing that sense of a capable self, Lia searches for a confirmation that she can do alone. She still needs help to re-find this confirmation but, once she feels secure in herself, she can continue to solve problems with a sense of agency. Lia seems to have achieved some capacity for symbolization: she is not eating food in order to make herself feel well, for example, but she eats in pretend a lovely image of herself. In this way, Lia is strengthening her ego and her identity. The capacity to relinquish the mother will foster the development of language: in the absence of mother, I can call her; I can express my needs; I can think my own thoughts; I can grow, become independent. This is a very difficult moment, the caesura between letting go of the marsupial space and acquiring the capacity to become separate: able to know one's own emotions, needs and desires, and learn how to express them.

The incapacity to manage this transition has terrible consequences for the developing child. He remains trapped in the phantasy of living in the womb, which is order which is known. Chaos, the unknown, remains unmanageable and with it creation, creativity, expansion and discovery. The child needs to go on creating what is unknown, what is chaos, the same way he did it after birth, go on figuring

Continuous becoming 167

Figure 11.3 Caravaggio. Madonna and Child with St. Anne, 1606 (Rome, Galleria Borghese)

Source: Courtesy of Borghese Gallery/ph.Mauro Coen.

out, finding ways of representing what is unknown and chaotic. This is the capacity of the artist, the infant that goes on discovering the world.

Becoming a person in one's own right: discovering the world around us, and the role of the father

In this phase, the mother has to let go of her child, allow him to become separate, allow him to develop his own potency, to do what he can do, discover what he can discover. So the child is going to go away from mother, discover, observe, give up the illusion that he possesses mother, that he has created her. Mother becomes part of the order that the child has created inside himself. His task is to continue his journey of creation, to be re-born again into new chaos, unknown, and represent it, order it, master it, in order to go on creating, representing, ordering, always at the limit between known and unknown as this child in the following vignette seems to show.

Rikako, 2 years old, came to a worm on the road in a puddle and stopped what she was doing. All three children gathered around to look at the worm, which was alive and moving. Rikako moved forward to stamp on the worm, but father stopped her. Rikako bent down to try to pick the worm up, but father took her hand and said, 'No'. There was a drain cover nearby, and the three children gathered around the drain cover to look down into the water. Rikako suddenly stopped, pointing up at the sky saying, 'Bird'. Father looked up but couldn't see any bird. They looked carefully at the trees and the sky for some time, as Rikako pointed at them, and saw a bird in the tree above. Then Rikako spotted a squirrel and pointed fascinated as she watched the squirrel swinging from one tree to the next. The other two children were moving on along the path, but Rikako didn't seem to notice them much and seemed in a separate space. Then they came over to her, and one of them pushed Rikako quite hard, so she almost fell over. But regaining her balance just in time, Rikako looked bemused and didn't retaliate. The father of that child said something, so the little girl went over to Rikako and hugged her; they kissed. The third child did not want to be left out, so she joined the two in a tripartite rather unstable hug. It was time to go, so they walked slowly back with several distractions such as another worm and another large muddy puddle which Rikako splashed in.

The role of the father becomes very important here. He points out to the child the future, the unknown, the task to go and explore. Orangutans do this in a very clear-cut way. Once their offspring are ready, more or less one year after birth, and have learnt everything from their mothers, fathers fight against them and send them away. They want their wives back. It is now the task of the young orangutans to go in search of their own wives. For humans, the process is much more complex. The work of the father is to push the child to move on, to go on experiencing the world, to study, to find out who he is and leave the world of the mother behind, go into the unknown yet again.

From lived meaning to representational form

The child has now to find ways of creating for himself objects or forms that help him contain experiences (playing with a doll and loving it, writing a poem, creating a hut in the trees). Eurydice has to be lost forever; Orpheus begins to sing and creates a form in which he can contain his feelings of sadness when she is lost. The infant needs to appropriate words now, words which are understood by everybody, but represent for him at best his own experience as in the following vignette.

Lorenzo, 4 years old, has to start school the next day and is afraid. He does not know how to do it. First, he sits on the couch, jumping up and down, maybe as a way of expressing his confusion and anxieties; then he sits on and transforms the couch into a car. He is now driving the car and with his mouth makes the sounds of a sports car, he is driving very fast, on top of things. So I say, 'Now that you can drive the car, it will be easy to go to school tomorrow'. He was showing me in pretend that he is a potent boy.

Creating a language: Alfi, 8 years old, a black boy who has been bullied, asks me, 'Do you think that colour-blind people are not racists? They might not see the colour of the skin'.

Finding a form: Maria, 11 years old, who suffers from multiple traumas, brings playdough to her session and creates a sort of breast without a nipple. Instead of the nipple, there is a hole. Together we understand how terrifying it is to live inside that hole, an empty hole without a mother.

These children are representing for me in a creative way a very charged emotional experience that seems chaotic to them. By giving it form, we were able to give voice to it so that the experience could become known, ordered and, hopefully, a way of handling it could emerge.

The journey of the hero

Every human being has to create their own life by being and becoming all the time, moving into the future in the same way the foetus moved out of a known space into chaos and the unknown. Like the baby who creates his mother, the human creates his future by opening up to the unknown, finding a form for it, creating a language and giving it meaning. Being and becoming means sacrifice. What you already are, for whom you could become, like the foetus who has to move out into the unknown and is guided by an internal knowledge that pushes him to go in search for what is needed, like Lia, who stops and reminds herself that she is capable, that she has already overcome obstacles and has to try again and again. Like Rikako, who openly explores the unknown, discovering the beauty of nature, and its ugliness, including the other children's attack. Each of us, day by day, has to repeat this pattern, the pattern of life. The child, like the artist, lives in a space which we could call chaos-order-chaos, similar to the space between womb and extra-uterine life. In order to go on developing, we need to investigate that link, that caesura; to approach it by knowing beforehand is here of no use. Unfortunately, those who have suffered multiple traumas and have lost a possible link to their internal guide are in danger of remaining trapped in horrible wombs, which by promising order protect from pain, chaos and growth. The price to pay for this protection is life itself, as those wombs are deadly, like hell. Life is always outside where the future is. The artist has to find the courage to be born again and again.

Note

1 This chapter is the transcript of a talk given at the conference on Childhood by the Alpine Fellowship in Venice, 28 June 2018. Talk available on YouTube.

Index

abandonment 25, 30, 107, 129, 143; and rejection 4–5, trauma of 5–11, 61, 113
Abandonment in Infancy (Fordham) 107
abuse as defence against (the pain of) containment 13–15, 44
act of birth 162
act of faith 29
affect to feelings 76–7; depressive position 86–7; emergence of third 83–5; idealization as necessity and defence 80–1; letting go of the hand-breast and the beginning of differentiation 81–3; parent's history 79–87; persecutory feelings 85–6; theoretical consideration 78–9
aggression 143
aggressive feelings 53
Alessandra 10
alpha function 15, 78, 147
anger and hostility 77
angry feelings 76
anorexia 64
antedate 'splitting' 101
antidepressants 87
anti-traumatic value 62–3
anxieties 36–7, 70, 101–2, 109, 127, 161
archetypal guiding force 87
archetypal law of the mind 1, 3; translating function 2–4
attacks on linking 40
attunement 8, 9, 17, 49–50, 53, 88
autism 52
autistic-contiguous mode 89
auto-satisfaction 77
avoidance 22

baby observation 35
Balint, A. 92

Balint, M. 92
Bavarian penalty code 32
bearing witness 60
befriending street children 120
behaviours of infants 90
Bick, E. 34, 50, 90, 92–3
Bick's and Ogden's hypotheses 98
Bion, W. R. 3, 34, 40, 49, 51, 60, 63, 78, 92, 147
Bion's beta 105, 115
Bion's O 105–7, 116–17, 142, 144
blank moments 109
bodily mental act 58
bodily mental contents 50
body-mind conglomerate 149
Botella, C. 63, 106
Botella, S. 63, 106
Bowlby, J. 92, 98
breast crawl 162
breastfeeding 35–6, 94–5
Britton, R. 73

caesurae 162
capacity: for reflection 85; for understanding 22
Carvalho, R. 10
catastrophic anxiety 34
Cavalli, A. 2, 6
chaos 70
child's communications 64
Clark, G. 12
clinging reflex 92–3, 98
complexio oppositorum 17
confusion 109
connectedness 161
Connolly, A. 61, 73
constitutional psychic fragility 49
containment 119

continuous becoming 161–2; beginning of ordering 162–4; caesurae 162; person in one's own right 168; representational form 169; space between mother and infant 164–8
coping strategy 70
core self 89
countertransference 34–6, 69, 147; attack the 'breasts' 38–42; discussion 36–7; implication for technique 46–8; refusing the breasts 43–6; reverie 7; similarities 38; theoretical implication 37–8
crying 67
cumulative trauma 146
curiosity 24

dead-alive object 112
death-giving eating disorder 65
defence mechanisms 71
defences of the self 34, 101
degree of acceptance 41
degrees of maturity 106
deintegration 10, 34, 46, 49–50, 73, 78
delusional-illusional states 117
depression 33, 81, 86
depressive feelings 42
deprivation 44, 124
despair 143
destructiveness 41–2; assaults 39; manoeuvre 40; narcissism 40; phantasy 72
devil, symbolic experience 116
differentiation from unity 78
disintegration 60, 98
distortion 146
do-it-yourself defence 29
Dolto, F. 161
drawing and writing 26, 28
dreams 30

eating disorders 62, 64
Eliot, T. S. 47
emotional stress 53
emotions 26
encopresis 20
environmental mother 34
experiences into mind, integration 2–3
external trauma 49; event 67
extra-uterine life 89

Faimberg, H. 66, 72
fear of disintegration 113
fears 127
feelings 76; *see also* affect to feelings

Feldman, B. 105
feral child 19; analysis 20–1; case presentation 19–20; from Easter to the summer 24–6, 30–2; first meeting 20–1; first month of analysis 21–2; hypotheses 21–32; from January to Easter 28–30; second and third months of analysis 22–4; from September to Christmas 26–8
Ferrari, A. B. 3, 10
figurability 63, 106
foetal position 36
foetus 161
Fonagy, P. 10
Fordham, M. 2–3, 9, 34, 50, 90, 98, 101, 105, 112, 120, 131, 143, 148
Fordham's concept of deintegration/reintegration 2
Fordham's hypothesis 108
Fordham's model of self 50
foster mother 78
Four Quartets (Eliot) 47
fragility 70, 83
Fraiberg, S. 72
Freire, P. 119–20
Freire's theory 120
Freud, A. 143
Freud, S. 76, 105–6, 108, 162
Fundación JUCONI 120, 126

Garland, C. 60–1
ghost 61; friend 26–7
Green, A. 61, 76
guilt 143

hallucinations 25–6, 110, 164
hate 71
Hawkins, L. 6
heat orientation reflex 92
helplessness 113–14
Hermann, I. 98
Hesse, E. 64
holy spirit 84
homeostatic function 63
hopelessness 69
Hoxter, S. 120
human predictability 66
human seed 161
hypothetical depressive feelings 53

idealization 149
idiocy 21
imaginary companion 26–7
imperfection 41

inborn Tiresias 16
incontinence 21
infant clinging 103
infantile neurosis in children 76
infantile trauma involving separation 5, 105–7; clinical presentation 107–8; delusional aspect 115–16; separation and hallucinations 108–15
infant observation 35, 120; illustration from 91–4; method of 120; mother 47; seminars 49; vignettes from 94–9
infant's mental life 3
infant's physical space 89
instinctual synchrony 49
intensive pain 143
inter-generational transmission 61
inter-generational trauma 67
internal object 89
internal pressure 57
intimacy 28–9
intra-psychic trauma 49
intra-uterine life 162
irrepresentability 67

Jackson, M. 105
JUCONI 120, 126
Jung, C. C. 2–3, 51, 73, 76, 105–6, 117, 131–2, 143, 147

Kaspar Hauser (von Feuerbach) 19
Klein, M. 3, 51, 112–13, 148–9
Kleinian psychoanalysis 1, 9, 112
Knowledge 24
Kradin, R. 47

lacking sense of balance 21
language 21
Laub, D. 61, 67
Liber Novus, The Red Book (Jung) 105
Little Hans (Freud) 76

madness 21
Madonna and Child with St. Anne: Caravaggio *167*; da Vinci *165*; Masaccio *163*
Main, M. 64
mania 45
manoeuvres 34, 81; emotional impact of 45
marsupial space 89
mastectomy 6
masturbation 26
maternal failure 47
Matte Blanco, I. 2–3, 10, 77

maturation 88
McGilchrist, I. 76–7
ME *see* myalgic encephalomyelitis (ME)
meditation (vipassana) 47
mental (izing) capacity 50, 78
mental crisis 105–6
mental excursions 65
mental functions 2
mental health 63
mentalization 10
mental operations 49
mental skin (articulating) 58
mental vulnerability 83
Meredith-Owen, W. 105
mindful attention 47
mistrust 21
moment of meeting 8
monosyllabic words 21
Moore, Y. 63
moral certainty 30
Moro (startle) reflex 92
motherese 56
mother-infant bond 98
mother-infant interactions 58
mother's insecurity 37
motor activity 100
mourning 72
mutual identity between mother and infant 50
myalgic encephalomyelitis (ME) 19
mystical man 27

nameless dread 34
nastiness 42
nausea 24
near-death situation 113
near-uterine state 89
neglected children 13
NGOs *see* non-governmental organizations (NGOs)
Noah's Ark 2, 6, 9–10, 151–2, 158
non governmental organizations (NGOs) 119
non-symbolic act 58

obsessive-compulsive disorder behaviours 150
Odgen, H. T. 89–90
Oedipus complex 11–13
Ogden, T. 51
omnipotence 8, 124, 126, 142, 149
omnipotent defence 40
Operación Amistad (Operation Friendship) 120

Index

otherness 12
over-stressed mother 6
oxytocin 162

pain of separation 30
Panksepp, J. 76
parents' sexual intercourse 77
'penis-to-penis' collision 22
phantasy 26, 39, 43, 46, 76, 102, 116
phantasy of unity 98
physical stress 53
Piaget, J 100
placenta 162
pornography 28–9
power cut 39
powerful defences 16
pregnancy 72, 76
primary object clinging 93
primary self 78
primitive attachment 101
primitive capacity 58
primitive identity 49–50, 112
primitive phantasies 116
private incomprehensible language 58
projective identification 49
proto-conversation 56
proto-thinking 26
psyche 60
psychic conflict 15
Psychic Conflicts of a Child (Jung) 76
psychic development 80
psychic energy 26–7
psychic pain 119; development 120–1; double deprivation 126; institution as family 129; omnipotence 126; from protection to containment 119–20; running away, being found 122–6; separation 128–9; special time 121–2; trauma and repetition of trauma 128
psychic recovery 63
psychodynamic thinking 119
psychological matrix 65
psycho-physical development 127
psycho-physical needs 92
psycho-physical reciprocity 90
psychosomatic unity 50
psychotherapy 31
psychotic episode 84

Raphael-Leff, J. 72
reflex 92
regression 24

reintegration 10, 34, 50, 73
repetition compulsion 122
reverie 49, 65
Rey, H. 64, 72
Rosenfeld, H. 40
rug-skin shrank 58
rumination 69
Rytovaara, M. 8

sadness 143
Satinover, J. 105
school counsellor 62
seclusion 21
second-skin defences 10
sense of identity 89, 141
sense of me 90
sense of self 116
sensorial experience 22
sensorial perceptions 24
sensory emotions 50
sensory motor preverbal stage 90
separation 23, 30, 128–9; defence against 42; pain of 30
sexual abuse 13, 79, 82–3
sexuality 76, 86
sexualized thumb-sucking 127
shame 71, 143
silences 7
silent voice 66
social services 86
Special Time (ST) 120–2
split 45
split-off emotional experience 117
split-off experience 37, 58, 66
ST see Special Time (ST)
Stevns, M. 6
street children, British-Mexican connection on vicissitudes 119; development 120–1; double deprivation 126; institution as family 129; omnipotence 126; from protection to containment 119–20; running away, being found 122–6; separation 128–9; special time 121–2; trauma and repetition of trauma 128
suffering 30
suicidal attempt 43
survival anxieties 126
survival attachment 93
survival reflex 92
survival reflex and the development of capacity to separate: clinical

implications 100–1; discussion 99–100; illusion of being all wrapped up with mother 101–2; infant in marsupial space 89–91; infant observation, illustration 91–3; infant observations, vignettes from 94–9; phantasy of being at breast 102
survival reflex for babies 103
Swan-Foster, N. 3
symbolic attitude 51
symbolization 27
Symington, N. 122

Tavistock Certificate 122
Telescoping of Generations, The (Faimberg) 66
theory of liberation 119
thinking skin 10, 50
transcendent function 2
transference 80, 147
transformation 6, 58, 103
transgenerational transmission of indigestible facts: clinical cases 61–4, 67–72; differentiating and ordering 64–7; trauma 60–1
transgenerational trauma 6, 72
transitional experience in relation 98
transitional movement 98, 100
transitional object 98
translating function 2–4
transmitted trauma 72
trauma 60–1, 109, 128; abandoned children 5–11, 61; chaos 66; external 49, 67; infantile 5; inter-generational transmission 73; intra-psychic 49; parent functions 64; repetition of 128; rupture 103; transgenerational 6, 61; transmitted 72
trauma, metaphor in treatment 146; circumscribing the traumatic event 147; differentiation and reparation 157–9; discussion 151–7; integrating and transcending the opposites 149–51; reactivation of primitive mental structures 147–9
Tustin, F. 92, 101

Unconscious as Infinite Sets, The (Matte Blanco) 77
unconscious communications 51, 55
unconscious fears of losing parents' love 76
un-mentalized events 10
unmetabolized psychic events 10
unpleasurable experience 45
Urban, E. 50

violence 4, 7, 28, 30
violent emotions 34
violent feelings 25
violent intolerable affects 64
vomiting 62, 66, 73
von Feuerbach, Anselm 19
vulnerability 70

Wiesel, E. 61
Williams, G. 121–2
Winnicott, D. W. 92, 98, 105

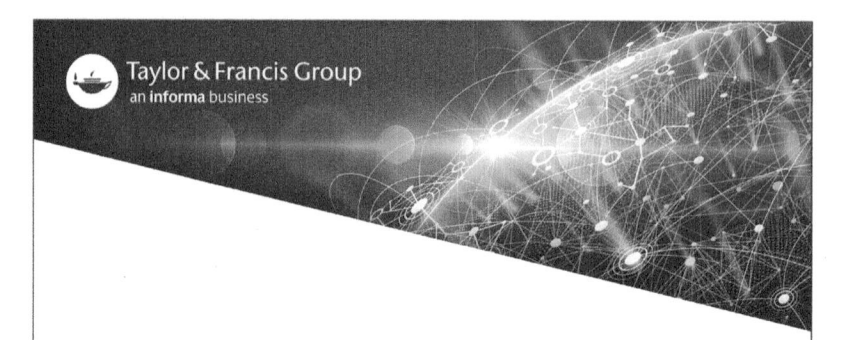